AND YOUR DAUGHTERS SHALL PROPHESY

AND YOUR DAUGHTERS SHALL PROPHESY

STORIES FROM THE BYWAYS
OF AMERICAN WOMEN
AND RELIGION

ADRIAN SHIRK

COUNTERPOINT · BERKELEY, CALIFORNIA

Copyright © 2017 by Adrian Shirk
First Counterpoint hardcover edition: August 2017

Grateful acknowledgment is made to the following for permission
to reprint previously published material:

Excerpt from *Ceremony* by Leslie Marmon Silko. Reprinted by permission of
Penguin Random House.

Excerpt from *An American Childhood*. Copyright © 1988 by Annie Dillard.
Reprinted by permission of HarperCollins Publishers.

Excerpt from *Teaching a Stone to Talk*. Copyright © 1982 by Annie Dillard.
Reprinted by permission of HarperCollins Publishers.

Library of Congress Cataloging-in-Publication Data
Names: Shirk, Adrian, author.
Title: And your daughters shall prophesy : stories from the byways of American
women and religion / Adrian Shirk.
Description: Berkeley, CA : Counterpoint Press, 2017.
Identifiers: LCCN 2017015896 | ISBN 9781619029538
Subjects: LCSH: Women—Religious life—United States. | Women and
religion—United States. | Religious biography—United States. |
United States—Religion.
Classification: LCC BL625.7 .S55 2017 | DDC 277.30092/52—dc23
LC record available at https://lccn.loc.gov/2017015896

Jacket designed by Jarrod Taylor
Book designed by Elyse J. Strongin, Neuwirth and Associates, Inc.

COUNTERPOINT
2560 Ninth Street, Suite 318
Berkeley, CA 94710
www.counterpointpress.com

Printed in the United States of America
Distributed by Publishers Group West

1 3 5 7 9 10 8 6 4 2

For my grandmothers

And if my experience in that church did nothing else for me, it accustomed me to strange outpourings of the Spirit and gave me a tender regard for con artists and voices in the wilderness, no matter how odd or suspicious their messages might be.

—DENNIS COVINGTON, *Salvation on Sand Mountain*

The force behind the movement of time is a mourning that will not be comforted. That is why the first event is known to have been an expulsion, and the last is hoped to be a reconciliation and return. So memory pulls us forward, so prophecy is only brilliant memory . . .

—MARILYNNE ROBINSON, *Housekeeping*

The future is female

—T-shirt for Labyris Books,
NYC's first women's bookstore, 1975

· CONTENTS ·

A DECLARATION OF SENTIMENTS

I will start as close to the end as possible.

In February, I took a train up to Rochester from New York City to visit two friends. They howled at me from their Subaru parked outside the station and waved me into the warm car. A few minutes later we were sailing over the Frederick Douglass–Susan B. Anthony Bridge, and Sofi turned to me and said, "So I've got a project for us tomorrow: We're going to Seneca Falls."

In the morning we had breakfast and then pinned our hair into nineteenth-century updos: ear braids, topknots, and tight, low buns. We tore muslin into matching white collars and fastened them together with brooches from Goodwill, tucked into dun-colored dime blankets we'd turned into shawls, and then we drove the fifty-seven miles to the Wesleyan chapel.

When we arrived, it was cold, and the chapel was empty. Bright winter light fell in panels across the twelve rows of pews. The gleaming sheetrock belied the chapel's authenticity: It was, to my quiet disappointment, only a simulation of the original. I ran my fingers along the far wall. Here and there an old beam or two was on display, but the rest was mirage. We split up and cased the interior for a good place to put the camera, finally setting it on a tripod just below the pulpit. Then we sat in the front row clutching our shawls and recited the Declaration of Sentiments as we imagined they'd been delivered 170 years before:

Resolved, That such laws as conflict, in any way, with the true and substantial happiness of woman, are contrary to the great precept of nature, and of no validity.

That because your laws are bullshit, because they are *at war with the interests of mankind*, they are without authority—

(I was startled, as we began to read, by how deeply theological so many of the resolutions are, for a document primarily associated with suffrage.)

That woman is man's equal as intended by the Creator.

It is not just her right to vote, but her sacred right.

(The language, of course, is borrowed from that other declaration.)

It is a perverted application of the Scriptures and other corrupt customs that have been the yoke of her oppression, and it is time to overthrow the monopoly of the pulpit.

Man has usurped the prerogative of Jehovah himself, telling woman what to do and where to go and when to stop, when that belongs to her conscience and her God—over and over again.

At one point, a young couple wandered into the chapel and then quickly out again.

At closing time, a park ranger in full regalia came and stood beside us until we'd gathered all of our things and left. But we weren't finished with the action yet: Outside, we stood on the sidewalk against the brick of the chapel and continued filming and reading the Sentiments in tension with passages about fitness and facial care regimens from *Real Simple*. (For some reason, that afternoon, *Real Simple* embodied to us the ways in which America had betrayed the suffragists.) As we read, I felt that age-old double-bind described by Professor

Naomi Greyser in her article "Affective Geographies: Sojourner Truth's Narrative, Feminism, and the Ethical Bind of Sentimentalism," that all "the 'men' who, Thomas Jefferson declared, 'are created equal' shed their gender and their race" that day they signed the Declaration of Independence. "The problem . . . was that women and blacks could never shed their bodies to become incorporeal 'men.'" The Declaration of Sentiments was trying to make an intervention, but no black women were invited to that first convention in Seneca Falls. Across the street and over a little river, I could see a collapsed wool mill, where on that summer afternoon in 1848 some women, mothers of a thousand children, had had to work for low wages while some other women, mothers of few or none, were stating their resolutions. The river was so narrow and dribbled by so quietly that members of the two groups may even have heard the other—the clang of her machinery, the appeal to her God.

I did not ask my friends what we were doing there in Seneca Falls, what we hoped to make or make contact with, because in some unspoken way I knew. During graduate school, when the three of us lived in Wyoming, we occasionally observed Witch Night. This included tarot readings, chakra clearings, making soup, workshopping our writing, smoking cigarettes, giving thanks to the Virgin of Guadalupe, troubleshooting cures for ovarian cysts and other reproductive woes—really anything that needed doing, ritual or otherwise, under lamplight, with other women. We never codified what should happen on these nights, but it made a sort of internal sense. Winters were long in Laramie, and there was always some burdensome masculine energy of the Mountain West that needed counteracting.

Meanwhile, my instinct toward the magical, the occult, the feminist ran up against my participation in various patriarchal churches: During the years of Witch Night, I found myself attending a nondenominational church plant, the liberal synod of the Lutheran church and a Catholic Newman Center (though without a Confirmation, the

Catholics had refused me the most magical of the mass's gifts). But it had always been that way, my compulsion toward and resistance to religious institutions always rendering me somewhere in the fray. There is a needlepoint above my kitchen table of the Last Supper and an Indonesian fertility goddess hanging on a nail right next to it, and sometimes I pray and go to church, and sometimes I do not. When a new friend or colleague asks me if I am religious, I never know what to say: theologically Christian, culturally pagan, aspirationally heretic? Heretics work from the inside. Heretics, being radicals, don't bear the politically dubious connotations that come with the word "Christian." (I have also recently heard that early followers of Christ were referred to as "wayfarers." I could be a wayfarer, too.) But this is still weird for me, a child of the New Age, raised in a family of deeply secular musicians and social workers in the Pacific Northwest.

Like so many Anglo Americans, my family's religious history is amorphous—especially being from Oregon, where long ago those pioneers had thrown off the mantle of the old dogmas for new ones. Plus we had been Americans for eight generations already, on both sides (whatever that means), and by then my flaky ancestors had tried out every American religious fad you could think of, an experiment that ended (though how egocentric to think of the present as the end, or even a culmination) in atheism. Growing up, religion did not especially matter, and it was anathema to my own social education about what it meant to be a liberated woman. And yet, by the time I found myself, at twenty-seven, in the Wesleyan chapel, I had long since begun to interrogate this. For years I'd cycled rockily through one cosmology to another: secular humanism, New Age paganism, Lakota shamanism, Unitarianism, Protestantism, Catholicism, and a handful of nondenominational church plants—small, localized, often urban congregations that have been "planted" by a larger church organization or network—that congregated in the basements of high schools and beat-up storefronts, only to find myself again, nearly a decade later, in the same weird spiritual no-man's–land in which I had begun.

Or was it the same? It seemed this time around that religion did matter, must matter, in America and elsewhere, especially where women are concerned. Since the 1960s, the fastest-growing U.S. Christian movements have been the most virulently conservative, throwing their energies into vile, insipid causes mostly having to do with women or sex in one way or another. And it is Christians, so often the least religiously literate of all, who are fueling all the Islamic fearmongering. (After 9/11, when asked whether he was religious, theological essayist Richard Rodriguez started saying, "I'm Christian-Judeo-Islam.") Fundamentalism is its own religion entirely. It understands the Bible as a divinely inspired document to be read (with great incoherence) literally, rather than as a very old library. During my lifetime, fundamentalism has monopolized American religious thought, tearing it from progressive action where, historically, Abrahamic theology has seen better days, mostly, maybe always, within the most marginalized communities: the civil rights movement, the sanctuary movement, the suffragists, the abolitionists, the leftist Jewish diaspora.

So the monopoly of the pulpit, whatever kind it may be, cannot remain uncontested—not ever, but especially not now. Religious literacy is one way out from under the thumb of fundamentalism; constructing new literacies is another.

For American women, there has always been a strange call to holiness, to divinity, somewhere else. They've had to find their own ways there outside the prescribed patriarchal orders. Where did they end up? During those cold Wyoming winters, between Witch Night and church, I began to amass a casual archive of American women who had made or revised a theology, more or less as I encountered them: the Spiritualists in upstate New York; a hushed-up Mormon prophetess in Utah struggling to explain what she saw and heard, beyond the established revelation; the pop–New Age pioneer, channeler, and astrologer Linda Goodman; the New Orleans high priestess Marie Laveau, who, in the antebellum South, ministered magic to an interracial public that was, as they say, 30 percent Baptist, 70 percent Catholic, and 100 percent Voudou; Aimee Semple McPherson and her Pentecostal media empire; the prophetic vision of intersectionality as preached by Sojourner Truth. These official divergent prophetesses, and also "saint" Flannery O'Connor; the radical feminists of the Fifth Street Women's Building; the Calvinist Indians of the Hamptons; the woman behind Christian Science who sought to understand a God in bodies and with bodies; and the hidden messengers and messages within my own old American family.

It is a totally idiosyncratic list, deeply revealing of my own haphazard interests, problematic and incomplete by nature. But perhaps there is something useful about those qualities, too. Because women were not invited to participate in the creed-making and exhorting and politicking and debating of official religion-making, it has been necessarily true that, as American religion scholar Catherine Brekus puts it in *Strangers and Pilgrims*, throughout most of American history, the ways in which women mete out spiritual authority has been "characterized not by upward progress, but by discontinuity and reinvention." And while reinvention was a consequence of erasure, it may have always been a hidden strength.

That there has been a long tradition of women being cut off from their own history is no surprise and nothing new. Our lives were not considered worth keeping record of, and then when they were, the means by which to transmit those records were few and late— especially if we were poor, immigrant, or darker-skinned. Then, of course, there is the persistent belief that powerful women are frauds, and if not frauds, then crazy or bitchy or snobby or greedy or *bad*. How, then, do you write about them? When Djuna Barnes sought her friend's advice about how to ethically novelize one of her ex-lovers, her friend said, "Think of her in as detached a way as you possibly can—not as a saint or a madwoman, but as a woman of genius, alone in the world, frantic."

If I have learned anything, it's that the truth shifts. The modes by which to interrogate it must always change and are always changing. This doesn't indicate an absence of truth, but rather its elusiveness. If there is anything hopeful about these women's histories, it's often not their righteousness, but rather their sense of the spiritual avant-garde.

So I stood outside the Wesleyan chapel door, looking at my friends reciting the Sentiments, still steadfastly costumed, the orange sunset against their lovely scrubbed-clean faces. I thought of all the wrong stories I had told, or had been told, up to now. What were we doing? We were communing with the dead. We were having fun. We were trying to remember what no one had remembered for us. We were devining a future. We were imagining the past. We were retelling the story. We were telling the wrong story.

AND YOUR DAUGHTERS SHALL PROPHESY

WE ARE ALL SCIENTISTS

Mary Baker Eddy

There's a marble bust of a stately Victorian woman sitting on my grandparents' hearth in Seattle, and for part of my life I thought she was Mary Baker Eddy. The bust's craftsman detailed each ruffle in her collar, the fine downturned corners of her mouth, a neck tendon—handiwork so thorough and lifelike that, as a child, my mother's cousin was regularly inspired to jam his finger up her nostril, whispering, "Pickin' Gramma's nose, pickin' Gramma's nose . . ." The reasons for my confusion were complicated and have to do with the way my family tells and does not tell stories about itself—but these were Eddy's problems, too.

Reverend Mary Baker Eddy, the founder of Christian Science, is recorded as having been sick for most of her life: anxious, erratic, doubled-over, her frail body racked by mysterious intermittent pains. Eddy's temper tantrums and day terrors alienated her siblings and forced her parents into a lifelong tiptoe. She required constant rocking as a child, and when she was an adult her family commissioned an oversized cradle in which she spent many of her days.

Harold Bloom describes Eddy as "a kind of anthology of nineteenth-century nervous ailments," though I suppose many Victorian women could have been characterized that way. Female nervousness was being written prolifically into diagnostic manuals at the time, one strain of which was even called "Americanitis." Is it surprising? The cognitive dissonance of the 1870s was sharp: the blitz of postwar wealth, a booming middle class, half a million young men dead, and 3 million freed slaves expected to begin anew and forget—along with the emergent progressive majority—that anything had happened at all. We were tripping on the heels of the Industrial Revolution, which had sped everything up, and we were struck dumb by the realization that all Western powers were in cahoots and had been for a long time, and that millions were perishing in their colonial crossfire. Women were indoors getting splinters, dying in childbirth next to the window through which they'd watched the world pass them by. Time was no longer linear, but fragmented. So when Eddy established the Church of Christ, Scientist in 1879, she offered an irresistible alternative: Life, as you suspected, is happening elsewhere. Disease and death are metaphysical glitches. Maybe the members of this new religion could feel it in their marrow, maybe Eddy more than others. After all, as scientist and novelist C.P. Snow asserted in his 1959 Rede lecture "The Two Cultures," it is scientists who "have the future in their bones."

It was Eddy's lifetime of illness, and her subsequent encounters with newfangled medical therapies, that poised her as an instrument of revelation. The Christian Science hermeneutical stance is that the whole Bible is a literal guide toward psychic and physical restoration, and that Eddy, as evidenced by the prophesied "little book" mentioned in Revelations, was uniquely appointed to reveal it through her explication of the Bible, *Science and Health with Keys to the Scripture*. In it, she writes that "health is not a condition of matter, but of mind," a conviction undergirding all of Christian Science—the controversial principle blamed for the deaths of those who refused hospitalization for their ailing parents or their kids. But Eddy's call issues from the belief that Creation is inherently good, and that every physical or psychic aberration is an illusion that can be willed out of consciousness, vaporized by prayer. She saw all manner of disease as requiring only a "re-alignment between Mind and God." Any perceivable darkness or disorder is the consequence of wandering, as in a dream from which you cannot wake. And rather than believing in the divinity of Jesus, she held that "Christ" is a spirit which flowed through him, and through all men and all women, granting everyone the potential to "demonstrate the Christ," to be a healer.

The marble bust on my grandparents' hearth was made, of course, not in the likeness of Eddy but of Mary Stevenson Semple, my fifth-great-grandmother, whose husband founded the shoreline city of Elsah, Illinois, which—for no particular reason having to do with his governance—became the site of Principia College, the world's only Christian Science university. Maybe this was the source of my confusion. The Semples were Methodists when they arrived in Illinois and Episcopalians later on. And then their only daughter, Lucy, converted to Christian Science following the death of her business-tycoon husband.

Her family worried she'd joined a cult, but Lucy didn't give a shit. She was rich, a businesswoman in her own right, summering her last decades on a rolling estate overlooking the Missouri River. Meanwhile, her younger brother Eugene had left Illinois, gone farther west, starting but failing to complete all of his entrepreneurial endeavors on the Pacific Coast, as large and optimistic as they were: cedar mill baron, filler of tide lands, canal builder, state printer, police commissioner, appointed governor of the Washington Territory, and three-time Democratic loser for elected offices. When his wife ran off with a businessman and the new baby, Eugene filed as a widower and sent his three young daughters to be raised by Lucy in Illinois. She brought up her nieces, Maude, Zoe, and Ethel, in the Church of Christ, Scientist. Then Ethel begat Lulu, and Lulu begat my grandfather George, who begat my mother. I know all of this now.

But which of my ancestors believed what, and for how long, and how those beliefs faded—in one lifetime, in one generation?—is still unclear to me. Did Eugene's daughters cleave to Science to salve the wounds of their father's abandonment? Was Lucy's conversion to this rather egalitarian religion a radical response to Victorian restrictiveness? And how has the irreligious thrust of my immediate family been informed by the inheritance of a religion whose optimism allows for a near-complete disavowal of pain, of disorder, of chaos? Because there is no spiritual continuity in my ancestry to speak of, and because no one really knew why Lucy converted to Christian Science, I imagine unbroken lines of connection wherever they've never explicitly been debunked, and so when I was younger, having Christian Science relatives might as well have made me Eddy's descendent.

And what if Eddy was my relation—my grandma, even? Being too weak to hold me, she'd ask a relative to set me beside her in a chair designated for children, her cold, thin hands folded in her lap. She wouldn't even pat my head or crinkle a smile, and she'd be rocking, still rocking, as she had been doing her whole life. I'd listen to her chirp about the various miracles and revelations that had led to the founding of her church: the monastic fasts of her childhood, her experiences in mesmerism, a slip on the ice in Lynn, Massachusetts, that, by one account, left her paralyzed, cured only by reading one of Jesus' healings—after which she sprung from bed in full form. But origin stories are unstable. Even the New Testament accounts for this. There are, after all, four gospels. Some biographers claim that after the fall in Lynn, Eddy was treated with morphine, and that the injury was not a dire one. In her autobiographical writings, Eddy claims that the revelation happened when she was a child, bedridden by stomach ulcers, and later that it was some other sickly girl, then woman, then man, who'd revealed to her the true spiritual reality.

But that's all make-believe. It was my wealthy ancestor Aunt Lucy who had the marble bust made of her mother, and it was passed down from household to household until it was set in my grandparents' living room—a place which, before my lifetime, held all-night parties, endless packs of Pall Malls, jugs of Carlo Rossi on the coffee table, bespoke packing cubes for the VW van, great American novels and psychology tomes, my grandfather's endless stories, and my grandmother's tipsy, intellectual wit, which kept everyone from going to bed when they otherwise ought to have—and which is now a tomb of cobwebbed furniture and old bicycle parts. The bust, however, sits in the same place it always has and is, at best, a prompt for jokes and tall tales about the religious zealots from whom we descend.

I am visiting my grandparents in Seattle during winter break from graduate school. My grandfather and I are sitting at the kitchen table, plates scraped clean from dinner. I've recently grown interested in Mary Baker Eddy, and Lucy and her brother Eugene—I'm not sure which first—and plan to casually excavate the "Semple Papers," a trove of correspondence kept deep in a library at the University of Washington. I've come, too, in hopes of asking my grandfather what he knows about the Science that trickled down to his mother's generation before disappearing entirely. But when I ask, he only shrugs and changes the subject to something more pressing.

"GMC is offering me thirteen grand for my Suburban," he says from behind a tall plastic cup of scotch. "They've been sending letters." Out the window, I can see the giant twenty-year-old rig parked halfway on the pavement. "But I'm not giving it up. Why do you think they want those transmissions so badly? I'm keeping hold of it just in case I want to run off into the mountains . . ."

When he says this, I'm not sure if he's talking about an apocalyptic flight or just a summer excursion, of which he still imagines there are many to come. He laughs at his own frugal genius, his lifelong pride in beating "the system," and shifts his eighty-five-year-old body in the chair, uncrossing his bloated ankles, the shattered hips intact only by an intricate act of balancing bones.

"Yeah," I say. "That's crazy. But—did your grandmother ever talk to you about Christian Science? She was Eugene's daughter, wasn't she?"

"Mmh," he says. "Now—*Robert* Semple, Eugene's eldest brother, *he* was interesting. He helped start the California Bear Flag Revolt in 1846 . . ."

I listen to the full twenty-five-minute account of the Bear Flag Revolt and the capturing of Alta California before rephrasing my question about Christian Science. I keep hoping that he'll tell me some story about this grandmother, her undiagnosed schizophrenia, her devotion to Science, or maybe a story she told him about the years when she and her sisters lived with their Aunt Lucy in the mansion on the Missouri River. But his mind wanders to more exciting adventures: the feats of the "Great Mizners," Eugene Semple going north to the Yukon Gold Rush, his own cross-country bike rides.

When my grandfather was twelve years old he bicycled around the entire perimeter of Seattle, and then later Washington State, and by fifteen he and his friends were hitchhiking out to the new Olympic National Forest and hiking over the pass for days, weeks, after which they'd hitchhike home.

"One time we were coming back from a hike and got a ride, five of us, really squished into the back like sardines." He chuckles, miming the closeness of the quarters. "And the car lost a tire and rolled over four times. But we were all packed in so tightly that no one was hurt. So I yelled, 'Everyone OK?' and then we kind of scooted out of the wreck and thumbed for another ride." While we've been talking, he's dug up an old photo album out of the back room, and he opens to the first page: There's a photo of him just after the accident. He's cavalier, shoulders thrown back, grinning through a shock of black beard, a virtually invincible young man clutching a cardboard sign that says SEATTLE.

The funny thing is that, despite his adventurousness, my grandfather's body has always been fragile. He was born with a degenerative joint condition. After a childhood of failed reconstructive bone surgeries, his body started really falling apart in his twenties, and he's lived in denial of this ever since. He speaks now of his exploits very casually, as though everyone in 1948 was cycling from coast to coast for no particular reason. When, at twenty-one, he mounted his three-speed Peugeot with a bedroll and his camel-colored loafers, he wasn't worried that his hip bones might grind against each other from Seattle to South Salem, New York. He was fearless, and he was looking for something, but unlike his forbears it had nothing to do with God. Instead it was strength, immortality, a way to will his frailness out of existence—something like that.

What did he care about Eddy's Science? His mother had left Science as a young woman for the more formal pastures of the Episcopal Church. Her husband left their family, so she raised her two boys alone and—the way people talk about it—presided over a life so gentle and without expectation, she never urged either of them to heed any doctrine. She put on her little blue shift and matching jacket and went to church; alone or not, it didn't matter. So, by my grandfather's generation and thence on, no one in our family was healing by prayer, nor insisting that their children retain any kind of spiritual education. Religion, it seemed, was a perplexing recessive gene whose raison d'être was not worth remembering. In fact, my grandfather found that one could live a productive and ethical life without it, abiding instead by some inner voice. It was inevitable, really—in his blood. You ended up in the West only if someone in your family was looking for escape, or had gone on some impossible adventure, hauling all of their worldly belongings over the continental divide, or were otherwise looking forward, beyond, away from whence they came: erasing their trail or letting it disappear into the wilderness.

If, any time between 1955 and now, someone asked my grandfather what he wanted for Christmas, his answer was always the same: "Improved human relations." This was his Apostles' Creed. And my grandfather's secular humanism was handed down, tacitly, to my mother: I was raised to value tolerance and pluralism and to believe in the native and potential goodness in everyone. It was a privilege, really, to grow up in Portland, Oregon, and never think twice about the sanctity of gay marriage, women's reproductive rights, or social safety nets, or to doubt the systemic oppression of American minorities. I was taught to recycle, to distrust the free market, and to eat local produce. If I was sick, I went to counselors, naturopaths, and acupuncturists. If I was healthy, I told other people about how they should go see a counselor, a naturopath, an acupuncturist. I was expected to be healthy. I wanted to be healthy. Health and kindness were the marks of moral superiority.

If my distant Aunt Lucy and Mary Baker Eddy ever met, it would have been on Lucy's property in Elsah, Illinois, a conference of two wealthy nineteenth-century widows in frothy white tea gowns, praying that the other realizes her nerves are fine, that nervous disease isn't real, and that there's nothing really to be nervous about anyway.

Christian Science doesn't espouse such healings to be miraculous but "scientific," methodical, an ultimately "proven" rediscovery of Christ's methods as apparent in the Gospels. Jesus laying his hands on the blind man didn't restore his sight; it showed, through the correction of spiritual thought, what he could see all along. So Jesus is not the son of God (any more than any of us are God's sons or daughters), but the model Christian Science practitioner, those individuals who, even today, provide healing services in American business park offices and the like.

But despite her interest in restoring Christ's first-century healings, Eddy's accomplishments were much more nineteenth century: trustbusting, free enterprise, dissolving an anthropomorphic God, installing women in positions of leadership. By the turn of the century, some 70 percent of Christian Scientists were female, and the world had risen up to meet them.

The frontier had now been scaled and just as quickly secured, the occasion of its endlessness lasting only as long as the momentary hope that it truly might be. More Americans were running away, looking for gold, land, fur, time, freedom. They believed in God, though belief was more tenuous than ever. Frontier women were hanging out in parlor halls or rearing children in small tar-roof cabins in the woods, all by themselves, while their husbands sought nebulous fortunes. It wasn't great, but maybe it was better than the civilized yoke of Victorian life—a modern period nearly unparalleled in its restrictiveness, in the stripping away of places for women in public *and* private life. More women lived farther and farther away from their birthplaces, so, if they survived, they could be anyone. They could run off with businessmen. They could convert to a different religion. Or they could make one. During a time when women were excluded from seminaries, pulpits, and medical and scientific professions, Mary Baker Eddy's religion created a way that they could occupy nearly all of these roles at the same time.

In a way, there are some strange similarities between that religion of secular humanism I grew up with and Christian Science's deepest convictions: a self-selecting responsibility for one's emotions and well-being, and a wholesale rejection of certain evil, not to mention a wariness of Western medicine. And sometimes I wonder if my grand-father has some predisposition for not believing in his own maladies. He never goes to the hospital. He walks with two canes and yet, every summer, makes a point of tilling his entire property into "supersoil," and he climbs ladders to pick the plums, and the stairs five times a day—one set to the second floor and another set to his tower, a small room he built on the roof the bungalow in the early 1960s.

I remain at the kitchen table after my grandfather leaves, and I clear our plates and scrub the dishes with a one-thousand-year-old sponge. The cabinet doors are splitting and stacked full of unused in-struments and expired parmesan cheese. I listen to the house creak as my grandfather lurches to his tower, where he'll listen to the classical station, mull over the Dow Jones, and thumb through every sheet of paper he's ever collected just to make sure it's all still there, until he goes to bed.

I wander out of the kitchen and through the living room, where my grandmother has fallen asleep in her chair with the TV on and her legs elevated, then through the musty front hall, with the ancient dictionary on a book stand, and out the front door. I find my mother sitting on the front porch among empty flower pots, plywood, stacks of newspaper. She's sipping a cup of tea, looking off into the distance.

"Did you get any good information?" she asks.

"Not really," I say. "He just kept telling these stories about the Mizners."

She nods and laughs.

I pull up a seat next to her. "Has he always been hard to keep on track?"

"More since he's gotten older. But he's always just, you know, talked like this—" she motions a hard, straight line from her face. "In his own world, on a mission."

I look at my lovely, slight mother, sitting there in her green fleece, quiet and smiling. We're high on the hill in Ravenna and the radio towers blink peacefully from the north. She was raised in this very house by these jolly alcoholics. Nowadays, in her fifties, she casually describes their general denial of family dysfunction as a consequence of their drinking, but I always thought it was the other way around. Wasn't the drinking a cipher for the dysfunction?

She is a flutist, and she has spent her entire adult life working with emotionally disturbed kids, mostly in residential treatment programs, and both her parents were social workers, too. She is a teetotaler, yes, but my mother's remoteness and tranquility seems also to be her way of keeping inexplicable evils at bay.

"You know," she says, "in junior high one time, I was invited to compete in Walla Walla for a regional honors student orchestra. And the morning I was going to leave—now, you're going to think this is just goofy—I woke up and the house was empty, right? So I went down to the kitchen, and on the table there is this tiny note from him folded around a five-dollar bill—" She pauses for effect. "'I hope it is a trip to remember!'"

And now she looks at me, her mouth agape, as though this were the most extraordinary gesture, Excalibur rising from the lake. She laughs. "I kept it in my wallet for twenty-two years."

She doesn't elaborate, but I think I understand: It was a moment when, in a very small and practical way, her father acknowledged the daily, regular world and her own place in it.

Later, when she goes inside, I stay on the porch and call my husband Sweeney on the phone. I tell him about coming up short on ancestral information, and about the echoes of Science I see in my own family. He's silent at first.

"What?" I say. "Is this not making sense?"

"No, no, it is. But you know," he says, "the missing piece of this is that *you* don't really believe in illness either."

I feel my neck stiffen.

"That's the funny part," he says. "Even though you don't ever say this outright, you always wear any illness you have—even a cold—as a moral failing. You actually get angry with yourself. And, you know, there *is* a part of you that believes cancer is caused by repression, and that depression can be solved by bananas and herbal tinctures. You can't even accept the possibility of your brother's illness in medical terms."

I don't know what to say. I feel an unnamable fury and am also close to tears. "I do accept his illness," I say, "I do, I do. I just feel like there's more to it, like there's more going on than illness alone."

I hang up.

The subject of my brother feels shrouded in silence, especially between my mother and me, except to comment on how great he is doing, what a long way he's come, how lucky he's been. When I was sixteen, Aaron was arrested for arson and armed robbery. Or, first he went AWOL during basic training and later cut off his fingers, and then came the arson and robbery. Or, he had done a lot of hallucinogens in high school and thought he could start a cult, and then all the other stuff happened. Or, he had always been angry and destructive, and no one knew why. Regardless, he was arrested, that's for certain, when I was sixteen and he was twenty, and after a year in holding and scrupulous work from a high-profile defense team that required all of our family's savings, he was sentenced to the Oregon State Hospital and diagnosed with paranoid schizophrenia: the inability to discern between what is real and what is not.

For most of my adult life, the lines drawn around that illness and my brother seemed too simplistic, or didn't seem to illuminate the complicated guy I knew, whose entire life couldn't, as far as I was concerned, be described away in a sweep of psychosis. Where was the margin of error? Where was agency? And where did it all fit into the larger ecology of our family? And what—I felt Sweeney's voice creeping back to admonish me—what *was* illness anyway?

I do have to face that, much to my chagrin, there is an unchecked part of me that views health as a moral metric, whether or not I mean to, or think consciously about it that way. At the center of my interest in Christian Science and my ancestors are, perhaps, my own reprehensible ideas about health being one's own responsibility, within one's own control, and somewhere this overlaps with mental health as it relates to my brother—whose out-of-court diagnosis I'd dismissed early on in the heat of teenage rage. It was a diagnosis that implied helplessness. Helplessness seemed easier to live with.

M ary Baker Eddy is a complicated figure. She's portrayed sometimes as a narcissist, a plagiarist, and a hack, whose own account of her life shapeshifts and doesn't match up with those of others. It's known for sure, though, that Eddy was married three times—divorced, abandoned, widowed—acquiring three different names before, at sixty years old, her Christian Science "association" became a church, at which she was installed as the universal pastor. Then she started the Massachusetts Metaphysical College, wherein anyone who had what was then the exorbitant fee of $300 could train to become practitioners. She funded new newspapers, not least of which was the *Christian Science Monitor*. And the religion proliferated as a brand-based operation, with lots of literature, rings, brooches, photos, and even commemorative Mary Baker Eddy spoons, and 423 different editions of *Science and Health*, which all members were encouraged to purchase—or purchase a dozen of each "if they could afford to." And despite Eddy's messianic march toward health, she herself never ceased to be sick.

In his 1907 book-length satire of Christian Science, Mark Twain says, "I was assured by the wise that Christian Science was a fleeting craze and would soon perish." He says that if Christian Scientists were arriving at their beliefs purely by intellect, rather than by environment, family, or milieu, then the prediction would've been true, because eventually they'd realize it made no sense. But of course we almost never come to religion by intellect alone. Echoing a common opinion held by outsiders, Twain casts Eddy as not much more than an infantile, illiterate, potentially deranged theologian and a successful snake oil peddler who scammed her followers until she was very, very rich. But if we can suspend our doubt and allow, for a second, that Eddy did start her church based on genuine belief, that she was the prophet she claimed to be, then she needed money to do the Lord's bidding. Ministers of other sects are supported entirely by the church body, and Eddy, a woman initially without a following, a presiding order, or an income, didn't have that option.

But her prophecy, especially as a self-described Christian one, leaves lots of questions—in particular, for me, about good and evil. In the earliest book-length biography of Eddy, coauthored by Willa Cather while she was still a grad student, she's presented as both business-minded and lunatic, a charlatan and a trailblazer—at best a pragmatist more than a prophet, and at worst an all-around crappy writer and spiritual thinker. Cather looks at the complexity of Eddy's character: She relies enormously on her friends and mentees but then turns them out, ruins their names. She copies the ideas of the famous mesmerist Phineas Quincy, but the accusations deepen her martyrdom. Abandoned by her husband, she hands her son over to her childless neighbors, denying later—even to him—that she'd ever had a son at all. But even this changes. The biography moves through these elements as the stuff of life, not scandal. Still, Cather wonders if this religion has anything to do with Christianity. Where is the talk of sacrifice, charity, love? And how can all of creation be good? If Cather is disturbed by anything, it's Eddy's theology, not her life: "No philosophy which endeavors to reduce the universe to one element . . . can admit the existence of evil unless it admits it as a legitimate and necessary part of the whole. But the keystone of Mrs. Eddy's Science is that evil is not only unnecessary but unreal."

There is something familiar to me about that inability to court the possibility of evil, or whatever you want to call it, to accept that it may exist, that it may be in you or me, or down the road somewhere, or in the trees. I guess it's that almost lethal optimism that binds the Christian Scientist and secular humanist thing together: a hope, a belief that everything in this life will, or at least can, turn out OK, and that all the bad stuff—war, famine, rape, abuse—is accidental, aberration, a deviation from what could otherwise be a perfect world.

The afternoon following my conversation with my grandfather, I trek to the library at the University of Washington to dig through the Semple family correspondence in the special archives. In the archive's careful silence, I fill out a liability form and give the librarian my driver's license, and then he motions me to a table where I wait for someone to bring me the letters.

I'm excited. I feel like a sleuth about to crack a case. When the letters do finally arrive, in weathered archival boxes, I stare at them for a long time before finally taking one out.

In short, they're incomprehensible. Each one is as inscrutable as the next. Most of them are written in a wet, loping cursive that's impossible to read. And even when I make out a passage or two, they're references to money that Lucy, the optimistic Christian Scientist, wired her brother Eugene for some failed project or another—exact sums, suggestions for its use, and occasional notes about his daughters' health.

I take out another and stop looking for anything in particular, instead attaching to things that seem to make contact with common experience: "My dear Edwin died tonight," "Did you go to the Feast of the Annunciation?" and (in one from their mother) "We all agree with you in thinking Eugene a splendid man, and [who] with judicious management will make his mark in whatever he undertakes. Eugene was always inclined to be a little extravagant . . . you must admonish him not to go beyond his income." Finally I come across one from Eugene to his daughter Maude: "I've made it to the Yukon," he says, and then he begins to tell of the gold rush, on and on, in this excited, sloppy script. Did he think she cared, this girl he'd abandoned years before with his sister in Elsah, Illinois? Or did it not matter either way, his excitement being so solipsistic that he was oblivious to the fact that she must have felt alone, beached, dispensable, that she might only be scanning the letter for one more mention of her name? "Oh, Maude, how I miss you."

Under the auspices of his rich sister Lucy, who saw no limits in the divine reality, Eugene more or less abandoned his daughters for his dreams, or even dreamed them away. He was a stubborn man, hypnotized by that soft ghostly glow of the Pacific horizon, missing everything that was immediately in front of him. His children came of age without him. And he failed to complete, at great expense, all of his undertakings, and he finished out his life in cheap rented rooms in Astoria, Oregon, continuing to scheme about how to industrialize the coastline, how to open the tidelands, with plans that proved always too expensive, always the laughingstock of the legislature. He eventually died penniless in an old folks' home. These days, my mother says she's pretty sure he was an alcoholic.

It's raining when I leave the library. My pursuit of the letters now seems ridiculous. I tried posing as a scholar and got nothing—didn't have the patience to see any of it through, didn't even know how to use archives. If I'm being honest with myself, I expected to sit down in that library and pick out the letter where Lucy described her conversion to Science in crystal-clear detail, or where Eugene confessed, in perfect nineteenth-century prose, to the creed of manifest destiny, or where either of them echoed Eddy's words, or my grandfather's words, or my own.

When I get back to Wyoming after winter break, I contact an archivist at Principia College—the Christian Science university in Elsah, the town my great-great-great-great-great-grandfather, Eugene and Lucy's father, founded—to help me track down information about Lucy's former property on the Missouri River, which has since been absorbed by Principia's campus. She doesn't have much information and knows nothing of Lucy being a Scientist, but she does know a lot about her philanthropy and her business exploits. She eventually sends me a scan of a very old photograph, about which she says, "I think you will find this of particular interest." It's of two marble busts: Mary Semple's—the one in my grandparents' living room—and one of Lucy, facing each other from a tabletop and a windowsill respectively, as though in conversation.

There's something droll about it. For one, they no longer live together—the busts, that is. Lucy's sits in the dark archival reaches of Principia College, while Mary's is in Seattle, dusty and forgotten in my grandparents' living room. One woman was a Methodist who had to face the necessity of evil in order to believe in redemptive goodness, and the other saw only the divine light, all the time.

The busts, the way they were situated in that musty parlor, closed-mouth on nearby surfaces, face-to-face, remind me of my mother and me.

The thing is, my whole interest in Lucy and Eugene and Christian Science started with my mom, though I'd forgotten this. It was between the cool pink sheets of a bed-and-breakfast in rural Oregon that she first told me about them. We were in the middle of a long open-ended road trip across Oregon following my high school graduation, just she and I, alone at length for the first time in years. We were tucked into twin beds on opposite sides of a room, cheeks to pillows, facing each other. She was talking about a college boyfriend of hers I'd never heard of, and how one day he was just "done" with her, and how she was confused and humiliated and never really spoke to her mother about it. Then, out of nowhere, she said, "Have I ever told you about Eugene Semple?" I shook my head.

"Well, Eugene Semple was your great-great-great-great-grandfather, the governor of the Washington Territory. And when his wife left him for a businessman, he filed for the status of a widower. And he sent his three daughters to live with their rich Aunt Lucy, the Christian Scientist, in Illinois . . ."

I fell asleep that night thinking about Eugene and the scandal of a public figure being left by his wife in such a salacious way, and also our connection to a rogue Protestant sect that still exists in the margins of American life. It seemed like we could still be Scientists, in one way or another, though neither my mother nor I had been given any education in the nature of the atonement, what a messiah's sacrifice might mean, or, moreover, how it might be related to restoring physical and mental health. If we'd been Christian Scientists, we wouldn't be lounging around gossiping about our ancestors but would instead be praying over my brother, whose illness would be simple, and who was—at that moment, while we were on that road trip— interned in a state hospital in the city where my mother and father had lived in college, and where, 150 years before that, Eugene Semple wandered into a local tavern for a nightcap and quickly found himself in a fistfight with one of his constituents. (That I know from a book, so maybe my mom is right about the drinking.) If we were Christian Scientists, we wouldn't have been thinking about any of that. We would have been kneeling by my brother's bedside, helping him will his mind into alignment with God's.

My grandmother has been going through all of her old correspondence, including everything I've ever written her, but also things from my brother, my uncle, and my aunt, and tying it into bundles with twine and sending them to me. It's the kind of liquidation that precedes death, though I cannot quite tell from where or when the end is coming. She sits in her old wooden pew at the kitchen table, sunlight coming through the window and shining through her colorful bottle collection, and handpicks which ones I'll like the most. They arrive in chronological order.

In the most recent bundle, I take out a letter from my mother. It's from September 1975. She's nineteen years old. "Dear mother Gale," it starts out cheekily.

> I have been anticipating the writing of this letter for two days now. The reason why I've put this off has been to make sure it sounded sane when I wrote it—and three days ago it would have sounded incredibly unstable.

She describes this boyfriend who's been slowly breaking up with her and hints at a nearly psychotic pain she feels over it. It's the boyfriend she told me about in the bed-and-breakfast, I realize. She then reveals that she's writing the letter from Astoria, Oregon, where she's getting ready to play the flute at a wedding gig with her friend. And she goes on and on about the effect of the ocean on her, the "crazy energy that is transmitted into your body," and that Astoria "satisfies a romantic part of me."

> There is something about Astoria and Bellingham and Seattle that I feel definite "roots"—Seattle is more home and familiar secure feelings. Astoria and B'ham get me thinking about water + fish—people + history. I start getting an urge to learn about Indians from the area, the very beginning. And (this is crazy) I think about Eugene Semple—my family + the Pacific Northwest and to me it is an important combination. I am intrigued with these ideas of history coming to Astoria—it is such a source—the confrontation of the rivers and the ocean.

My mother knew these stories about our family, about our ancestors, only because my grandfather had been telling them unceasingly her whole life. As a kid, she probably sat next to him on a chair designated for children as he talked and talked without ever looking down, and maybe she was happy just listening. But that note she folded into her wallet for two decades—"I hope it is a trip to remember!"—still rattles in my brain, or rather, it's the idea of my twelve-year-old mother standing in that silent Formica kitchen, thinking, *My God, I exist, I exist.*

OUR BODIES, OUR SMOKE

The Moon Lodge

M y acupuncturist scribbles some final notes onto her clipboard and smiles at me. I'm seated under the vaulted ceilings of her immaculate office suite near Union Square in New York City. Next to us is a vinyl exam table, a single potted orchid, and a tall street-facing window. Beyond that are the gabled steeples of an old Episcopal Church whose steps I tripped over hurrying to this appointment a few minutes before.

"Let me see your tongue," she says.

I try scraping it clean against my teeth.

She considers it, iguana-like, from across the room, and then asks me about my diet ("Red meat, yogurt, whole grains, leafy greens"), bowel movements ("Firm, I guess"), and tobacco intake ("About a pouch per week").

"A pouch?"

"I roll my own," I say. "That's about fifty cigarettes."

My acupuncturist is Chinese American with bright, pick-like eyes, and when I confess my daily coffee intake ("Five cups"), she raises her thin brows and says, "Impressive."

I tell her that I'm looking to curb my habits—but even to my ears this sounds insincere. It's the plea of a burnout, a middle-aged man. What habits? I become suddenly aware of the smoke smell rising from my wool coat, the circles under my eyes. Under the tepid winter light, my hair is brittle and dull. I think back to a week before, when my stepmother sent me an email: "Your references to smoking are making me want to steal your lungs in the middle of the night and adopt them out," to which she'd attached a photograph of black lungs.

That wasn't the reason I ended up at the acupuncturist's, but it was that same night that I made the appointment. My life in New York had changed. I was in a weakened state. Many of my friends had moved away from the city, college was coming to a close, and all the energy I'd once gleaned from a vibrant social life I began drawing from tobacco. I smoked with abandon and spent much of my time writing and lighting up in solitude. On the phone with my friend Lily one night, I'd said, "I wonder when this smoking streak will end," and she'd just laughed at me. In the meantime, I'd grown chronically fatigued. This bothered me because the West Coast dogma of my childhood demands that I feel healthy by default.

"It's good you had a chance to go a little wild," my acupuncturist says, gathering her papers. "That's what college is about. Testing your limits." She leaves the room. I listen to the lively click of her boots from behind the door and relax onto the table.

I consider what she said and begin to doubt that I or anyone has natural limits. It seems more accurate that life is about imposing constraints, rather than arriving at them. And yet, from my first self-destructive freedoms of early adulthood to the kitchen table pedagogy of my well-meaning parents, the hope persists that I, or anyone, will reach their instructive "limit." Staring into the mood-lit gloom of the office, wooden flute music playing from a boom box nearby, I think about the roots of my tobacco gluttony.

When my acupuncturist returns, she says, "We're going to get you back on track." She approaches the table and gently locates points on my feet, shins, and arms. As the first redemptive needles break my skin, I realize that what I didn't express to her or myself is that I adore smoking cigarettes, in spite of my West Coast piety, black lungs, and my own better judgment. There's the obvious physical and mental stimulation, addictive chemicals and oral fixation, but that's not what I—or probably anyone—am dwelling on when I light up. So what is it that's so pleasurable about this time-tested vice?

It's hard to say exactly. Each situation modifies the smoke. For one, a cigarette provides a visceral and cerebral pause that lasts as long as it burns. On the contrary, and for the same reason, it prolongs conversation. Deep silences between friends become communal. Communion is made with strangers. As a writer, smoking commits my focus to the piece I'm working on, or binds my attention to the story I'm reading, or focuses an ongoing conversation I'm having with myself. It is instant gratification in a life punctuated by activities with very long-game outcomes. In that way, the relationship between smoking and the solitary acts of thinking and art-making resembles a kind of prayer. For almost every American Indian nation, and especially for the Lakota community I grew up around, tobacco is smoked as a means to send prayers to ancestors and the Great Mystery. The smoke can literally travel to the spirit realm, to where it carries the intentions of the smoker. I can't help but make the connection, when smoking is a part of the writing act, between these inclinations. It puts thoughts into a concrete form and sends them into the ether, and there is great comfort in that.

In a lot of First Nations origin stories, it's a woman who brings tobacco to Earth—like the Sauk spirit who emerges from the mist, hungry for the venison that two young hunters are roasting, and who leaves them the plant in thanks for sharing their meal. Or the Iroquois' Sky Woman, who falls through a hole in the clouds and populates Turtle Island, giving birth to a daughter who dies in middle age and from whose grave sprouts the "life-givers": sweet grass, strawberry, and tobacco. For the Lakota, tobacco is the tangible presence of Wóhpe, or "the Beautiful One"—the daughter of the sun and the moon, both.

Of course, white people changed all of that, mostly men. While the plant originated in the Americas, America is also where it sours. The Europeans loved it; they brought it home to cultivate themselves, and their methods turned it colors the natives had never seen: brown, gray, black. It became the only commodity to be exchanged cross the Atlantic both ways, and its addictive properties increased, a new organism altogether, which tribes of the north traveled great distances to obtain when they heard about new arrivals coming in from Holland, England, or Spain. And later on, it becomes the crop propagated by slavery in the American South, and later still, in the arm of conservative lobbyists, laced with irresistible poisons, it was brought back across the ocean to grow (as my father once put it to dissuade me) "in China next to nuclear plants that leak."

When my acupuncturist finishes setting the needles, she puts a space blanket over me and turns out the lights. "You know," she says, "the fact that you're this attuned to your health in your early twenties is a good sign for the future." Of course, she's unaware of the compulsory health-conscious culture I've come from. She says she'll be back in a half hour and shuts the door.

I arrived in New York in late August 2007, a week before my nineteenth birthday. I was newly enrolled in the Pratt Institute writing program, and the housing application I'd received a few weeks before allowed me to state several preferences, including smoking or non. On a whim, I selected the former, though I wasn't a smoker.

It was midnight when I landed in LaGuardia, with everything in the arrivals terminal cast in dirty yellow light. Rain poured down while I waited for a cab. Barreling along the expressway to a family friend's house in Park Slope, I watched the dark wastes of Queens go by, and the brief glimmer of skyline just before the exit. The next day I hauled my enormous suitcases through puddles across campus, having spent the whole flight imagining I'd escaped the perpetual dampness of the Pacific Northwest.

I spent that afternoon taping photographs to the cement walls of my freshman dorm and carefully hanging my dresses in the wardrobe. My new roommate sat Yogi-like on her bed puffing Camel No. 9s, whose packaging, that summer, had been reintroduced in an irresistible palette of turquoise and magenta.

"I don't smoke," I told her, wedged halfway into my closet.

She blew curlicues around her head and scratched at the shooting stars tattooed across her collarbone. "Then why did you choose a smoking dorm?"

At the time I just shrugged as though it might have been accidental, because I knew my reasons were dumb. I was drawn to smokers, or at least to the idea of smokers. There was an intensity, camaraderie, and frenetic brain activity I associated with them. I believed there were possibilities in the smoking dorms that didn't exist elsewhere.

Later that day, walking around Fort Greene together, I bummed a cigarette off my roommate.

"I thought you didn't smoke," she said.

"Well, when it's for a good cause," I said.

"What's the cause?"

"Saluting a new life."

During the first week of class, there were frequent fire drills in the dorms due to the highly sensitive smoke alarms. Idling on the lawn during one of these evacuations, I picked out a pretty, spectacled girl from the crowd. She had a shaved head and dramatic Italian eyebrows, and she immediately lit a cigarette. Later that week, we had class together. To break the ice, the professor asked us to pen the worst prose we could think of and then read it out loud. When he asked Lily what made her piece bad, she said in a deep, eloquent voice, "It's bad because no one should use the word 'soul' in a short story." Sensing that she was as serious about writing as me, I approached her after class. Practically a cradle-smoker, Lily had recently started rolling her own cigarettes because of high New York prices. We spent our first long conversations crouched in the grass on campus, talking about Diane di Prima, Salinger, our estranged brothers. She rolled me smoke after smoke, laughing at my hesitant acceptances. Each drag sent me into sublime, primordial dizziness that prolonged our meeting until dusk.

I was calling my new hobby "celebratory smoking," meaning that I only found myself with a cigarette when spirits were high. During parties, after shows, on the streets outside of bars, in the throes of a "New York adventure," which, at the time, included everything from passing over the Brooklyn Bridge to crossing the street. I got a job at a health food store. Someone at school asked me how I reconciled smoking with my health-consciousness, and the best response I could come up with was, "Choose your poison."

It wasn't that every new friend I made was a smoker, but I was drawn to many. During lunch a month into the semester, I listened to some peers discussing a biweekly open reading that a few upperclassmen held at their apartment. "It's crazy," a boy said. "One of the guys writes these poems that are just words, like, 'Refrigerator. Python. Front porch. Rectangle. Secular,' and he just goes on and on." This sounded like just the thing for me, and I decided, with a bravery I've never had since, to show up at the next one.

When I arrived, I buzzed to be let in. I watched a tall, whiskered boy in furry black boots come stumbling down the stairs. A second boy followed him. They overshot the doorway, visibly drunk, flying past me onto the sidewalk. The second boy was shirtless, his long wool coat open in the front. He had long dirty hair and a black beard, and he was smoking a rolled cigarette that he'd taken with him through the hallway. "I'm Sweeney," he said, and held out his hand.

They led me through the crumbling white hallway into the crammed apartment where the reading was in process before a captive audience. I took a seat on the crowded floor, and someone passed me a Basic. Still an unseasoned smoker, I could barely see straight after each cigarette. I went up and read a poem I'd written earlier that day about my grandparents' plums. And later Sweeney, the shirtless one, rolled around my feet on the floor like a worm, reciting "The Wasteland" at the top of his lungs. Then he disappeared for a month.

When he finally resurfaced, he'd sobered up some and was more able to court me. Too shy to ask me to a pre-Thanksgiving party, a friend of his arranged a bait-and-switch where I thought I'd be meeting him but instead found Sweeney waiting for me under the streetlamp in his ragged waistcoat and steel-toed boots. He was so nervous. He started telling me how he'd been reading *East of Eden*, and how Steinbeck says that "the triumph of man is his ability to believe that something is true, even after having been proved otherwise over and over again." We got to a bank of elevators to go up to the party, and he couldn't stop talking. "It's crazy that he calls it man's 'triumph' instead of man's 'plight' or 'pitfall.'" The elevator opened and I pushed him in, kissed him hard against the back as the doors slid shut. He tasted like tobacco, salt, and last night's whiskey.

This is when I truly learned to smoke.

We were inseparable that winter. We took walks in the blinding cold, read entire novels out loud, cooked steaks at his house, went to the movies, stayed up smoking and talking until dawn with friends or in bed, what seemed like every single night. We woke up next to one another each blue New York morning until spring, and realized we were barely looking at anyone else.

In February, he took me to Westchester to meet his parents. His father, a lawyer and Marlboro man, said, "So are you two dating, betrothed, or what?" As I grew closer to his Irish Catholic family, I'd find myself at Easter dinners or graduation parties, smoking and talking on some porch with an uncle, an in-law, a sibling. These were moments when the distance between this culture and the one I'd come from echoed loudest. Had I come from WASPs, even though we weren't religious? I found that the citizens of the East Coast were not as concerned about health, but with other things: stoops, efficiency, bawdy humor, success, loyalty, heavy coats.

We spent the rest of the school year driving back and forth along the Brooklyn-Queens Expressway, Taconic State Parkway, I-95; to the Catskills, Connecticut, Baltimore, Savannah; talking and smoking endlessly out the window. I loved these drives. I learned to roll my own. I was gorging on diner burgers, drinking truck-stop coffee, sending carbon emissions into the atmosphere, and I realized I'd stopped identifying with the West Coast consciousness of my childhood. I didn't even bother using public ashtrays anymore; I just stubbed the butts out in the street.

Sometimes I'd think back to the summer before I moved to New York. I'd spent a great deal of that rainy Portland August watching the entire *Sex and the City* series with my mom and my little sister Charlie. Carrie Bradshaw quit smoking during the second-to-last season, and that's the last television character I could remember smoking who wasn't a villain or acting in a period piece. In Brooklyn, I began noticing posters appearing all over subway stops, campaigning to incorporate smoking into the MPAA rating system. I found myself standing in contradiction not only to the place I came from, but to popular American culture, too. There was enough public consensus now to make the sensational PSAs I'd watched as a kid obsolete.

At the end of my first year at Pratt, Oregon outlawed its remaining smoking bars. Shortly thereafter, New York State put a moratorium on smoking dormitories (Pratt's was the last in the city), eventually extending nonsmoking laws to all public places, including parks and areas with heavy foot traffic, like Times Square. I remember, just before this happened, hurrying across 42nd Street through a weekend mob, looking for someone with a light. I finally tapped a woman on the shoulder who, upon my asking, looked horrified. That summer, Sweeney and I flew out to see my family, and I remember my mother wincing when I reached for my pouch of Drum, as if the whole West Coast was pleading for me to stop.

I grew up in southeast Portland, at the top of a lawn-flanked hill populated by earth-toned turn-of-the-century bungalows. The local elementary school was close by, and parents frequently took turns walking us to class. Everyone composted, kept health-conscious menus, strict TV-watching limits, and respectable used cars. My best friend's father, who worked for the Environmental Protection Agency, bicycled to work every morning. There was absolutely no smoking culture to speak of. I remember being six or seven and hearing a friend's mother say, "I can't think of a *quicker* way to kill yourself," after passing some teenagers outside of the grocery store one day, and I remember being already privy to the slogans.

The era ushered in national antismoking efforts of its own, with the force of Nancy Regan's DARE and the exposure of Joe Camel's appeal to children. But Portland was perhaps riper than most places for the politically correct bandwagon on the road to better health. The parents in my community almost never drank around the kids and believed in the preservation of our bodies and our forests. These parents were also of the first generation to identify, on a large scale, the relationship between cigarette smoking and innumerable diseases. Collectively, they witnessed the slow, grueling deaths of peers and national icons that, for the first time in the twentieth century, every public medical and media source had concurred were preventable.

Fear of death by smoking was ingrained at an early age. Saturday morning cartoons were regularly interrupted by public service announcements: An adolescent sporting a neon baseball hat approaches his ne'er-do-well friends in the park to say that smoking "isn't cool." Another, tempted after a stressful night of studying, is stopped by a cartoon head that pops out of his textbook saying, "You're Too Smart to Start." A girl lights up at her mother's makeup table and watches herself morph into a shriveled hag ("It'll suck the life out of you"). And then there's one I remember particularly well, wherein animated skeletons, spiders and pus oozing from their eye sockets, smoke cigarettes while flying menacingly around an underworld, finally reaching the earth's surface only to force the cigarettes into the fingers of a teenage posse. "Don't smoke. It'll drag you down" is the tagline flashing across the scene as a skeleton reaches through the dirt and pulls one of the girls to Hell.

In the fifth grade, my school sponsored a series of sex ed seminars called FLASH wherein the perils of peer pressure, particularly in regards to smoking, were introduced in tandem with the marvels of menstruation. Sometime during those lectures, I remember watching the school nurse beam as promisingly and white as a flight attendant as she finished her demonstration by removing the Maxi pad's tape and extending its wings. "Some of you may start your menses by the end of this year," she said, somewhat excitedly. Supporting the pad's flight with two manicured fingernails, she circled the room, presenting it to each girl before resuming her place behind the table of props: an open package of Always, a popped tampon, a beer bottle, and an empty pack of cigarettes, about which she'd said earlier, "As you get older, your friends will start to use peer pressure. Just say no. Statistically, one in ten of you will be addicted by the end of high school."

In retrospect, it seems deeply problematic to freeze the two in collusion forever. Those first days of sex ed promised the end of all innocence. Ovulation was the gateway to addiction.

When we were finally excused, I looked to my friend in the seat next to me. She was white-faced. We lined up for a bathroom break and she said, "My greatest fear is that someone's going to tie me down and force me to smoke, and then I'll be addicted forever," expressing a paranoia that echoed beyond elementary school hallways and into the PSA-riddled Northwest psyche of the 1990s.

But that it was especially horrifying for women to smoke—that's old news. It was true then, true now, and true in 1929 when a cadre of early feminists volunteered after "the father of public relations" Ed Bernays and feminist Ruth Hale incited them to light their "Torches of Freedom" on a New York Easter Day Parade. But even Bernays was riding the coattails of a zeitgeist: As early as 1916, *The Atlantic* commented that for some women, cigarettes had become "the symbol of emancipation, the temporary substitute for the ballot," and we saw the same rhetoric again in the 1970s campaigns of Virginia Slims, Eve, More, and others. Why does vice, especially smoking, look so powerful, political, and perhaps scary on women? If it's death that's so unbecoming, then it's the same damn death men are subject to. The PSAs of my childhood really put the emphasis on how it might make girls ugly ("Who cares about a pretty face when you've got ugly breath?" croaks the narrator of one ad that depicts a pretty young teenager slowly turning into a troll, set to Pachelbel's Canon), but also how uncool it was. It's a hard message to sell for a product that, for so many decades, symbolized male social authority and savvy. I mean, of course a cigarette, whatever disgusting work it's doing physiologically, suggests power, sophistication, autonomy, allure, and mystique, and it threatens all fantasy of what might be ladylike.

In general, though, in Portland, the quiet conviction was that no one but the very aged, deeply troubled, or otherwise trashy smoked. I never once felt the desire, nor experienced the pressure, that I was promised. Even now, the city seems to ring with a humorless mantra that one of Carrie Brownstein's characters in the parody show *Portlandia* gives voice to. In a recurring skit, she plays a feminist bookstore clerk who, when her friend remarks that she's "practically hooked" on a particular kind of herbal tea, peers sternly over her thick frames and says, "Addiction isn't funny."

Growing up, I knew only two adults who smoked, and, weirdly, they were my father and my stepfather Leo. But both were such exceptional cases, for different reasons, that they almost didn't count in my mind. My father became an occasional smoker the year he started running with Lakota spiritual circles, and Leo was from the East Coast and had been a smoker his entire life. He grew up in a rough blue-collar neighborhood in Hartford and was always an exception to many of Portland's niceties. He drank instant Folgers, swore a lot, and wore a black fedora. He was the only adult who'd buy me Cherry Coke and Dunkin' Donuts outside of the context of a birthday party. He let me sit in the front seat of his truck, and I would listen to stories about Hartford that he repeated over and over again. He used the F-word a lot. He told me a story, multiple times, about being a teenager and taking his friend to a Dunkin' Donuts after the guy had turned green from heroin. It was the only place open twenty-four hours: "The coffee saved him," Leo said, nodding like a dashboard figurine each time he said it. Even as a kid, I knew he didn't fit in in Portland.

Shortly after the unlikely marriage to my Northwest-native mother, he went back to school, and during that time he was my stay-at-home caretaker. On our way to grab lunch or a movie matinee, he'd pick up packs of Kools at the Clinton Street Market. He kept a toothbrush next to the front seat to keep his breath from stinking, and I could never tell what mood he might be in. There were days we'd get in fights—about my dirty room, back-talking my mother, not playing enough with my sister—or he'd just fall into a dark mood, and in response he'd spend the afternoon spraying down the sidewalk with our garden hose, biting a smoldering filter. When the ghostly traumas of his past came back to roost, he couldn't find communion with anyone but Kool. It's the one thing that bridges his past to his present, that reminds him of a life that nothing in Portland, Oregon, suggests is even possible.

Leo was born in Hartford in the early 1950s and spent the first part of his life in a housing project across the street from a foundry. Over the next two decades, white flight, middle-class flight, was in full effect, and East Coast cities were quickly plummeting in population as suburbs boomed. Hartford was nearly bankrupt. Leo, like a number of children in his project, got polio, and, with little access to thorough medical treatment, those who survived learned to walk again only by physical therapy methods implemented by their parents. Leo's mother strapped his feet to a tricycle until his muscles came back. His father was unemployed for most of his childhood, and he was a heavy drinker, a hitter, and a screamer. Leo dropped out of the public school system in the fifth grade and dabbled in crime until he left home at fifteen.

He worked odd jobs, saw a thousand terrible things, quit drugs, and finally hitchhiked across the country to Portland, where, at twenty, he started a new life. He passed the GED, got married, became a dad, and started doing menial jobs at a residential treatment center for emotionally disturbed kids. After earning his associate's degree, he became a teaching assistant in my mother's classroom around the time my parents divorced. He followed that line of work until he was forced into retirement ten years later as a result of debilitating muscular dystrophy from his childhood polio. I was halfway through high school at that point. He slept for what seemed like an entire year, then woke up bored to a drawer full of Social Security checks. Between spells of fatigue, he'd kill the pain by finding pipes and vents that needed fixing, hunting shoelaces and scrap rubber to remedy things around the house. These pastimes were strenuous, so he eventually took up drawing, too.

The first picture of his that my mother had framed was of a green pear, and she hung it above our kitchen table. Before putting it behind glass, Leo peeled the USDA Organic produce sticker off the picture's model and affixed it to the picture as it had sat on the real fruit. For the next several months, whenever he found himself in the kitchen with somebody—anybody—he took the opportunity to talk about how hypocritical he found the sticker to be.

I remember him lurching into the kitchen one day while I was eating lunch. He banged his mug on the counter, a familiar signal that he was about to speak, and he stood admiring his labor out the window: He'd been cleaning the back deck for the past several hours with a piece of steel wool.

"That deck looks fuckin' *clean*," he said. I nodded but remained silent. "I mean, just look at it!"

When I still hadn't responded, he spun around and fixed his gaze on the green pear, considering the drawing. I already knew what he was going to say.

"You know, they make such a big deal about the apple being organic," he said. "But do you know what that sticker's made out of? *Petroleum*." As in times past, left uninterrupted, he continued on the horrors of petroleum. "You know what else they use petroleum for? *That*," he said, pointing at my tennis shoes and polyester shirt. "And *that*." He motioned to the Tupperware and then to his car in the driveway. Each new example made his knuckles white. For as long as I'd known Leo, since I was about five, this was how he dealt with whatever he was currently haunted by, a kind of emotional exorcism to which I was frequently the audience.

"I'm so ashamed of my generation," he said. "I really am. Oil has really fucked up the world. I wake up some mornings and think about donating my car. I do." Then, having made himself sick, he stepped out onto the spotless deck for a cigarette.

* * *

My father didn't start smoking until he embarked on the Red Road. In his early forties, unable to shake a familiar low-grade depression, he sought shamanic healing. He took a series of "soul retrieval" workshops and quickly became interested in the movement's Lakota-Sioux roots. After attending some sweat lodges held by communities around Portland, he left the workshop setting and was taken in by the Whitedeer family, a Lakota hoop—"hoop" being an imprecise word referring a small community or band, regional or tribal, organized around sacred principles and activities. Being a fair-haired, blue-eyed white dude, it was a shock both to my father and the hoop how naturally and powerfully he was able to sing traditional songs. Soon he was being called on to lead singing for various ceremonies. Traditionally the community offers gifts to the singers, and the most common token is a pouch of tobacco.

I was ten or eleven years old, and rather than having it explained to me, I simply watched him change. He pierced his ear, learned to build animal-skin drums, and started rolling his own cigarettes. He reserved them for ceremonies, though I occasionally caught him in the backyard after dinner in a wreath of smoke.

The summer before I turned sixteen, I agreed with some reluctance to accompany him to southern Oregon for a Sun Dance, a Lakota renewal-of-life ceremony where three dozen men and women carry out a commitment to fast, dance, and pray in a nearby arbor for four days. An additional three dozen people from the community, including my father and I, came to camp out and support the dancers. At the time, I was more or less restricted from doing anything after a recent confrontation about drinking and smoking pot.

During a record-breaking heat wave, we packed camping gear into my father's camel-colored 1980 Mercedes and spent six hours making our way down I-5 without air-conditioning. I was in a foul mood. Whenever I uncrossed my legs, my skin stuck to the leather. I started to complain.

"Open the window," he said.

"No," I said. "It'll mess up my hair."

"Suit yourself."

"What am I even gonna *do* there, anyway?"

"You didn't have to come," he said.

We drove on in sweltering silence. I felt isolated and doomed. At home, my brother Aaron was going slowly and conspicuously crazy, coming out of his bedroom only in the evenings to chain smoke on the back porch, a habit he'd picked up during basic training, from which he'd recently returned. I looked out at the arid valley walls and regretted coming.

When we arrived at the remote campground on Pilot Rock I was still in a foul mood. Then I was informed that menstruating women are believed to carry an energy that has a powerful effect on the ceremony, and as a result, they'd constructed a camp about a half mile into the woods where they could participate in their own way from afar. The next morning I started bleeding, and to my deep dismay, I was to be whisked away to the Moon Lodge.

A petite gray-haired woman in hiking boots and a long denim skirt came down from the mountain and met me by my father. I was white with irritation as I slung my backpack over my shoulder.

"No," she said. "Let me. This is your time to rest."

With the single savvy swoop of a pioneer woman, she hoisted my backpack, tent, pillow, and sleeping bag over her shoulders, then motioned for me to follow her up a steep wooded trail.

"This is going to be fun," she said. "You'll be their youngest one!"

At the end of the trail was a meadow where a handful of women of all ages had pitched tents. Next to the meadow was a dusty tree-shaded clearing where a few others wandered barefoot or gathered in a circle of camping chairs, smoking cigarettes under a lean-to. I crouched down to help the escort pitch my tent, but she held up a hand. "Please." In the same mountaineering manner as before, she set up my camp in five minutes flat, then brushed off her hands and smiled at me. "You're going to like it here," she said. Then she hugged me, mashing my face against her neck, and left me alone in my patch of grass under the trees. I sat in my tent, crying at first, then I blew my nose and wrote in my notebook, all the while listening to the women talking outside, cigarette smoke wafting toward me.

Finally I emerged, grabbed a granola bar from the common cooler, and joined the circle. When I took a seat, a fleshy, freckled woman turned to me and said, "Oh, a child!" She handed me some beadwork to finish, and they continued the conversation they were all having about Depo-Provera and other rogue forms of birth control.

Over the week, women came up from the main camp three times a day to cook the Moon Lodge meals, deliver notes from friends and family, and generally make sure we were comfortable. Otherwise the women and I were left to do with our menstrual powers what we wished. I spent most of the time I was up there sitting in that circle, under the shade of scrub oaks, listening to the women talk about the trials of their lives. One was an anarchist living in an abandoned church in Brooklyn. Another was a stripper from Hawaii who was in the process of breaking up with her boyfriend. Another had spent four years in a correctional facility outside of Seattle. Another hailed from a Washington reservation, and her youngest daughter was about to have her second baby. Another was a Sioux woman from South Dakota who'd grown up on the Rosebud Reservation and served in Desert Storm, and whose husband committed suicide on Christmas morning, 1988. All of this was shared while they chain-smoked in that oak grove.

However, most of the women weren't ordinarily smokers. In the same manner that a cigarette is enjoyed, its glorification can last only for an instant. Smoking tobacco was part of their ceremony, passing-of-the-peace style, but snaring cigarettes into your writerly or otherwise daily routine is dangerous. I'd be lying if I said it didn't scare the hell out of me. After all, death's dark threat bore on me heavily enough to compel a preventative visit to the acupuncturist, reducing my intake to three a day and causing me to make near-future plans to quit. Cancer has so many correlatives; everything is a carcinogen, so I often dismiss studies, but the rest is indisputable: emphysema, blood clots, brain aneurysms, heart attacks, cataracts, strokes, bad skin, shortened lifespans. But then there are people like Kurt Vonnegut, who smoked unfiltered Pall Malls his whole life as a decidedly "classy way to commit suicide," but in a 2006 *Rolling Stone* interview threatened to sue Brown & Williamson Tobacco because, at eighty-three years old, their products hadn't killed him as the packages promised.

When I came down from the mountain after the ceremony ended, my father met me at the trailhead and we smiled at each other. I felt lighter. In the evening around our campfire, we ate buffalo burgers and drank root beer in the dark, and he looked at me and said, "You're a good girl." It was a gesture of fondness or acceptance, but I didn't like hearing it then—I felt like I was being rewarded for being dutiful, co-operative, a good sport. But I had just been cracked open. I'd sat on a thousand-foot slope in the shade rolling tobacco into prayer ties, on a rock face with a woman who listened to me talk about my brother's recent arrival home from the military and about how no one was listening to me. Later, she stubbed out her cigarette and bemoaned that she'd picked up smoking because of "those late nights studying and writing in college," and I pictured her hunched over a notebook in some seaside garret, and I thought that sounded just great.

Falling asleep that night back in the main camp, I thought of the women in the Moon Lodge, their sturdy grace, good advice, stained fingers. Being so young, I had not been invited to smoke, nor brave enough to ask. And anyway I hadn't had any real desire to, really, save that smoking seemed to reinforce these otherwise impossible bonds. It certainly could have happened with some other substance, but it happened with cigarettes.

* * *

Long after I've moved away from home and years since my last
Lakota ceremony, a service at my church in Providence, Rhode
Island, has just ended. Everyone is eating cake and coffee, talking
about their jobs, their week, the election, their mortgage, and some
people are even talking about the service, but only to say how much
they'd liked "the message," which that week might have been about
how we are all recovering idolaters, or how Christ meant for us to
live as communities of worship. (And "worship," a word that always
seemed so strange for Christ to have ever used in relation to himself—but the thought is interrupted, and doesn't return for a long
time.) If I really want to talk about religion, to face the difficulty of its
paradoxes, the moral ambiguity of what all the bright-faced congregants refer to as the "gospel-centered life," I have to step outside, on
the wheelchair ramp leading up to the front doors, where I will find
Tamy. She'll be standing there, tired, her long dark hair falling heavy
down her back, smoking a Marlboro No. 27, talking about the recent
adoption proceedings with one of her foster children. She'll laugh,
and her laugh is raspy, and it is the laugh, I understand, of someone
who has really tested the limits of belief.

THE LAUGHING VIRGIN

Flannery O'Connor

I n the winter of 1949, Flannery O'Connor took her first and last trip to New York City. She was fleeing from an "upset at Yaddo." Two friends of hers— sweethearts Robert Lowell and Elizabeth Hardwick—had enlisted O'Connor in their attempt to oust the colony's executive director for harboring a communist. There was a sort of petty hearing in Yaddo's common room headed by Lowell, after which not even the FBI, all puffed up from the Red Scare, remained interested. Instead, O'Connor and the other informants were attacked by friends in the literary community. Lowell and Hardwick felt wounded by the backlash, but O'Connor felt justified, "detachedly judg[ing] the assault to be an evil." She narrowed her eyes and crossed her arms and wrote to her friend with that wry certainty that inflects every syllable of her fiction: "As to the devil, I not only believe he is but believe he has a family . . . Yaddo has confirmed this for me." So the Lowells proposed a weekend of solace away from the scandal in their Manhattan apartment—which turned into a week, a month, a season.

Even though O'Connor ultimately hated New York, it was where her life opened in the many permanent directions she would be pulled until her early death fifteen years later. During that first rainy weekend after they arrived, Lowell introduced her to Robert and Sally Fitzgerald, a pair of intense Catholic converts, a literary critic and painter respectively, with a growing brood of children. All evening, O'Connor sat by the big window looking out at the Hudson piers and listening to Lowell bellow on to the Fitzgeralds about the Communists at Yaddo and his fine cross-examination at the hearing, while she maintained the signature stony stare she'd been bringing to parties since she was young, when she had been known to sit with "her face fixed in a look of utter boredom."

The Fitzgeralds remember seeing in her that first night in their apartment "a shy Georgia girl, her face heart-shaped and pale and glum." Sally notes in retrospect that this face did not prepare her for the ferocity of the girl's stories, which she read later, and which left her hair "standing on end." O'Connor, too, recorded impressions of her new friends: "Mrs. Fitzgerald is 5 feet 2 inches tall and weighs 92 pounds except when she is pregnant which is most of the time. Her face is extremely angular; in fact, horse-like, though attractive, and she does have the pulled back hair and the bun." The Fitzgeralds immediately loved this twenty-three-year-old writer, her inscrutable Southern accent and general lack of apology, her unwillingness to please or to smile, her "thirteenth-century" theological outlook. When O'Connor mentioned to the Fitzgeralds that she was trying to finish her novel, they invited her to their house in Connecticut to use the apartment above their garage as a private writer's retreat.

O'Connor thanked them, took a rain check, and tried to tough it out in New York. The only thing she really enjoyed in the city was the Cloisters, that old monastery crumbling above the West Side Highway in a little spit of forest. She'd walk the halls of Medieval art for hours but was less interested in the stoic tapestries and paintings. Instead she found herself always at "a smaller, four foot high statue of Virgin and Child, with both parties 'laughing; not smiling, laughing.'" Biographer Brad Gooch notes that the statue embodied "a profound spirituality that could accommodate humor, even outright laughter—a recipe [O'Connor] was working toward in her own novel," *Wise Blood*, which she labored over every morning after mass, the tale of a prophet for the Church of Christ Without Christ.

But she was growing desperately lonely. By then, Lowell, her one truly close New York friend, was already beginning to show signs of a psychotic break. He had been showing those signs with the manic energy he'd thrown behind Yaddo's Red Scare, but no one voiced alarm until he started showing up at Manhattan parties trying to convince his friends and confidantes that Flannery O'Connor should be canonized.

She was the last to hear about it: It was March 2 when he "received the shock of the eternal word"—the revelation of Flannery's sainthood—and after several years as a lapsed Catholic, Lowell re-baptized himself in the cold waters of his New York bathtub. Then he'd gone out looking for a book about St. Thérèse Lisieux, Flannery's birthday saint, and ended up buying her a book about a Canadian girl with stigmata. This, too, was a sign. And he thought of his brilliant young friend in her bobby socks and housedress and envisioned her suddenly in sackcloth, like the Medieval monks she identified with, and he knew he had to tell someone else, and eventually, of course, the church.

When O'Connor finally heard about Lowell's brief campaign to canonize her, he was already interred in an institution in Massachusetts. It was spring, and their mutual friends were tittering: Saint Flannery, Saint Flannery.

Shame on you, she'd said, for making fun of this friend whom she loved dearly, who had been just "three steps away from the asylum" when he was saying all of that. Absurd. All of it.

And yet right now, sixty years later, there is a wish among some Catholics to make O'Connor not only a saint, but a Doctor of the Church—a station of sainthood occupied by the likes of Augustine, Thomas Aquinas, and Teresa de Ávila, who get this distinction not only through the right number of miracles occurring in their name, but by being great teachers for the church, and for their profound theological witness. O'Connor would probably be horrified if she knew.

I first read Flannery O'Connor when I was a teenager, maybe sixteen. A selection of her stories appeared in one of those ubiquitous anthologies of female Southern writers, with a folksy black-and-white cover photo of kids playing on a farm, poking sticks into a mud hole. I sat on the heater vent in my parents' kitchen reading "Good Country People" while delicious, scalding heat forced its way up from the basement furnace below me.

My mother walked by, holding reading glasses and a folder of Independent Education Plans for her special-ed students, right as I reached the final scene.

"Woah," I said, looking up, "she's *crazy*," as the Bible salesman made off with Hulga's wooden leg.

My mother nodded. "Grandma's a big fan of hers."

The next time we visited Grandma Gale in Seattle, I sat in my usual spot on the burgundy sofa beside her reading chair, both of which faced the big picture window overlooking the street. We had been in the habit of exchanging book recommendations for my entire life; even when I was younger and only had YA novels to offer, she still read everything, took fastidious notes, and administered opinions through our regular letters and phone calls. So when I told her about reading O'Connor for the first time, she looked at me, nonplussed.

"Well, shit," she said, and gave me her copy of O'Connor's collected stories—a big ragged clothbound tome in a paper sleeve printed with a peacock—which I read in one sitting a dozen times over the next decade. Sinister Bible salesmen, prophetic children, gossiping moralizers, blank-eyed psychopaths, self-righteous PhDs, racist sharecroppers, bitter women, monstrous men—all of whom meet some violent spiritual awakening that, if they survive it, alters them so profoundly they may never be able to live in polite society again. That this writer could be famous for both her piety and her mercilessness was thrilling to me.

Years later, in college, I walked into my first day of Critic Practitioners, a small tutorial that focused on the reading and writing of literary criticism about one writer's body of work—whoever you wanted, for the whole semester. I was the only registered student. Professor Ben Lytal sat lithe and alert at his desk, helming an empty room, flanked by neatly organized reading packets, and we stared at each other from our single desks, and he said, "Well, let's see what we can do—"

We worked our way through a bunch of different takes on John Updike, who had just died, written over the last forty years, and decided that if we could enlist one more student before the end of the week, we would continue.

At Mike's Diner the next day, I sat with a few friends over breakfast, watching Amber debate furiously with someone else about the red-herring quality of the fight for gay marriage, an issue that she feared absorbed all the other issues for queer people: job security, healthcare, economic justice, suicide. I didn't know Amber very well yet—I knew she was a queer poet in exile from Tennessee who had almost gone to music school. I watched her refusal to relent in this argument, her laughter when her rhetoric got critiqued, the way she pulled her long blond hair into an elastic only to launch into her next argument long after her opponent thought he'd already said the last word. I knew that she volunteered for Radical Women, a New York feminist organization started in the 1970s, and spent her Sundays defending the entrance of an abortion clinic in the South Bronx. I thought, *If there's anyone I'd like to be a in a two-person class with, it's her.*

So how did I ask? "Do you want to enroll in this class I'm taking about writing literary criticism, with just this one guy and me?" She said yes, basically without blinking, and we remained the only two students for those four months, in a giant classroom, poring over books. It was riveting. We collaborated on reading sequences, work-shopped our writing, sparred, fought, and laughed, and Ben Lytal ended up designing the class entirely around our tastes. Eventually this meant we were learning exclusively how to write criticism about Flannery O'Connor.

New York, needless to say, fell apart for O'Connor quickly. Oddly, her only stories to have ever taken place there were her first and her last. "The Geranium"—a revision of which, called "Judgement Day," she would be finishing on her deathbed—is about an old Tennessee man in ill health who has been moved to his daughter's Manhattan apartment, bemoaning God's will at the end of his own grim life, and New York is dreary, inhumane, rendering its inhabitants anonymous and gray and hopeless. The story ends as the old man witnesses the destruction of his one last pleasure, a pot of geraniums on a windowsill across the airshaft, when it falls and smashes "at the bottom of the alley with its roots in the air."

By spring, O'Connor had gotten her fill, and with her novel-in-progress in tow, she finally left the city to shack up with the Fitz-geralds in Redding, Connecticut. There she "spent her days writing and her nights relaxing with Sally and Robert, discussing movies and literature while sipping on martinis" and joining them in elaborate Latin prayers before dinner. During the afternoons, she and

Sally took walks to the mailbox and tended the growing number of Fitzgerald children. At night, the "master of the house" retired to his study, in a move that is so timeless it makes me want to vomit, and Flannery and Sally split the dinner dishes. But it was OK: They talked about the nature of original sin, the consequences of grace, the language of the Nicene Creed, her stories, and Sally's paintings, which were all the kinds of things Flannery discussed in letters to other female friends over the next decade, developing together an understanding of theology that would become the foundation for her stories.

It's not as though she and her friends were reinventing or subverting religion—she was bearing continual, rigorous witness, through her letters, stories, and conversations, with the mastery of a theologian. O'Connor's Catholicism remained orthodox, in that she honored the papacy, received hermeneutical instruction from her priest, observed saint's days and drank the literal blood of Christ at every communion. Contrition was to be embodied, spoken in confessionals; messages between man and God were mediated by saints; the spiritual world had rank and order. And yet, literacy begets subversion—it must. The more religiously literate she becomes, the more desperate and deranged her characters. And how could her orthodoxy not have been affected by the charismatic Christianity of poor Southerners? Growing up, she was outnumbered by congregations that, belting cheerful spirituals, raised their arms to the sky, clapped her on the shoulder to say "Jesus loves you," and might, at any moment, have let some babbling vagrant waltz in off the street to enjoy the holy supper with them.

In addition to finishing *Wise Blood* in Redding, O'Connor wrote her first three stories after graduate school: "A Good Man Is Hard to Find," "A Late Encounter with the Enemy," and "The Life You Save May Be Your Own." The protagonists are an old woman embittered by the changing South, an obsolete confederate soldier, and a snaky farm wife who gets outsmarted by a drifter, respectively—all angry characters, believing they were owed something they did not get for their goodness, their sacrifice, and above all their hard work, leveling a critique that makes O'Connor, when I think of her now, sound kind of like a commie.

That first summer we knew each other, Amber and I went to an opera, or maybe it was an aria, in Greenwich Village that dramatized the trial of Matthew Shepard's murder. Our friend had composed it, drawing from the transcript language of Shepard's bereaved parents, and as we watched, I remembered news images of the "angels" who wore wings of white muslin to block out the Westboro Baptist Church protesters at his funeral. Afterward, we wandered around Lower Manhattan, talking. Is friendship, *philia*, the most communist of all the loves? Unlike marriage and family, it offers no structured economic gain, not directly. I use "loves" in the way that C. S. Lewis uses it in *The Four Loves*, which I was reading at the time: "Friendship is unnecessary, like philosophy, like art . . . It has no survival value; rather it is one of those things which give value to survival." We talked about Lewis and we talked about Marx.

Amber's grandmother had just been diagnosed with terminal leukemia, and in the gloaming, we walked to an Episcopal church on whose steps we sat and talked, about her grandmother, our families, baptism. She'd grown up gay in a family of Baptists and the Church of Christ, and she had all but left the church by that point. We drifted to a bar and ordered Coronas. I told her that I couldn't explain my conversion, or even whether or not what I'd done was convert, to most of my friends or my parents, and how I didn't want to get baptized until I could. I think the real impediment was that I couldn't explain it to myself. What had changed in me? How can people change? She laughed, this wonderful, devil-may-care sound, her eyes in a squint, and sort of waved her hand and compared it to the coming-out process: "You have to give them as long to accept it as it took you to realize you were gay—er, you know what I mean."

Then we read lines to each other from *Mystery & Manners*, or was it *The Habit of Being*, that near-religious book of O'Connor's letters that Sally arranged and published posthumously? O'Connor writes to someone—a teacher's college in Georgia, her best-friend pen pal—that she had always wanted to write a novel about a Simone Weil–like character, saying about the idea, "What is more comic and terrible than the angular intellectual proud woman approaching God inch by inch with ground teeth?" We laughed and laughed at this—it *is* funny!—and we were the only people we knew who'd find this comic. Then we walked east, caught a train back to my apartment, and sat on my living room floor and talked until dawn, and just never stopped talking. When my roommate woke up in the morning to find us splayed out and still awake on the knotty rug, he squinted at us and yawned. "What are you on?" he asked. When we admitted that we were on nothing, we looked at each other and laughed harder than we had all night.

Sometime after that Amber came to a service at my church in Williamsburg. We sang "Amazing Grace." We sang "Joy Is a Fruit." We listened to the parable about the laborers in the vineyard. In the parable, the master of the house goes out and hires laborers early in the morning. They toil away all day, and right before sunset the master finds another set of laborers who've been idle until then, and he sends them into the vineyard, too. At dusk, he lines up his hires and doles out an equal day's pay to everyone, even to the ones who came late. So the ones who've been there since sunup begin to grumble about fairness, but the master says, "'Friend, I am doing you no wrong. Did you not agree with me for a [day's wage]? Take what belongs to you and go. I choose to give to this last worker as I give to you. Am I not allowed to do what I choose with what belongs to me? Or do you begrudge my generosity?' So the last will be first, and the first last."

A little tremor went through our pew when the minister uttered "So the last will be first, and the first last." And Amber remembered this parable from her childhood days of the hateful Baptists—and she realized this story was why she'd become a Marxist.

But then, in an attempt to illustrate the parable's meaning, the minister made a disheartening analogy and the magic was lost. He knew a college professor once, whose students had done poorly, so he gave them extensions on their final papers. They complained about their grades, and so he threatened to fail all of them—"Or do you begrudge my generosity?"

We went back to Amber's apartment and poured whiskey into dirty glasses and agreed on one thing: The parable's charge is to take what God has given you and be glad, not to take what God gives you *or else*.

In late May 1952, after a long respite from her homeland, O'Connor was forced, due to a slipped kidney, to return to the South. She left some belongings at the Fitzgeralds' home, expecting to come back soon for a visit, and boarded a train to Georgia for the winter. At the farm in Milledgeville, her mother had just finished sewing a set of brown gingham curtains for the guest house as she gleefully awaited her daughter, as well as the arrival of a displaced family from the Soviet bloc.

A year later, O'Connor published a story in which Mr. Shortley, a live-in field hand, is replaced by refugee laborers. His outraged wife demands that their family flee their disgraced position, and then she drops dead from a stroke on their way out of town. The widowed husband returns to the farm and runs a tractor over the displaced person's spine while the man is crouched at work in the horse stables. The farm proprietress looks on at the attack but doesn't step in, "freezing them in collusion forever." The United States was late to accept displaced persons after the war ended, but by the time

O'Connor arrived at her mother's estate, more than six hundred thousand had been deposited around the country.

O'Connor was not thrilled to be homebound in this way; she was still very young, not ready to give her life away so quickly to illness. The doctors pumped her full of cortisone, still not sure what exactly was wrong with her, and then she returned as quickly as she could to a strict writing schedule, even in her weakened state. When she wasn't writing, she hosted visiting friends or maintained deep exchanges of correspondence that lasted the rest of her life.

After a two-year convalescence that was supposed to last only a couple of months, doctors finally determined that O'Connor had lupus, the disease her father died from, and only then did she send for her suitcases and books in Redding, order a pair of peafowl, and begin "getting home in earnest."

That first December, several months into her "short trip" home, she received a prayer card in the mail. It was included with her Christmas gift, a *Catholic Worker* subscription, which had been given to her by the only man she'd ever kissed, an ardent admirer of Dorothy Day (Flannery admitted a fondness for her later, too). The prayer card was "A Prayer to Saint Raphael," beginning, "O Raphael, lead us toward those we are looking for." Raphael was often thought to be the saint of friendship and marriage, and Gooch records in his biography that "Flannery would recite [the card's] invocation daily for the rest of her life," and that she was known to have said to friends that Raphael "leads you to the people you are supposed to meet."

Redding is a small village near the weird, woodsy heart of Connecticut. Its ribbon-like roads cut through forested neighborhoods where big Colonials have been rutted into the rocky landscape. During college, I used to take the Metro-North to Redding where Chanelle had moved, somewhat miserably, back to her parents' house, and one time I arrived in the throes of a nervous breakdown. On the train, I couldn't stop reading *Last Exit to Brooklyn*, which was horrifying, and though it hadn't happened yet, I knew I was breaking up with Sweeney, who was at that moment on a reactionary religious quest I had been closed out of.

I was crying by a tiny creek next to the train depot when Chanelle emerged from the trees on her bicycle, her blond hair and woven bracelets and linen scarves fluttering behind her. With a canteen of white wine in tow, we walked through the woods. As we passed a beetle rolled onto its back, she plucked it up, turned it over, and said, "It's things like this that make me believe in God." Then we lay down on the blacktop of a conservatory nestled just beyond the trail and listened to the breeze.

Chanelle and I first met years back through Sweeney, when, one night, the three of us made a drunken pact to drive to Savannah— and then did so the following week. I was nineteen, fresh to college, and I barely knew either of them yet. We drove through the night, stopping only to eat meals at IHOP and camp out in the sand dunes of the Outer Banks. We bought a carton of Basics, brown and red packaging, for $25, and by the end of the trip, they were gone. We listened to Elton John from a dying laptop because the car radio had been ripped out by thieves and we still had flip phones and no iPods. Chanelle sat in the back with a little notebook, scribbling, and Sweeney and I sat in the front, and sometimes the three of us would talk and tell stories of our lives, what seemed like every last one, which is what you do when you're on an endless car ride with two people you barely know, and then sometimes we'd fall silent.

One night we pitched a tent on a beach in North Carolina, then sat around the fire drinking Magic Hat we'd bought at a drive-through liquor store that looked like a barn. Then, later, the three of us were all snug in the tent, Sweeney and I whispering, zipped into a single sleeping bag, still getting to know each other. And on that night I got mad—mad enough to jump out of the bag, out of the tent, onto the sand. What was I mad about? I remember stepping out by the fire in my underwear and Sweeney following after me apologetically. It must have started innocently ("All our friends, everyone we grew up with, are, like, post-post-anarcho-liberals," we agreed, "committed to FREEDOM, but what the fuck does that mean?"). And then he must have told me that I was like that, too, didn't know what I wanted, "all over the place," no sense of loyalty, no commitment. I liked him, but I was sleeping with other people. I really did like him, but I wanted to be free. (From what?) And the fight seemed so serious for a second, the waves crashing, our arms waving by the dying fire, until Chanelle yelled, muffled from inside the tent, "SHUT UP shut up at least you can TALK to each other. At least you can talk! GOD."

The next afternoon, as we were getting off a commuter ferry to South Carolina, we each popped an Adderall and, still working through that carton of Basics, sped through marshland at sunset and were suddenly really high. We were interpreting passages about troubadours and romantic love from philosopher Alain Badiou's *Saint Paul* or C. S. Lewis's *Mere Christianity*, which I'd found in the dumpster outside of our apartment the week before. I kept shrieking, "I get it, I get it!" Somehow Sweeney was driving and reading simultaneously, and I was holding this little diagram he'd just sketched out of the way Ancient Greece had arranged its cities, with the temple literally highest above ground, visible from all parts of the city, a symbol of unity. For some reason this was astounding to me.

We arrived in Savannah just before dawn, in that post-speed metallic scraped-out lull, very tired and very still, and were more moved than we'd ever been by a place. It was sparkling. It was saturated, beautiful. We stood within the thick, sky blue walls of a cathedral. It was Palm Sunday and a homeless man from Serbia was folding fronds into roses, and we bought one. The air was dewy and warm, having come from the still-freezing north. Sweeney and I lay under a live oak in a graveyard and kissed and he said, "Did we just drive a thousand miles to make out under a tree?"

The next day we walked by Flannery O'Connor's childhood home, though I didn't realize it until years later: For my twenty-fifth birthday, Chanelle mailed me a volume of O'Connor's linoleum-block comic strips that she'd published in her college newspaper in the late '40s, and the book opened with a photo of that antebellum building, her childhood home. I couldn't believe it. We'd been so close and missed it! When we found out that she'd been in Redding, too, it began to feel like she'd been with us all along.

In 1955, at the onset of the worst years of her lupus, O'Connor was speaking at a women's college in Lansing, Michigan, when the peacocks back in Milledgeville got into the strawberry plants: "Mother took a dark view of them and I have to reestablish relations—as next year I plan to have twice as many birds as last." By now, she knew she'd never be able to permanently leave her mother's care in Georgia, and she'd garnered a menagerie of birds to keep her occupied.

In preparation for the Michigan talk, O'Connor had asked the woman who'd invited her about the audience there:

> I have made a good many talks in the past year, but all in the South, which is like talking to a large gathering of your aunts and cousins—I know exactly what they don't know—but talking to Northern ladies is a different thing. I can't imagine that there's anything they don't know. Maybe you could enlighten me a little on this.

Her problem was as follows: Are Northern girls unimpressed by blunt theological inquiry? Because, you know, she'd visited the *Mademoiselle* offices once while she was living in New York, "full of girls in peasant skirts and horn-rimmed spectacles and ballet shoes."

Despite her feeling of cultural separation, and despite her increased reliance on double-crutches clipped to her wrists, she began to give these kinds of addresses more and more, speaking about theology and fiction, art and God.

O'Connor spent some of her career shuffling up and down the Eastern Seaboard but the majority of it holed up on her mother's farm. She was a writer entirely "within and without" the rest of the country, her stories constructed from the raw materials of her homeland but with the unforgiving eye of an alien. Whether the stories take place in New York or Georgia, a grotesque character manifests, someone who has been supremely, at times cartoonishly distorted by their brokenness, their sin. O'Connor calls them freaks: "It is when the freak can be sensed as a figure for our essential displacement that he attains some depth in our literature." And by displacement, she means the one from Eden.

In another address, "The Fiction Writer & His Country," O'Connor writes, "I have heard it said that a belief in Christian dogma is a hindrance to the writer, but I myself have found nothing further from the truth. Actually it frees the storyteller to observe. It is not a set of rules which fixes the way he sees the world. It affects his writing primarily by guaranteeing his respect for mystery." As she gets sicker, her fiction sharpens, though her characters continue to have the same kind of realizations and violent ends. The mysteries get stranger, more subtle and more gruesome, and her final collection, *Everything that Rises Must Converge*, is the apex of this.

In the story "Revelation," Mrs. Turpin sits in the lobby of a doctor's office all afternoon, mentally and verbally judging the other patients: a woman and her daughter visiting from college, a white woman from a trailer park, and a young black mother. Unable to stop talking, Mrs. Turpin is finally attacked tooth and nail by a teenage girl who's been glaring at her for the duration of their wait. Mr. and Mrs. Turpin leave the office in a daze and go back to their farm, where, for the rest of the afternoon, Mrs. Turpin anxiously returns to her attacker's—the girl's—condemnation right as she'd launched herself across the room: "Go back to hell, you old warthog." She discusses this with her black farmhands, looking for someone's witness to her being "a good, respectable woman" of the South. Of course, it is her feeling of supremacy over the workers that prevents her from feeling consoled. She walks and rants and fumes. Finally, night falls and she goes out to feed her pigs. In the pen, Mrs. Turpin has a vision of a procession of people making their way toward Heaven: white trash, black people, "and battalions of freaks and lunatics shouting and clapping and leaping like frogs" in line on the bridge to God. It is not until the very end of the procession that she sees people she identifies with:

> They were marching behind the others with great dignity, accountable as they had always been for good order and common sense and respectable behavior. They alone were on key. Yet she could see by their shocked and altered faces even their virtues were being burned away.

The first shall go last, and the last first. This troubling of order and rank and class intensifies in the American 1960s, as O'Connor got closer to death. "You shall know the truth, and it will make you strange," she said—and it did begin to make her stranger.

The very last story Flannery O'Connor published was a revision of her first. "The Geranium" was that story about the old man in his daughter's apartment, bemoaning the end of his grim life, and it was the title piece in her 1946 Iowa graduate thesis. Its revision, "Judgment Day," she was still editing on her deathbed in 1964. In both versions, the old man stumbles in the hallway of his daughter's decrepit New York apartment building and runs into a young black man who attempts to help him from falling, to which this elderly white man slurs and complains. In "The Geranium," he then returns to his spot by the window to wait for his neighbors across the way to put the flower out on their windowsill, but at the end of "Judgment Day," he does not return to his window—in fact, the geranium is entirely removed from the story. He simply sits down and dies.

It appears that O'Connor used the geranium to write her way into this world—the world of religious irony, of dark comedy—and, upon arrival, no longer needed its assistance. In 1964, weak from lupus, a typewriter on her lap, maybe she was saying, "No more lengthy metaphors—this is about hubris and *death*. Always was."

But she wasn't done with symbols. Symbols were her greatest gift, those things, she said, which "are details that, while having their essential place in the literal level of the story, operate in depth as well as on the surface, increasing the story in every direction." While she was more famously quoted for saying, "If it's a symbol, to hell with it," the only thing she was referring to was the Eucharist.

One of my favorite biblical "moments" is when God visits Abraham and Sarah in the form of three men. It reads like a chapter that Flannery O'Connor would have written if she'd been around in the days of scrolls. As usual, God must arrive in a weird disguise so that the humans' heads won't explode. Anxious Abraham rushes to greet Him/them, tripping over his feet, fetching food and cattle and water—it's God! (Or is it three men?) Moments before, Abe had just been picking his teeth outside the tent in the horrible heat, feeling weird about the whole thing with Hagar and Ishmael. (Hagar is off-stage pounding roots into flour, shaking her head.)

God accepts the drink of water, the bit of bread, and squints at Abe's shabby digs. "Where is your wife, Sarah?"

Abraham says, "Sarah? Oh, well, she's in the tent."

And then God/the three men just come out with it: He's going to come back one year from now, and Sarah will have a son.

From behind the tent door, Sarah bursts out laughing and says, "Me? A ninety-year-old woman? Are you out of your fucking mind?" then slaps her hand over her mouth. *Shit shit shit.*

> Then the LORD said to Abraham, "Why did Sarah laugh and say, 'Will I really have a child, now that I am old?' Is anything too hard for the LORD? I will return to you at the appointed time next year, and Sarah will have a son."
>
> Sarah was afraid, so she lied and said, "I did not laugh."
>
> But he said, "Yes, you did laugh." (Gen. 18: 13–15)

What are you going to do, argue with God? Yes, actually, yes, because it is the only thing to do. O'Connor's characters are always picking these impossible fights, making the wrong choice (because, again, it is maybe the only choice) and O'Connor laughs—at them, with them—as she wastes away at thirty-nine years old. She sits in the kitchen with Sally, writes letters, makes jokes at the expense of God until God says, *Why did you laugh?* And O'Connor clams up: *I did not laugh.*

Yes, you did laugh.

Most of what I know about theology, or ways of approaching theology, I have learned from talking with friends, mostly women. The theology makes way for all kinds of the most beautiful things, but the culture that forms around the theology is broken. Dorothy Day knew this, and even though a young Flannery O'Connor once got swept up in the Red Scare, she eventually knew this, too. Jesus had a lot more in common with Marx and Dorothy Day than with the people Amber fought off outside of that abortion clinic in the South Bronx. So why keep caring? Because we haven't gotten to the punchline yet?

I've been to the Cloisters, too, though just once. I went looking for the laughing Mary and Jesus that had captured Flannery's attention during her lonely season in New York. And I've seen it—at least I think I have. Looking into one of the main halls, I could see a large Catalan statue of a healthy, plump-faced Virgin and child, both with open smiling mouths. But when I walked in and looked around, I realized that there were three other statues of the Virgin and the Child, and they were all laughing.

DEAR LINDA

Linda Goodman

Toward the end of her life, Linda Goodman's favorite movies were *Gone with the Wind* and *Brother Sun, Sister Moon*, both of which she regularly screened for her friends in the rambling Cripple Creek, Colorado, home she lost to bankruptcy just before her death. A giant stained-glass window depicting St. Francis de Assisi cast blues and oranges across the carpeted parlor where, once a week, this famous American astrologer would mouth "as God is my witness" along with Scarlett O'Hara. Following the films, she'd cart everyone off to the Palace Hotel on Main Street for a three-course dinner that she'd cover with a combination of estate jewelry and the small fortune she'd amassed from her astrology books' sales.

Goodman was a beautiful woman. In her earliest public portrait, a black-and-white author photograph for *Sun Signs*, she is leaning forward, her eyelids heavy with makeup, her high cheekbones defined by shadow. She's wearing a turtleneck and her hair does a Nancy Sinatra flip at the shoulders. In a press photo ten years later, she's redheaded with a raised eyebrow and peach skin so smooth it looks painted on. Then there's a point-and-shoot photo from her late Cripple Creek days, in which she stares directly at the camera wearing a Navajo-print T-shirt, her palm planted on a golden bust of Osiris sitting before her on a coffee table.

I remember sitting at my own coffee table one night in Brooklyn, flipping through *Love Signs* and finding an appendix I'd never noticed before that brought the weirdness of Goodman's worldview into sharp relief. My copy of *Love Signs* shared shelf space with the English Standard Version Bible and *The Collected Stories of Flannery O'Connor*, and though it was weathered from reference, here was this thing I'd never noticed before, like a hidden track on an old album: a reproductive treatise in the appendix called "A Time to Embrace." In it, Goodman argues for all forms of modern birth control to be replaced with a family-planning method called "astrobiology." She allows that "whether abortion is right or wrong is not the Aquarian issue," then, in the next paragraph, writes, "The Catholic Church has taken the view that abortion is an act against Nature and against spiritual Wholeness. The Catholic view is correct." It was funny, that lack of self-awareness, an idiosyncratic style so complete she could thread Christianity and references to the planet Vulcan into the same world, the same cosmology. It was funny, yes, and emboldening, considering my own awkward position transversing secularism, the occult, and American Calvinism.

During those years, because of my apparent interest in the subject, I was frequently asked to interpret astrological charts for my friends and friends of friends, and I eventually learned to read tarot as well. Both the Western zodiac and the tarot are constructed from similar forms, archetypes, and patterns, and can be used to interpret one another. If I found any use of them for myself or others, it was not because of their predictive powers, but rather the way the zodiac organizes things that are already happening, that have already happened. I often felt compelled to say, "I am not telling your fortune. I'm showing you what's going on and what you might be inclined to do next. If you don't like your current inclination, it's up to you to change it."

Soon I was being hired to read cards at art openings and book launches, and I even had a few clients. My roommates and I were hosting regular literary salons at our apartment, and a young man who sometimes arrived on uppers dressed as Arthur Rimbaud and read excerpts from his sinister, mystical poems invited me to a service at his Presbyterian church in Williamsburg, which I ended up attending every Sunday until I left New York.

I sometimes picture Linda Goodman in her final years, standing in the glow of her stained-glass windows, and I wonder how she knit it all together—the magi, the magic, the church, the channeling of ancient wisdom, the writing on the wall—or didn't.

If you've never heard of Goodman, you'd likely recognize her book jackets anyway, if only because of the sheer number that remain in print. Her second *New York Times* bestseller, the 900-page *Love Signs* written in 1978, bears the iconic Alphonse Mucha portrait of a priestess orbited by the Western zodiac. Flip over the book and you'll find the sorts of teasers you see on monthly horoscope booklets in grocery store checkout lines:

"Can a Gemini man find happiness with a Virgo woman?"

"Will it be smooth sailing or perpetual fireworks between the Scorpio female and the Libra male?"

"If you're a Taurus, you will love or hate Scorpios, nothing in between."

But inside, *Love Signs* is perhaps the weirdest, most verbose, conversational mishmash of astrological writings to ever have graced commercial bookstore shelves. In a chapter detailing the various incarnations of a Virgoan-Aquarian relationship, Goodman writes:

> The Aquarian male's eccentricity often stops just short of the altar. In his choice of a lifetime mate, he tends to be slightly old fashioned. Maybe that's because there's room for only one cuckoo in a clock . . .
>
> Since a Virgo female won't compete in the cuckoo-clock Olympics, you can see that a mating between these two can work out nicely . . . For one thing, she's too discriminating to flip over all the odd, assorted friends he may bring home at various hours. (I know one Virgo wife whose Aquarian husband expected her to play hostess to a snake wrestler from Pakistan for two weeks while he practiced with his reptile in the basement in preparation for the worldwide Python Tournament Match—and that's a *true* story.) For another thing, she's not a torrid sex symbol. But let's face it, he might not know what to do with Raquel Welch if he had her.

This casual style is consistent throughout all of Goodman's books, each of which is penned in the first person. Every chapter in *Love Signs*—most of which are lengthy insights on astrological pairings (e.g. Scorpio woman and Taurus man)—is introduced by an excerpt from J.M. Barrie's original *Peter Pan* script, with secondary sources spanning the Gospels, Plains Indian cosmology, Henry James, and "Dear Abby."

In that slim addendum I stumbled upon, "A Time to Embrace," she opens with a verse from Ecclesiastes: "To everything there is a season . . . a time to embrace and a time to refrain from embracing . . ." She charges readers to heed the scripture's message and find ways to make their actions "*harmonize* with the flow of cosmic currents, rather than timing them to *oppose* these powerful forces." She goes on to dismiss the use of birth control, artificial insemination, and other reproductive innovations on account of being against "Universal Law":

As the ancients who planned the conception of Kings knew well, a woman can conceive only during a certain, approximately two-hour period of each Lunar month, when the Sun and the Moon are exactly the same number of degrees apart as they were at the moment of the woman's first breath at birth . . . Without exception, a woman can conceive at no other time than this approximately two-hour period, easily determined if her birth data are known. Each individual woman's "cycle" is different, bearing no relation to the generalized, and consequently inaccurate, so-called "rhythm method." It's absolutely foolproof. And awesomely profound.

The book is peppered with these polemics. It begins with several title pages of quotations from the Bible and one from a fifteenth-century pope. These introduce a long letter to Goodman's daughter Sally, who overdosed on speed in 1973—a death Goodman believed was a cover-up by the government—which she addresses openly and in good faith to a Sally she's convinced is alive and reading it in 1978.

Since its first printing, *Love Signs* has sold over eight hundred thousand copies. Goodman's total sales, according to the *New York Times*, amount to more than 30 million. Accompanied by other mystical uprisings of the 1960s and 1970s, Goodman's books uniquely suggested that astrology was for everyone. How such unusual texts became an American blockbuster is no surprise: Most people scan astrological books as quick and affirmative reference, reading only the parts they believe have bearing on their own lives. Thus the birth chart's complexity is reduced to cartoonish archetypes, and Goodman's rambling meditations and appendices are lost to obscurity, remaining as unexamined as the woman who administered them.

The United States might be the only nation to have made its astrologers both famed and tawdry, with dual statuses of celebrity and hack. While earlier Euro-occultists like A.E. Waite and Aleister Crowley had formed brotherhoods, ministries, and esoteric origin stories, their midcentury American counterparts were advising movie stars and presidents, writing columns, and generally benefiting from the free market according to their calling. And while the U.S. government dignified the practice with a federal union in 1938, any public understanding of the tradition has been diminished by the print news demand for two-sentence horoscopes with our morning coffee, affirming harmony and passionate sex.

After reading hundreds of near-identical obituaries of Goodman as well as a handful of magazine features, the only non-book-jacket-type biographical information I could find came from a now-defunct website called Colorado History Chronicles, where a local historian had been selling articles for fifty cents apiece since the 1990s and happened to have written one at Goodman's passing in 1995. This is where I read about her community standing in Cripple Creek as a generous eccentric who kept her friends closer, perhaps, than they wanted be, and also of her neighborhood screenings: two films that seem to express the strange place she occupied as an American writer and occultist. One is the story of the lavish fallen antebellum heroine, the other an affectionate biopic of St. Francis. Somewhere in the hang of Scarlett O'Hara's dreams of "better times," Goodman's acute sense of victimhood, the communion of saints, the American Indians, the resurrection of the body, and casual encounters on the astral plane is the sum of this unlikely celebrity's legacy.

Goodman migrated to Cripple Creek, the site of the last Colorado gold rush, shortly after *Sun Signs* reached the *New York Times* bestseller list in 1968. It was her first book. She was forty-three years old then and had already, reportedly, cycled through twin careers as a radio personality and a copywriter, reading aloud soldiers' love letters during the Korean War and, somewhat inexplicably, speechwriting for Whitney Young, the black American civil rights leader who, during Goodman's reported tenure, served as president of the National Urban League. Born Mary Alice Kemery in Morgantown,

West Virginia, "Linda" created the pseudonym during her years broad-casting *Love Letters from Linda* for Parkersburg's WCOM. Goodman was her second married name, which she took on in her early thirties.

This is the gist of what's available of her pre–*Sun Signs* life, digested and repeated ad infinitum from cyberspace to microfilm. The rest of her legacy has been hijacked by a Tumblr of excerpts, a Twitter account operating in her name, and what appear to be forums run by compulsive-posting New Agers—and no book-length biography exists to date. When I asked her former agent, Art Klebanoff, how he interpreted her low profile, he said, "Linda was basically opposed to dealing with the media. The one interview she granted to *People Magazine* during the years I worked with her ended up focusing on the death of her daughter and did not cast Linda in a favorable light . . . Indeed, the fact that Linda was inaccessible was probably a marketing plus." While reports of her work with Whitney Young are printed in all of her obituaries, Klebanoff said he is not even sure this is true.

In that 1979 *People Magazine* article, which opens with a portrait of Goodman tending the woodstove in her Cripple Creek home, reciting the St. Francis prayer ("Lord, make me an instrument of your peace . . ."), her late husband Sam O. Goodman attests to her interest in astrology beginning when he brought home John Lynch's *The Coffee Table Book of Astrology* in 1962. She pored over its pages while the children were at school and Sam, a disc jockey, was at work. "I think she stayed in a nightgown studying astrology twenty hours a day for a year," he recalls. Once everyone was out the door, she'd sit at her cane-back chair, slumped in that tiny kitchen with the lights off, her Victorian nightdress still smelling of sleep; she wouldn't change positions, not once, and by sundown she'd be surrounded by legal pads wrinkled from note-taking.

Perhaps Sam silently agreed to start cooking dinners, taking charge of the kids' hygiene so his wife could carry out her vocation. He was an even-tempered man, Linda's wary but dutiful supporter, who, while never quite believing in what she did, gave her the benefit of the doubt.

When news reached them of Sally's death in 1973, Sam was the first to fly out to New York, where Sally had been studying at the American Academy of Dramatic Arts. Linda and Sam were already separated then, though still friendly, and she was holed up in Cripple Creek, caught in a fraught publishing debacle that had frozen her advance for *Love Signs*, rendering her temporarily penniless. When she was finally able to join him (on a friend's dime), she spent seven months couch-surfing and sleeping on the steps of St. Patrick's Cathedral while she tried to debunk what she believed was a corrupt investigation. The suicide note, she swore, was not in Sally's handwriting. There was no empty pill bottle in the apartment. And above all, she didn't "see" death in Sally's birth chart, but instead, as she mused in *People Magazine*, "shock, amnesia, seclusion, and a convent. I've heard the government hides lots of witnesses."

What were those nights like on the steps at St. Patrick's? Did she slip into a green nylon Coleman sleeping bag, surrounded by candles and a small St. Francis figurine? I picture Sam, as I imagine he always behaved in these situations, with a dark furrowed brow, saying, "Now come on, Linda, let's get a hotel room," or "As upsetting as this is . . . ," pacing around the church's landing, meeting the eyes of concerned passersby so as to assure them that everything was fine, everything was going to be OK.

My father's second wedding was officiated by an astrologer named Joanna Mitchell. This was in the mid-1990s. The ceremony was held in a deconsecrated church in Northwest Portland, and the guests—a mix of Catholics, rogue Episcopalians, and Old Order Mennonite descendants—fell into a confused hush as Mitchell began calling in the four directions, her big, shimmering body swathed in purple cloth. My new stepmother habitually referred to the zodiac in conversation with me, occasionally giving me doe-eyed pats on the shoulder when she'd remember I was a Virgo. I was seven then, and I'm not sure how I knew what she was talking about, but I did, and it stuck.

This was in elementary school, when Scholastic book order forms were passed out every month, with four-page newsprint pamphlets featuring kids' books available at competitive rates. These were highly honored in my mother's house. I was allowed to circle whatever I wanted, and she would clip out the order form and mail a check. In the third grade, among my selections was a blue paperback astrology book with "early reader" profiles of the twelve sun signs and accompanying cartoonish portraits: a Capricorn girl wearing furry boots and a headlamp; an Aquarius boy with a SAVE THE WHALES T-shirt.

I hauled that thing around with me for years, and I began memorizing the sun sign of every single person I met. Immediately I'd arrange their detectable characteristics in my head, cross-reference them in the book, and file it away for later use. This grammar-school astrology became a lens through which I acquainted myself with the world. It was, for the most part, a silent practice, barring the ingenious ways I'd weasel out birth dates from unsuspecting subjects. And somehow, through this, I created a Rolodex in my head of all the signs' nuances. Gemini: angular face, "nymph-like," quick, funny, rapid-fire decision-making mistaken for fickleness, holds a spoon like *so*. Taurus: shapely arms or legs, rooted, warm, well-behaved though contrary, unperturbed by all manner of taboo conversation. Leo: a striking or plentiful head of hair, friendly, hyper, "devil-may-care" demeanor, down for just about anything.

Around the time I first acquired the astrology book, much to the confusion of my parents, I'd begun attending a local Baptist church with my neighbor Kelsey and her family, a group to whom astrology was sacrilege. I don't recall why I'd gone—maybe I'd slept over and the family had invited me as a matter of course. Either way, I remember only a glimpse of the thick orange glow of the sanctuary, a young Southern minister and his chubby wife sitting in the wings with a new baby in her lap. Then Kelsey and I were sent upstairs to Sunday school, where an old woman with a curly brown perm taught us a psalm and then we played games and filled out word puzzles. There's a Polaroid she took of me, standing beneath my nametag on the door, clutching my *Pocahontas*-themed sweater. The room was small and carpeted, and the gray Portland light clashed with the buzzy yellow fluorescents, and for some reason, for many years, I kept going. My mother, who'd attended at most a few Unitarian services as a child, tolerantly came to my Christmas pageants, while my stepfather, a traumatized ex-Catholic, once-born-again Baptist, and brief Scientologist, would offer an unsolicited "Yep, there's no God, no aliens, no God" when he drove me to school in the mornings.

I kept both of my spiritual interests private for many years, examining charts and saying prayers I didn't understand until I started hanging out with punks in the seventh grade. Then, at thirteen, I denounced Christianity as a capitalistic hoax—a rebellion unnoticeable to anyone but me.

For my sixteenth birthday, my father and stepmother took me to Joanna Mitchell to have my birth chart read. Her practice operated out of a brightly painted Victorian cottage on the outskirts of Eugene, and she met her clients in its A-frame attic. We arranged ourselves around a card table, and she pushed her long brown hair behind her shoulders, clicked record on a small tape deck, and said, "What do you want to know?" What did I really care to know at sixteen, or rather, what was I capable of even articulating? I asked some vague questions: Where would I be in a year? How were my prospects for international travel that summer looking? Should I let go of my ex-boyfriend?

She focused, instead, on the fact that something to do with my parents' early divorce would cause me to spend a great deal of the next few years "building a toolbox," that I was obsessed with fairness, that I could expect to feel the obstinate and frightening pressure of Saturn until 2009, that I was particularly prone to health problems from narcotics, that I'd spend a great deal of my life in pursuit of familial belonging, that I was a writer—or a dancer. "Are you a dancer or a writer?" she asked.

In college, I was given *Love Signs* by a girl whose friendship I sought mostly for her beauty, and who handed the book to me saying that the writing was great but it was heteronormative and made a lot of references to the Equal Rights Amendment and had outdated ideas about "career women." "Otherwise it's great," she assured me. One of the last nights we spent together was over a dinner in Midtown, and on my walk back to the train on 5th Avenue, I passed the entrance of a giant office building engraved with the twelve signs of the zodiac and, above them, what appeared to me in that moment to be the twelve apostles encircling Christ. Shortly after, I read that Goodman identified the beginning of her astral pursuit at the moment she was baptized, in third grade, in the Parkersburg, West Virginia, Episcopal Church.

It's hard to find people willing to talk about Goodman. I reached out to her two youngest children and got silence. The publisher at Taplinger, who first put out *Sun Signs*, said he could not share any biographical information that was not already available. Many of her friends were celebrities, or are now very old, or dead. I finally was able to track down a man named Mark Aulabaugh, who grew up in Goodman's neighborhood and used to work at the station where she broadcast *Love Letters from Linda*. In her early twenties, his mother had been among Goodman's closest friends in Parkersburg. Aulabaugh now runs a local station in central Texas, and he took my call between programs.

"She was one of the first people my mother met when she moved to West Virginia as a newlywed," he said.

It's funny, my mother always referred to her as "Mary Alice," not Mary . . . At that point, I believe Mary Alice was working for the newspaper, something small, like the obits.

They hung out all the time. On Fridays and Saturdays, my folks would invite people over to drink, and she was always a part of those get-togethers . . . I remember Mary Alice always looking really, really gloomy . . . In old photographs, everyone is smiling and having a good time, but she was always frowning, like she had a chip on her shoulder. But then somewhere along the course of the evening they could cheer her up and she'd be real fun.

I was good friends with her old boss at WCOM, Jack See, until he died a couple years ago . . . He always had so much respect for her. He used to talk to me about how they'd go out and get coffee somewhere after work and talk philosophical stuff. Jack said she was one of the best writers of commercials he'd ever met, and also that she intimidated people . . . I don't know, maybe because she was kinda weird?

I asked if he recalled whether or not she was writing then.

"There used to be a little bar called the Car Barn she'd go to in the daytime, and she'd take her portable typewriter and sit in a booth in the back and write. No one really knew about what."

She wasn't writing about astrology in 1953, so what was it? Metered poems or short stories? Perfecting her top-notch copy? Coming of age in postwar America, during the years women were being filtered out of the workforce and into the suburbs, into a domestic ideal most closely resembling the Victorian era, I wonder if she knew in advance that she'd have to write something larger than life, that in order to do anything professionally creative, she'd have to make a spectacle of herself, or be spectacular.

I can see her smoothing her rumpled work clothes as she settles onto a vinyl bench in her favorite smoky corner of the Car Barn, clacking away on that portable typewriter, hiding out from a marriage that would soon dissolve, from boredom, from babies, from

weekly parties where no one talked about anything she found interesting. She'd continue to seek hiding places, even after publishing
her wildly successful *Sun Signs*. All of her subsequent contracts subsi-
dized the completion of her future books to take place in a particular
second-floor room at Hollywood's Roosevelt Hotel, an inn whose
renovations were long overdue, where Art Klebanoff visited her once
and remembers "the towels covering [his] body in color."

But it's not as though Goodman disowned all of that culture she
came from. For instance, she remained a member of the Daughters
of the American Revolution until she died, purportedly winning
West Virginia "Daughter of the Year" in 1971. She also took seriously church history and her own early experiences among the Episcopalians, a church that formed right after the American Revolution,
when once-Anglicans refused, or were forbidden, to keep pledging
allegiance to the British monarch. She was never fully willing to
admit the mutual exclusion of occultism and patriotism, motherhood
and fame, Christianity and astrology. These are powerful paradoxes,
and paradox is the substance of almost all religion, all those sacred
contradictions: barren women who conceive, prophets born as peasants, kings as slaves, the meek as brave, the poor as rich, the enslaved
as free, granted a will but only by the grace of God.

From the inconsistent information available publicly and from her
own books, I know this: Linda Goodman was a woman of paradox.
She was a proud mother of seven, though only five survived beyond
infancy, and she was possibly estranged from most of them. She was
intensely patriotic, though she believed the U.S. government was
behind a cover-up of Sally's death. She was a Franciscan lay scholar
and a Vatican enthusiast despite having been raised in an American
tradition that developed, more or less, in revolt from the Catholic
Church—not to mention that she was otherwise considered a heretic. She was a critic of astrologers and advisers who charged for their
services, though she was among the highest-earning authors of her

era. She sold the paperback rights to *Sun Signs* for a record-breaking $225 million but died bankrupt. Among friends, she was considered both needy and reclusive, often asking her confidants to spend the night so she didn't have to be alone. She was a celebrity and a hermit. She was born in the East and died in the West, ten thousand feet above sea level. She was part of the first generation of diabetics to have access to insulin but opted instead to become a "fruititarian," which may have led to the mid-leg amputations toward the end of her life and her death at age seventy.

On July 14, 2002, seven years after Goodman's death, her remaining belongings were auctioned from the Colorado home she'd lost to foreclosure. In the descriptions from the Colorado Springs *Gazette*, it sounds like the slim pickings of a garage sale. Among the detritus was a "bronze ram's head, four pairs of white Minnetonka moccasins, [an] avocado-green blender and [a] dented blue tea pot." Fans flocked to the auction from all over the region but were disappointed to find not much more than cheap furniture and kitchen goods, a cache of Sweet'N Low hard candy, a few coins in an Almond Roca container labeled "petty cash," an old photo album bookmarked with a cigarette stub, and a roll of toilet paper. The *Gazette* quotes a scavenger saying, "I guess I expected to see more stars and moon sculptures, cool stuff like that . . . It's typical stuff my grandmother would have in her house."

As with any person survived by children and grandchildren, Goodman's loved ones probably sweated out her last days together, then collected her precious belongings according to a will. But even that's unclear: Klebanoff doesn't even know who inherited her copyrights. He said she had "what was described at the time as one of the larger personal bankruptcies in Colorado history. The earning power of her books ultimately meant that nearly all creditors were paid off one hundred cents on the dollar—nearly unheard of," and that ultimately her intellectual property was invested in a literary trust overseen by a Colorado bank. "I have no information about the underlying beneficiaries," Klebanoff concluded.

Neither her most ardent fans nor her closest professional peers could conceive of the human realities of Goodman's life, but because the narrator of her books was so intimate and personable, the auction-pickers felt entitled to her relics. As Klebanoff told me, "She got a never-ending stream of mail, all of which was addressed, 'Dear Linda.'"

WHO WANDERS UNENCUMBERED

Aunt Robin

hite light from the motion-censor bulb strikes her narrow figure, hunched over a paperback. She reads standing up, lighting each Pall Mall off the last. Her hair, a yardstick-length for sure, swirls with smoke. It's nighttime on a public housing balcony, thirty identical cubes overlooking the Atlantic.

What might it have felt like for my Aunt Robin to read some version of her own words in what was, in 1986, the newest novel by her favorite author? She'd owned the book for a few months, but, too excited to read it straight through, had read only sections at random. On this night she flips to page 123 ("One two three!" she says now, astonished) and yells to no one: "Fuck! He stole my line!"

The book is Tom Robbins's *Jitterbug Perfume*, and my Aunt Robin's line, from her graduate thesis in psychology, was a long and glittering "drink list" masquerading as Diagnostic Question #28:

28.) You are sitting in Webster's doing your "Go-do-something-alone-that-you-wouldn't-normally-do-by-yourself" assignment, for this class. You've had two sloe gin fizzes, three martinis, one shot of tequila, two beers, four rum separators, one flying tiger, two coffee nudges, two scotch-on-the-rocks and a gin and tonic to quench your thirst. You haven't eaten all day. You are slightly inebriated. You are trying to write in your notebook about your alone assignment when Prince Charming/Princess Delight comes up to your table with two Kahlua sours and asks if he/she can join you. You:

A) Throw up.

B) Pass out.

C) Tell him/her you don't drink.

D) Other (PLEASE EXPLAIN)

   (Clue: It's not A, B, or C.)

The line in *Jitterbug Perfume* is:

Two slow gin fizzes; two fast gin fizzes; three martinis, dry no starch; twenty-eight shots of tequila, three beers (a Bud, a Tree Frog, and a Coors lite), seven rum separators, five coffee nudges, two Scotch and waters, five vodka and buttermilks, a zombie, a zoombie, four tequila mocking birds, thirteen glasses of cheap white wine, a mug of mulled Burgundy, nine shots of Wild Turkey (hold the stuffing on three), one Manhattan (with eight cherries), two yellow jackets, fifteen straitjackets, thirty-seven flying dragons, nine brides of Frankenstein, and a green beret made with sweet vermouth and in place of grenadine, banana liqueur. Amen.

At the time, Robin was thirty-one years old and was living on Block Island, a small community just off the New England coast, in the island's only public housing facility. For money, she sold quilts and hand-dyed greeting cards, was a dispatcher for the island's only taxi service, and cooked at the Barrington Inn. Recognizing her words in that drink list was among the most edifying moments of her life. She'd been writing letters to Tom Robbins continuously since 1972, initially in response to an ad he'd posted in *Rolling Stone* calling for a research assistant, preferably "female, ages 18–25." Though she didn't get the job, she continued writing to that address in La Conner, Washington, all through college, and even afterward. She told him about her life, her story ideas—"everything," she says. "I probably told him things that were too personal, way too personal." Naturally, this included her entire graduate thesis, the origin of Question #28.

The thing is, he never wrote her back—not once—but she couldn't stop herself. This phantom pen pal had become her touchstone, her gauge of a life lived. After rereading page 123 a few times, and a pack of Pall Malls later, she plunked down by her typewriter and wrote him again. Shortly thereafter, she received her first, and only, response:

Dear Robin;

Okay, I think I get it now. Someone—obviously you—did send me a long list of drinks that they'd promise to buy me if we could meet in a bar, something like that. And then a few days later I was writing about a waitress placing her order with the bartender, it was fresh in my mind and I decided to fashion her order after that list in the letter. However, I think I'm correct when I say that I invented a lot of new items and changed about 90% of the list, so that it was more a case of being influenced by an idea than wearing somebody else's underwear. In any case, T. S. Eliot said that the difference between an amateur writer and a professional is that an "amateur borrows, a professional steals."

And then he wished her "a cozy winter on [her] island," signing off with, "May the snowmen sing Latin love songs outside your window."

Of course, hers was never a concern of intellectual property. It was that, in the most extraordinary and accidental way, she realized that Tom Robbins had actually been reading her letters all along, that writing to him for fifteen years wasn't all for naught, that life might still have purpose and measure of some kind.

I can't help but think of Franny Glass in Salinger's largely epistolary novel, whose nervous breakdown is catalyzed by the fact that her brothers didn't see her Summer Stock performance, rendering her art in vain, all of it for nothing but "ego." At the very end of the book, Franny rises from her weeklong stupor on the family sofa to answer the telephone in her late brother Seymour's room. On the other end of the line is Zooey, who, unable to get along with her face-to-face in the living room, finally decides to phone her from inside the house. He tells her that he and Buddy had, in fact, seen her perform that June, and that the crowds were too thick to find her afterward. He says, "And I'll tell you, buddy. You were good. And when I say good, I mean *good*." After that moment, Franny, like my Aunt Robin, knew everything would be all right, that all the major promises would be kept.

My family history is punctuated by its men performing larger-than-life acts and then waiting for their fruition for a very long time. It's not a lineage of dashed hopes and abandoned dreams but rather a delirious optimism. For instance, my grandfather George built a tower on top of the family's bungalow in the early 1960s, where he holed up tirelessly, following the stock market through two recessions, convinced he'd make millions. In the 1970s he bought a dozen bundles of shingles with which to re-roof the house by himself, and those shingles sat on the porch from the summer my mother first brought my father home from college until 2003, when they were all finally thrown away and a contractor was hired. By then, an intricate series of tarps were keeping out the rainwater, my parents had divorced, and my grandmother had moved out.

But she eventually moved back in, after those outstanding repairs of nearly thirty years were completed. And my grandfather did eventually make a lot of money in the stock market, although he's lost most of it now. He's in his mid-eighties and uses two canes to get around the house, but he still goes up to his tower every night to listen to those numbers, waiting.

Before that, George's father abandoned him to start another family not too far away, and his mother, serene, unwilling to impose on anyone, was happy to let my grandfather go on statewide bicycle trips by the age of twelve, traverse the new Olympic National Park by fifteen, ramble across the country with a bedroll and an old Peugeot at twenty. And her mother, a schizophrenic Christian Scientist whose husband killed himself before their children were grown, was raised by her wealthy aunt in Elsah, Illinois, while *her* father, Eugene, tarried after his frontier fortune in the Washington Territory, becoming its thirteenth, and notoriously failed, governor.

Eugene's father founded a midsize city on the Mississippi River, and Eugene's father-in-law still looms over the Portland, Oregon, Park Blocks in the form of a bronze statue, oblivious to the city's eventual success. All through high school, my brother Aaron plotted to become an iconoclast, a sort of mastermind, learning how to hack, poring over *The Anarchist Cookbook*, jumping out of second-story windows after amassing a crowd, disassembling classroom chairs and tables so they collapsed when the next group came in, doing lots of drugs, and generally building a lone-wolf mystique among his brooding peers in haunts like the Burnside Skatepark—and then, at the end of it all, after going missing for two nights, he came home to announce he'd joined the army. And everyone said, *That's weird, but good for you!* And that was that.

A certain brand of obsessive compulsion mixed with psychosis is the cross my family bears, but as usual, the men are treated mythically, or at the very least affectionately, and the women as just crazy. By my seventeenth birthday I'd met my Aunt Robin only a handful of times and was just beginning to wonder why.

I knew that a week after her twenty-sixth birthday, Robin taped a note to the upstairs bathroom mirror, then boarded a Greyhound bus in downtown Seattle and headed east. It was 1978. Well beyond an age that necessitated it, and with no one, not even Robin, attesting to a particular trauma, she more or less ran away. Three days later, after crossing the entire country, she was let off in Providence and caught the next ferry to Block Island, where she lived for the next decade. Imagining both the journey and the impulse behind it, I think again of men, as essayist Annie Dillard also thought of men in her litany of "the culture into which we were born" at the end of *An American Childhood*. "American culture was Dixieland . . . was the stock-market crash . . . the World's Fair in Chicago, baseball, fancy nightclubs in Harlem, silent movies, summer stock theater . . . the sandhogs who dug Hudson River tunnels, silver miners in Idaho, cowboys in Texas, and the innocent American Indian Jim Thorpe, who had to give all his Olympic gold medals back." And then, "Above all," *above all*, she says:

> it was the man who wandered unencumbered by family ties: Johnny Appleseed in our own home woods, Daniel Boone in Kentucky, Jim Bridger crossing the Rockies . . . His heroes, and my heroes, were Raymond Chandler's city detective going, as a man must, down these mean streets; Huck Finn lighting out for the territories; and Jack Keroac on the road.

Back home, Robin's friends speculated that such brash decision-making was in her free-spirited nature, whereas her siblings linked the fleeing to her drinking problem. Those were two ways of looking at it, and another was that Robin had cut her losses and relinquished the frontier that her great-great-grandfathers had so fastidiously secured.

Ten years later, she and my mother both found themselves several months pregnant. My mother was living in New York at the time, and she took the Block Island ferry from Montauk to see what she could do to help, and also to see if Robin was considering adoption—which she was not, and they fought bitterly about this. Over the years, I've happened across a lovely photo of both sisters under that Block Island sunset. They're each plump-faced with long dark hair, wearing purple tie-dye and purple flannel maternity shirts, respectively, arms around each other at the ferry landing, a meeting to which they were the only witnesses, other than the mysterious photographer. After-ward, my mother returned to the city, gave birth, and named me Adrian, unsure where she'd gotten the name. A month later, Robin gave birth to Galen, who she thought looked disturbingly similar to his "paternal unit," who'd all but taken off by then.

Eventually we moved to Portland, and she moved to Astoria on the Oregon Coast, but my family only visited when passing through on our way to Washington. I remembered the rickety Victorians she lived in, the apartments full of books and trinkets and milk crates and hand-dyed greeting cards drying on a clothing line. And then I recall not seeing her at all for a few years. I listened to my family's stories about how, as an infant, Robin used to rock ceaselessly back and forth in her crib, how her first drinking buddies were friends from Young Life, how she got kicked out of school for wearing a hippie skirt, col-laged every square inch of her bedroom walls, wrote reams of stories, and made all of her own clothing. She was immensely creative, they'd say, visionary, but she was also erratic, needy, occasionally paralyzed by anxiety.

In the meantime, I'd started writing and reading and feeling increasingly separate from my family. My bedroom was a peeling shrine to my life: layers of wallpaper, painted over, curled at the edges; buckets and boxes teeming with every note I had ever been passed in class; scraps of newspaper; alluring magazine cutouts. Photos and books were squirreled away in cluttered systems of albums and boxes. Art postcards and old transit maps and a *Ziggy Stardust* poster and bits of wood were tacked to my walls, and scarves and necklaces I'd never wear hung on my desk chair, next to which sat a plastic wagon stacked with used printer paper, old drafts I was determined to recycle by writing letters, compulsively, several a week, to friends who were far away, or close by, or authors I loved who were still alive.

I was working part-time and watching my brother go crazy. Right before I turned seventeen, Aaron was sentenced to the Oregon State Hospital a year after he'd sliced off two of his fingers and doused his rental house in rubbing alcohol, then burned it to the ground. My family split down the middle—those who thought he was dangerous and those who thought he was helpless—and I felt unmoored. I remember it taking me forever to leave the house, gathering last-minute items, delaying, and then being on a bus with a friend and saying, "Don't you feel sometimes like you might just pass out?" and my friend did not. I remember visiting my grandmother and watching Todd Solondz' film *Happiness* together and feeling sickly certain afterward that the world was just as dark and arbitrary as I'd always suspected.

That summer I had not stopped moving around: I'd traveled to France, Seattle, San Francisco, and, finally, I was backpacking deep in Northern California's Trinity Alps with a friend, having reached a sort of stillness, and I was suddenly paralyzed by the thought that I might lose it, too. My mind raced, against my will, across every terrifying possibility. When I shut my eyes, all I could see was a future of sweaty isolation, great acts of violence, my brother's house going up in flames. As a salve, I started reading *Even Cowgirls Get the Blues*, a birthday present from my mother, every night before I went to sleep. When I got back home I started writing Tom Robbins a letter.

In the wake of this, unexpectedly, my mother suggested we visit Aunt Robin in Astoria. "She's not drinking right now," she said.

R obin's belongings were stacked in Chiquita Banana boxes, and bookshelves lined the walls, blocking her windows. She was waist-deep in Xeroxed pages from dictionaries, neatly preserved cereal box packages, and pencil cans. For the first time in my life, I saw myself in her.

"One more minute, just one more minute," she said, rushing from room to room, filling her purse with pencils, gum. "Sorry, just one more minute."

She'd been making the pencil cans for as long as anyone could remember: old soup or coffee cans hodgepodged with bits of magazine or wrapping paper. "It's my therapy," she said. "Galen's paternal unit said I couldn't have a baby because I'd lose it in one of my pencil cans. And you're too early. I'm not ready yet. I'm wearing my funny old jeans. Let me put on some nicer clothes."

We all went for a drive along the seashore. From one end of a tunnel to the other, I held my breath and wished that I would not become my Aunt Robin. As we roared into the light, Robin let out a huge, ragged breath and, one arm over the headrest, said, "Did everyone make a wish?" Only the two of us had.

We drove to the Circle Café on the Washington Peninsula, a sandy-floored cup-n-saucer on the edge of the beach, and ordered lunch. My mom smiled but didn't say much, and Robin told us stories, talked to the waitress about local history, drew pictures on her napkins, and ordered a Reuben.

"I almost named Galen 'Reuben,'" she said. "When I was pregnant with him, his paternal unit's mother used to take me out for lunch every week, and I'd always order Reubens, and she'd say, 'But wouldn't you like something else?'"

Back in the car, she turned to me and asked, "What have you been reading?"

"A Tom Robbins book, *Even Cowgirls Get the Blues*," I said. "I just finished it. I actually started this letter to him the other day——"

"Oh yes, Tom Robbins, Tom Robbins," Robin said. "I've been writing him letters since 1972."

My mother looked at me in the rearview mirror.

"Yeah, oh yeah," Robin said. Then she told me about the ad in the *Rolling Stone*, the years of unanswered letters. "I still want that job," she said.

After lunch, we drove back to her apartment and decided to stay for a cup of strong black coffee. While we were crowded onto her sofa, gripping our mugs, she grabbed a copy of *Jitterbug Perfume*—she evidently had eight—and said, "I didn't tell you the rest of the story."

She continued: "I was living on Block Island at the time. I was writing him letters but not as many. I still hadn't heard back. And, well, one of the letters I'd written him had included part of my college thesis. I was studying psychology—I know, *me*, right? One night, I flipped the book open to page one-two-three . . ."

On our way back home in the car, I turned to my mom and asked, "Do I remind you of her?"

"Oh, there's a little of Robin in all of us," she said, smiling out the windshield. But then she added, "There *are* some definite similarities."

That week, I sent my letter to Tom Robbins.

My friend Maggie and I have been working as back-up file clerks at the American Federation of Musicians headquarters for a year or so. We get paid under the table because when we started, we were barely sixteen and because they don't tax our paycheck and because we're cute and have straight teeth. And because my dad works there. About a month ago we were up there and Maggie threw down a stack of receipts written out to William Hunkapiller (or something) and exclaimed, "I want to be a prairie girl and Tiger Lily and an Earth-First hippie who clings desperately to trees, and I want to be valedictorian and an astronaut and a mermaid!" She collapsed into a box of files. "Do you see my dilemma??"

Because I was currently reading a book that starred cowgirls who, at one point, believed it impossible to be cowgirls, I told her she had no dilemma. Dr. Robbins, I hope you know what you're talking about. Right after I wrote the first draft of this letter, my mother and I drove up to Astoria to visit my aunt and cousin. We almost never visit them. When I told my aunt Robin I was writing you, she proceeded to tell me about how she's been writing you for twenty years about a paragraph you borrowed from a letter she wrote you in 1979 and published in "Jitterbug Perfume." A drink list to be exact. She makes pencil cans and sews and lives in small spaces with too many things. When she was fifteen, she sewed a dress made entirely of the tabs on the back of Levi's Jeans and sent it to the headquarters in San Francisco. They were so taken aback that they offered her an internship after she graduated high school.

Tom, she has this fantasy that if she were to work as your research assistant for three and a half months her problems would be solved . . .

I remember drawing hopscotch in the driveway of my mom and Leo's rental property when I was seven or eight years old, and hearing Aunt Robin call herself an alcoholic. It was during one of her rare visits. She was sitting cross-legged against the green garage, a can of Pepsi wedged in the crook of a thigh. She looked at my mother when she said it, waiting for a response. Robin's tan, knobby knees popped up and down like a pair of wings, and she twisted her long black hair into a single rope and then brought it over her shoulder to braid. It must've been when she brought her arms over her head, her shirtsleeves falling back, that I noticed, for the first time, shiny skin grafts left over from a childhood kitchen fire. They sagged and rippled on her otherwise slender arms. My mother nodded and said, "Mhm," relieving Robin's remark of its gravity. The only other scene I remember from this visit happened later in the car. I asked my mother what an alcoholic was and she said, "Someone who can't drink alcohol."

For many years after that, I imagined my aunt as being fragile, prey to this strange allergy. I even felt a little sorry for her, having to resort to Pepsi while the other adults drank wine, and I was subsequently disoriented a few years later when alcoholism was redefined for me as, in fact, drinking too much alcohol. I don't know who told me, but I remember feeling the subtle shift, though still maintaining a sense of her vulnerability. I thought of the way she tells the story of the kitchen fire. "I was in third grade, and I was leaning over the stove making soup, and my sleeve caught the flame for just a second, but I didn't notice. The next thing I remember is my mother coming in and trying to beat the fire out, but all I can think is, 'Why is my mother hitting me?'" Nearly fifty years later, she tells it exactly the same. "I mean, eventually I understood," she says. "But *why did I think my mother was hitting me?*" After all this time, what does it matter, and why can't she get this image out of her head—an image neither accurate nor indicative of the course of her life, yet ever-present, insistent, branded? This sort of cripplingly obsessive, frenzied engagement with the world and her life, this sort of seeing or feeling too much, or more than is useful, is what I recognize in myself.

In a 2015 *New Yorker* article published shortly after *My Life on the Road* came out, Gloria Steinem, who was raised by her single mother in the 1940s and 1950s, describes her mother's institutionalizations and subsequent pharmaceutical addictions:

It was only much later, when I began to understand how unjust the position of women was in this country, that I knew my mother had never been "ill," as the doctors claimed. It was that her spirit had been broken. Until then, I had always worried that I might have inherited something—that I'd start disappearing into the street in my nightgown, the way she had.

Years later, my mother and I found ourselves in Seattle, helping my grandparents clear out their own hoard of belongings. Buried in one of the old bedrooms was a thin hardbound volume called *Research, Reflections, and Recollections of Block Island*, filled with informal historical and geological facts, as well as personal anecdotes from the author. Folded in its endpapers were three cryptic letters addressed to my grandfather from Robin, dating from 1982 to 1984, with final sentences like, "I ~~apolozize~~ apologize for telephoning at the hour I did, but I don't regret the call." I'd continued to be frightened by my own certainty that I would turn out more like her than anyone else in my family, a fixed path toward unpredictable bouts of obsessive compulsion, mania, bridge-burning, and poverty. I opened the book and the first thing I read was:

In 1614, Block Island was charted by the Dutch explorer Adrian Bloch, which is why, until it became part of the first colonies, locals called it "Adrian's Island."

That July, I booked a room in the oldest structure on Block Island. I brought three notebooks, a package of pencils, old photographs, a pouch of tobacco, and that little green volume. At night in the Hygeia House, I read *Raise High the Roof Beam, Carpenters* and listened to foghorns from the parlor sofa. For three days I bicycled around the island, classifying plants, cataloging historical sites, wandering around the inns my aunt used to work at, drinking beers in the same places she might have. But the whole island seemed to conceal some essential piece of itself, and I felt none of the recognition I thought I would. I haunted her old haunts and wrote down every story I could remember her telling me about her life on the island, imagining it might reveal itself to me through this incantatory process. But I left understanding less of the place and my aunt than I ever had before. I condensed all worthwhile findings down to three pages, ending with this sorry, scrawled note:

> The first thing she saw from the ferry were the mud cliffs, sixty, seventy feet above sea level, and then housetops sticking out of the brush, one-by-one-by-one. Hollyhocks, rosehips and cypress trees made a dense wall that hid its contents. Then she docked in the Old Harbor, took a short walk uphill to The Barrington Inn looking out over the New Harbor, and started housekeeping: it must have been a mess. She frequently saw the same people, or no one at all. Most seasons, business was slow. The National Hotel stood three-stories high but swayed empty usually, its white sea-shakes flapping. There was a boat in the marina called "At Last" whose anchor line had grown thick with algae. The last abandoned building on the island was turned into a hostel in 1999. And anyway, she wasn't there then. She isn't here now.

Like any expedition, this accumulation of evidence said little about its topic precisely because it could only attest to what was visible, and further, what was visible to me: things that bridged me to a past I longed to understand. Each known fact acted like a star, the possible narrative imposed like a constellation. The mysteries of my aunt's life, the nature of the island, and my own familial inheritance still hung in the gaps. When I arrived at Block Island, I had trained my eyes to see only the ghosts and previously dreamed-of topography, and because it wasn't there, I couldn't see or write anything beyond that.

But I knew that she saw things, that she was openly angry at her mother and the rest of the family, that she was like the madwoman in the attic who'd come stuttering down the stairs telling some awful truth right as someone intervened to whisk her away, rushing to retie the gag. I remember watching her approach my grandmother at one of the last family Thanksgiving meals we ever had all together. She touched my grandma's shoulder with one hand, holding a glass of wine in the other, and she started to cry, started to say something, and my grandmother didn't turn to face her, just patted her hand and said, "Oh, come on, there now. I love you, too." That night, Robin slipped away from the gathering early, and after years of sobriety, she stayed out at a bar until four o'clock in the morning.

And while my concern about self-fulfilling prophecy faded, it was replaced with a deeper, quieter fear about the particular kind of isolation I saw in her, the paralysis of a mystical impulse, creativity overtaxed by frenzy. Is this what happens when you know too much?

Weirdly, I did end up living in Rhode Island, after all of that, though for reasons I never could have foreseen and which had nothing to do with her. I lived high up on Smith Hill in Providence for a little over a year, and all the while I kept the first letter I'd received from Tom Robbins folded in a book on my desk. He'd written it on stationary monogrammed with "Villa de Jungle Girl" and a cartoon of a leopard-skin-clad pinup girl. It's dated 2005. "Dear Adrian," it begins.

> In the past, when I would receive a letter written with as much charm and verve as yours of October 4th, I would respond by encouraging the sender to consider turning his or her hand to a novel or at least a short story.
>
> As you might imagine, many of them already had. In any case, the example of fiction which I later received from them invariably was devoid of that freshness, wit and originality that had made their

epistle sparkle . . . I've learned my lesson and where you are concerned, I'm just going to keep my mouth shut.

I do recall having fairly recently received mail from someone named Robin Adair. I also vaguely recall receiving, many years ago, in the context of a letter, a drink list, and that I took that list and improved it (expanded it, punched it up poetically, etc.) and used it in an appropriate place in *Jitterbug Perfume*. However, I did not connect the two, did not realize that Ms. Adair was the author of the letter that contained the original list. You must understand that I receive a great deal of mail.

My letter, that seventeenth summer, had reached him just before a major eye surgery that would be putting his "literary activities in limbo," and he apologized that he had no use for a research assistant, though he wished he could help my aunt. Tom Robbins and I corresponded for a couple of months until the complicated corneal surgery put his writing on the back burner, but not without first explaining to me that he had merely "borrowed" my aunt's drink list, and that writers were allowed to do that. But what he really meant was that *men* were allowed to do that.

MEET ME IN LILY DALE

The Fox Sisters

I hurry toward Lily Dale up a local highway edged in rows of corn dwarfed by drought. It's a sweltering summer afternoon. Each upstate town I wind through shares the shuttered look of has-been industrial communities or the eerie stillness of vampire covens. A teenager in a lone burger shack sells me an ice cream cone, and I inhale it against the heat on the hood of my car.

I prepare myself for a potentially disappointing Lily Dale, the colony of a Victorian religion probably made cheesy by the moneyed New Age: collections of crystal shops, deluxe motor homes, plastic angel mobiles, something like that. I get back in the car. I pass a rodeo field, an abandoned school, a pub called the Witch Hut, and I recall that Rod Serling grew up in this region. I can suddenly see *Twilight Zone* everywhere, its endless streets and existential conundrums: it's the end of the world but your glasses break; the streets in your town connect in an endless loop; you wake up in a dollhouse and your life is governed not by the hands of God but the hands of a little girl.

I turn off the highway onto a wooded road, Cassadaga Lake glittering through the trees. Finally, I'm at a toll booth: "LILY DALE ASSEMBLY—world's largest center for the religion of Spiritualism — est 1879." I hand my $10 to a young man, and he waves me through.

On the other side of the booth is a simple Victorian town made shabby by time and isolation. I pass a post office, a county firehouse, an old hotel, and gingerbread homes in varying states of disrepair, then I park in a gravel ditch behind a carriage house, its paint, at this moment, being chipped at by two uniformed men. A bell clangs for the two-thirty worship service.

The Old Assembly Hall provides cool, cavernous shade as I pass under its arched doors. There are large glassless windows but no electric light. Without a word of greeting, an old woman hands me a laminated hymnal, and I walk toward a congress of folding chairs. Once settled, I face a stage flanked by blown-up photographs of Lily Dale's grounds during the late nineteenth century next to a set of principles, the first three proclaiming:

The fatherhood of God
The brotherhood of man
Continuous existence

The last of those refers to Spiritualism's central belief: that the life of the soul, Spirit, is literally eternal, "continuous," after the decay of the physical body, allowing those who have passed away the ability to communicate with the living. The cornerstone of the religion is the practice of mediumship—communicating with the departed, who, in turn, can lead us toward a more perfect society on Earth.

A woman with a thick Eastern European accent explains from the stage that, because of the stifling heat, we don't need to stand during the service. Then she says, "We need to raise vibrations for our speaker today. Let's go to page twenty-three—'He's Got the Whole World in His Hands.'" So we sing this old spiritual, and as I flip through the hymnal, still singing, I notice that traditional songs have been slightly revised. Words like "Christ" are replaced with the generic "love," and "providence" with "angels." My favorite line in "Amazing Grace" is changed to "'Twas Grace that taught my heart to sing" rather than "to *fear.*"

A middle-aged male minister rises to the podium. "Who here knows much about the religion of Spiritualism?" Only six people, myself included, raise their hands. As I suspected, most guests must have come for the summer events, held from the solstice until Labor Day weekend, hoping to make contact with dead parents, children, ancestors, or looking for guidance during a dark night of the soul, or they're Catholics who told their families they were going to a spa or to the beach and instead snuck off to this metaphysical compound in the spooky rural reaches of the Finger Lakes. It's also then I notice that nearly all seventy or so people present are women, middle-aged or older, and white—and they look a lot like my tarot clients.

A year earlier, I was scraping by in Providence, Rhode Island, making part of my income reading tarot at a New Age shop called Andromeda's Alley. The guy who vetted me for the job was of old Boston Spiritualist stock and had spent his childhood in parlors with his medium grandmother. As a control, he had me read for a friend of his, a woman who had popped in during a lunch break. I pulled three cards: weird dreams, a feeling of inadequacy, a baby. She burst into tears and told me she was pregnant, unexpectedly, at forty-five years old.

In the weeks that followed, I noticed that my being a young woman was initially off-putting to clients (they'd see my smooth, hopeful face smiling at them from the back room), and then, a few minutes into the reading, my youth became comforting, inviting. I'd face them straight on and have them cut the deck a few times. I'd ask that they not tell me anything—not even ask a question (because it's always the wrong question anyway). I'd put my hand on the deck, recite the Lord's Prayer in my head—always the Lord's Prayer, I don't know why—and just get a couple of quick pictures in my mind, not the whole story of their life or anything, but enough to know how this person needed to be treated and a whiff of who or what was haunting them.

I read mostly for women—women who'd lost custody of their children, old women, young women, scorned women, depressed women, widowers, bankers, small-business owners, psychiatrists, beauticians, the recently fired, the recently sober. Catholics were my primary customers, and I often began readings by assuring clients that I was not telling their fortune but just seeing things—mostly the present and the past—and having a conversation about those things through the cards. This wasn't euphemism, but I also knew my audience, these wary people who'd sneak in after work or during lunch, feeling like heretics.

The church, and the Abrahamic religions in general, is openly dismissive and even damning of anything having to do with divination, as the fear is that some kind of idolatry is taking place, or a sort of blasphemous attempt to become God-like, to see "God's will," or posit God-like intercession, and this is especially threatening if conducted by women—all them witches, you know.

And yet, at that time in my life, every Sunday I was going to church in the basement of a vocational high school around the corner from Providence's historic Italian Federal Hill district. I'd sit in the middle row of a mess of folding chairs and sing these saccharine contemporary hymns and listen to the hour-long sermons, and I would cry, almost every time. It was a strange period.

But here I am at Lily Dale, back among a familiar set of people, a group that is by and large out of its element. The minister has begun his lecture, though I've missed the first part while taking in my surroundings.

"I'm from the Southern Baptist tradition," he says. "I didn't want to have much to do with church until I was an adult" excepting "funerals and weddings." He tells the story of the out-of-body experience he had in his twenties after a car accident, when he first learned to communicate "in Spirit." He says that, during the brief moments following the accident, he saw his "whole life, past, present, and future . . . and communicated with my relatives and ancestors." Sitting before him now is a big leather-bound Bible that he calls "an atlas," and then he concedes that, under different circumstances, he might be consulting any other book—this just happened to be Americans' primary religious text in the mid-1800s when Spiritualism came about. This admission seems extremely odd to me, and it undermines some of the urgency of the moment.

Early on in the movement, there was certainly serious anxiety over assimilation. In Sir Arthur Hill's 1919 *Spiritualism: Its History, Phenomena, and Doctrine,* he deliberately aligns the religion with Christianity but acknowledges sectarian dissent. He cites a contemporary Anglican bishop's remark on the movement: "There have been more people sent to Hell through Spiritualism than by all the bullets and shrapnel in [the Great War]," to which he asks, mocking that Protestant absolutism, "Has he been there to see for himself?" Hill argues, for his early-twentieth-century religious readers who are seeking permission to believe that spiritualist phenomena doesn't jeopardize their current beliefs,

It will be seen that there is nothing heretical about [Spiritualism]. Indeed, it is more Christian than many forms of modern Christianity, for it brings back into prominence those important facts, survival and intercommunion, which were taught by Christ, but which, as we have already noted, have in these latter days increasingly lapsed into a dim region of uncertainty if not actual disbelief.

Of course, these are not the kind of debates contemporary Spiritualism generally concerns itself with.

I drift back into observation. Not one person around me appears to be wearing the costume of mysticism, like I'd expected. They are dressed, rather, in tourist shorts or fanny packs or loose cotton T-shirts from J. Jill. As far as I can tell, I am the only attendee in my twenties, which is interesting, as is the fact that the minister is male. Because it was women, especially young women, who were the harbingers of nineteenth-century Spiritualism.

We should get this out of the way: In 1888, Maggie Fox gave a tell-all confession to a New York newspaper, admitting that the religion for which she and her two sisters had been patron saints for forty years was a hoax. When the interviewer probed for remorse, Maggie dabbed her eyes and said, "That I have been mainly instrumental in perpetrating the fraud of spiritualism upon a too-confiding public many of you already know. It is the greatest sorrow of my life . . ." She praised God for the courage to go public, slugged a bit of gin from a screw-top flask in her purse, and cried into the interviewer's lap.

Maggie and Kate Fox were twelve and fifteen years old when, shortly after the first day of spring in 1848, they ushered Spiritualism into the world. The Fox family lived in what was a notoriously haunted house in Hydesville, New York, where they often heard footsteps, doors slamming, and irregular tapping noises issuing from all corners of the building. Eventually, the two sisters took it upon themselves to attempt communication with the restless spirit through a series of responsive "rappings" on the kitchen table, after which they were able to determine the spirit's identity as that of an itinerant man who'd been murdered in the house not long before the Foxes had moved in. Those rappings, to use the now-departed Spiritualism minister Alice

Hughes's phrase, were heard "around the world." When the Fox sisters' séances started to attract neighbors, and then Quakers, and then the religiously restless from across the country, to demonstrate their powers of mediumship, a movement was born. All Americans, even WASPs, could talk to the dead, and teenage girls would facilitate.

But 1848 is an auspicious date. There was a lot of reform going on. It was the "Spring Time of the Nations," when Marx rallied the proletariat under the call that a "specter was haunting Europe"—not the ghosts of murdered men, but the specter of communism. That communism swept the continent at that moment not as an ideology but as a phantom, as something that haunts, is no accident. It implies that these uprisings abounded, not by the shock of something new, but of something revealed, a voice that had been whispering the secrets of the peasants' discontent for centuries. That same year, France abolished slavery, calling further into existence a burgeoning Western notion of human rights, making visible, as if a light had been suddenly switched on, the blood of black bodies on America's hands.

What's more, the Second Great Awakening was, in 1848, at its peak: an American Protestant movement that prioritized personal testimony and mystical revelation over institutional authority. Methodists and Freewill Baptists dispatched uneducated clergy, men and women, black and white, across the countryside to spread the news that all people were subject to God's messages. Inevitably, then, God was, it seems, revealing as many new ways to live as there were people interested in carrying out movements: Millerism, Mormonism, Jehovah's Witness; the Holiness movement, the revival movement, the African Episcopal movement, and a thousand brands of agnostic, pluralist, or Christian utopianism.

And just a few months after the Fox sisters' rappings, down the road from their home in Hydesville, the first women's rights convention took place. When Susan B. Anthony and E.C. Stanton stood at the pulpit of the Wesleyan Chapel in Seneca Falls, announcing that woman's destiny was up to "her conscience and her God," they were, as much as the Fox sisters, riding the Awakening's wave. The Awakening had arrived at the inevitable question, as put by scholar Ann Braude: "Why would God set men over women to guide and protect them and then choose more women than men to have wills perfectly attuned to Him?" Suddenly the disenfranchised—women, blacks, the poor—were all potential prophets, and everyone had better listen.

But things got strange for the Fox sisters rather quickly. Their elder sister Leah got involved in their Spiritualist celebrity, too, and for several years following, she leased their supernatural gifts to the management of P.T. Barnum, and, later on, a dozen other for-profit executors. Sir Arthur Conan Doyle, a Spiritualist himself, reported a sad scene involving the Fox sisters after a public séance ten years into their career. The three young women stood by as they were harassed by throngs of skeptics to prove their powers, and:

> poor patient Kate Fox, in the midst of a captious, grumbling crowd of investigators, repeating hour after hour the letters of the alphabet, while the no less poor, patient spirits rapped out names, ages and dates to suit all comers . . . Can one wonder that the girls, with vitality sapped, the beautiful, watchful influence of the mother removed, and harassed by enemies, succumbed to a gradually increasing temptation in the direction of stimulants?

The Fox sisters remained Spiritualist mediums, advisers, and orators off and on for the rest of their natural lives, drinking and sniffing doctor-prescribed powders, slowly turning on themselves and each other, spreading rumors and plotting to have each other's children taken away. They married men—rich men, controlling men, arctic explorers, Catholics, men who died suddenly from heart disease. They converted to other faiths, then abandoned those and returned to the Spiritualist lecture circuit when they were poor and had burned bridges. All three sisters were estranged by the end of their lives, and Maggie and Kate died in middle age, within months of each other, of alcohol abuse–related disease.

However, as important as they'd been to the religion's origin, their tragic ends went largely unnoticed by the Spiritualist community, and Margaret's late-life confession didn't affect believers any more than any prior refutations. As early as 1851, the Fox sisters had undergone tests that ostensibly proved that the rappings issuing from the rooms during their psychic meetings were being produced by one or another's double-jointed knees or toes, depending on the source. But by then the religion had spread like wildfire, with factions, newspapers, and hundreds of major and minor celebrity mediums holding court to a captivated public all over the nation. Anyone could own an Ouija board, and Spiritualism had produced a whole workforce of mediums, mostly young women, who were paid in spades for their vocations.

And anyway, a year after Maggie's confession to that New York paper where she claimed it was all a hoax, she gave an equally tearful retraction, saying that she had wrongfully defamed Spiritualism, that the rappings *were* authentic, that she'd only given in to diabolical pressure from her sister, her agent, her drink—but that the spirit world was real, as real as you or me.

Toward the end of the minister's lecture, he leads us in a long concluding prayer before introducing Mary Ockuly, the visiting medium for the day. Ockuly has short gray hair and has been sitting behind the pulpit with a slight silent smile for forty-five minutes. She says that she spent the first thirty years of her life as a nun among the Sisters of Humility of Mary in Ohio, and that her journey to Spirit has been a long one. She positions herself in front of the podium and, in a small voice, says to an older woman, "You—have you received a message today?"

The woman shakes her head.

"I have a message for you. A man is standing behind you. He says his name is Henry thank you. And his house burned down, I see flames thank you. He says he loves you, wants you to dig something, you know what it is, out of a sock drawer thank you. You'll need it. He says it's time that you started to think more highly of yourself . . ."

I wonder if these images, the image of this Henry, are as apparent to Mary Ockuly as a photograph, or a television screen, or if it's more like watching the live charades of a flesh-and-bone human. She squints. She interprets. She expresses gratitude when something comes through. She speaks in fits and starts. Does she see the man with her eyes or with her mind? Does she have to imagine, to some extent, before she can see anything at all?

And have I ever seen a ghost? If I have, what was it like? I am reminded of a whole year during my childhood where my dad's house smelled strange—musky, fishy—the source of which none of us could discern. I was eight or nine years old. One afternoon, one of my stepmother's friends was visiting, and while they drank tea and tuned their instruments in the living room, her friend looked at the empty futon couch and cocked her head. "There's someone sitting there," she said. "His name is Ted." The friend was already a known seer of things from the other side—this was just the kind of company we kept—so it was Ted's presence that surprised us the most. From then on, we joked that the smell was from Ted. And it was all fun and games until the sun went down, and the hallways and stairwells of the Victorian house grew dark, and I found myself skittering out of unlit rooms, watching over my shoulder. I always felt like I was about to see a ghost.

At the time, my dad was studying with Jan Englesmith, the Shamanic healer connected to his Lakota hoop. He came home one night and said he'd visited Ted in a vision quest that Jan had led. In the quest, he'd walked into the house, our house, but it was much smaller, there was no living room, and it had old, weathered 1930s wallpaper. And there was this middle-aged guy with thinning hair, looking very confused, standing in the doorway. He kept asking where his wife was. My dad told him that she was gone, she was OK, though. And Ted looked at him, more bewildered than before, and then—just like that—the confusion melted from his face, replaced with a softness. And then a sort of chariot appeared, with horses, and he got in—in the living room?—and it carried him away. This was how my dad told it.

Later that week we found a nest of dead baby possums in the cellar. They had apparently died because my dad had repaired a hole in the house's foundation, which must have sealed the mother possum outdoors. After that, the smell in the house went away.

I don't think it's quite that ambiguous for Mary Ockuly, but I have to imagine it's close.

The service ends and I walk outside to a hot bench. I dig out a copy of divinity scholar Ann Braude's *Radical Spirits* from my bag and flip to an 1857 daguerreotype of Cora Hatch, a world-famous Spiritualist medium at seventeen years old, gazing into distant light, a heavy pewter cross against her throat, golden ringlets falling below her shoulders. She was perhaps the second-most-famous nineteenth-century medium after the Fox sisters, her image appearing on mimeographed bills posted all over northeastern cities boasting of trance lectures wherein, with the help of spirits, she might deliver entire unrehearsed speeches about Darwin's theories or the daily activities of angels or Andrew Jackson's discontent with abolition or the history of Occultism.

Female youth was prized in these early Spiritualist circles, under the belief that it provided special innocence, ignorance, a lack of ulterior motive. For the first time ever, the nineteenth century "cult of true womanhood"—an assemblage of sentiments espousing that female virtue rested solely in the expression of piety, purity, submissiveness, and domesticity—rendered young women the perfect moral compasses and gentle receptors of messages, and so mediums, trance lecturers, and message ministers were often eleven, fifteen, seventeen years old, put up onstage in places like New York's Stuyvesant Institute or Union Hall, full of uncomfortable and expectant spectators. Because they were part of a new religious movement, Spiritualists had few public venues to display their practice, as most of the church's mediums worked one-on-one with individuals or families, and there were no educational institutions or centrally organizing bodies to spread the word. So trance lecturers were, as Braude argues, Spiritualism's missionaries.

Cora Hatch entered the assembly halls already in a trance state. Someone would usher her up to a podium, like a frail old woman with the face of a teenager, and she'd begin, eloquently. "The word 'occultism' is but a few months old, and bears no relation to Spiritualism. The occult presumes select individuals have access to knowledge that equips them with special powers; whereas God's gift of mediumship is meant for all the world to possess." A distinctive part of these "discourses" was their virtual impromptu form, wherein a committee or public figure would select a topic for her to speak on, after which they were published in the Spiritualist periodical *Banner of Light*, unedited, from the stenographer's speedy notes.

Within a couple of years of that 1857 daguerreotype, Hatch was a superstar. She divorced her husband, who was her manager at the time, and he dragged their split into the public sphere, raging, blaming her marital discontent on the unruly ideals and ministerial autonomy that Spiritualism instilled in American women. But it was way too late for that kind of talk. Spiritualism had long been partnered with the suffragists and other women's rights movements, and the community rounded the wagons, reporting on his abuse and exploitation of Hatch. In turn, she continued to rise in fame, on her own, gathering larger and larger crowds. When the suffragist Paulina Wright Davis spoke on a retrospective of the women's rights movement in 1871, she credited Cora Hatch with having "spoken more frequently and to larger audiences . . . than almost any other lecturer." For the most part, not only were trance lectures where most Americans first heard of Spiritualism, but also, Braude notes, where they first saw a woman speak in public.

From my bench, I look up from the book and watch congregants filter out of the Assembly Hall. Mary Ockuly comes last, her eyes full of light. I think about Cora Hatch with her eyes glazed over onstage. I think of Maggie Fox's confession and retraction. What if any or all of these people did have divine inspiration? I am not here to confirm or deny that. Is it possible that both happened at once, that divine inspiration occurred right when women were pushing for reform, or that the inklings of reform could even, possibly, have prompted or allowed for a receptiveness to such a message? In order to hear any call, there must first be some imagined future that makes it audible.

Eventually I decide to walk around town. There are multiple sites around Lily Dale's wooded perimeters where, scheduled throughout the day, four or five mediums gather to conduct Message Services. I go to one in the Forest Alter and sit on wooden benches with a hundred others in the dappled green light next to an entrance to the Fairy Trail. The mediums call mostly upon middle-aged people or older—I didn't see one person call on a child or a teenager or someone in their twenties. Some of the messages are very general ("I see a man who misses you") and some very specific ("I see a red toy airplane"). Spirits give warnings, exhortations, encouragement. "I see a red toy airplane thank you, and a man in a green sweater and he wants you to know you should increase your hourly rate thank you for your legal services thank you."

I drift off and wander around the neighborhoods. Lily Dale is made up of a lot of little paint-flecked Victorians built at ground level. I pass a man repairing the porch of a particularly dilapidated one. He turns out to be the fire marshal of the town and tells me that he and his wife moved to Lily Dale from Boston in 1999, and that the permanent resident count is 375—that's how many people stay through the winter. He wears Carhartts and a white T-shirt and has a thick New England accent. He says they'd moved to Lily Dale because his wife's family had history, property here, because her great-great-aunt was one of the founders. "Our church is over there," he says, pointing down the road to a smaller meeting house used during the off-season. "The Church of the Living Spirit."

A couple of houses later, I pass by a teenage girl, her hair cut short under a trucker hat, slouching in an old Adirondack on the porch. "Aren't you hot?" she asks me. "Why aren't you in one of the cafés?" I ask her what it was like growing up here and she says, "Boring." Down another street, there is a private beach on the lake, a beautiful two-bedroom house for sale for $77,000 (I pocket its glossy flier), and a Neighborhood Watch sign.

I had ended up in Providence in 2011, reading tarot to make ends meet, after having graduated into a recession, unemployed and broke. Sweeney was finishing graduate school, and so, with no other plan in sight, I followed him north and ended up in a shabby white walkup on the city's West Side, waiting for job interviews, waiting for revelations of the future—any future—and waiting for my clamoring heart to still. I felt haunted at the time by an anxiety so overwhelming I couldn't distinguish my fear of the future from my fear of the flickering lights in my apartment, the dry scrabbling that echoed from the empty units below my own, and the winding, unlit stairway I'd race down in the morning dark to catch my eight o'clock train to go read cards for people in North Attleboro.

There was a ghostliness to the region, to New England, and especially to Providence itself—a city from where much had disappeared: Native Americans, trees, barons, and one of the largest industrial economies in America, leaving the population to buckle under its absence. There were other things, too: a lot of garrets, towers, cupolas, the sense of being peered out at from behind glass. Hundreds of the houses on the West Side were abandoned. You could walk for miles during the summertime and barely see anyone at all—or maybe it was just that summer, maybe that was just me. A friend visited and said, "You can tell that a lot of witches were killed here," which seemed to reinforce my feeling, though he offered no further explanation. At night, I chain-smoked and squeezed out a paragraph here and there, and then Sweeney and I would watch episodes of *Six Feet Under* that we'd rent, season by season, from what appeared to be the last video rental store on Earth.

One night, shortly after Sweeney had started a dose of SSRIs, he drank two glasses of wine at a school event and then disappeared into a state of psychosis from which he did not emerge for several hours. He was standing stark naked on the landing of my apartment when I got home, and when my roommate and I tried to put him to bed, he kept waking up, wandering lustily to whomever was in reach, his pupils dilated. When we tried to guide him on the short walk back to his apartment, he yelled to passersby on the street, rolled around on the sidewalk in his rumpled dress clothes, charged an oncoming car, laughing.

I left him at his apartment with a couple of friends and wandered down to the Woonasquatucket waterfront, where a biweekly Providence ritual was underway. In that two-thirds of a mile of "reclaimed" river, once a month—and sometimes more frequently in the early fall—the city of Providence hosts WaterFire at the Waterplace Park amphitheater. It's a mysterious nonprofit community event wherein, at dusk, more than eighty bonfires are lit in elevated pyres in the river that runs through downtown. That night I sat on the grassy knoll with a thousand other onlookers as we watched fire tenders, cloaked in black, circle the river stoking the flames.

Despite how frightening it had been to see Sweeney that way, I felt free for a moment from the quivering fears of my own possible psychosis, having transferred all my concern on to him. The Providence populace and I sat on the banks and watched, wrapped in glow sticks, paper-bagging beer, listening to strange Euro-pop or New Age opera piped into the arena, while the fire tenders, looking like druids, receded into the darkness.

Afterward, I walked to an Irish pub downriver and sat with a friend until we got a call from the boys who'd been watching Sweeney. I heard the phone passed to him and then his voice on the other end, completely familiar, restored. I asked if he remembered any of the last few hours, and he said only a little bit—that he felt like he'd come out of a trance, a possession.

When I spoke to my parents on the phone during those months, I'd make oblique references to feeling anxious but insist that I was fine, everything was fine, graduating from college is crazy, you know. Right? Right. That's all.

My grandmother called me shortly after Sweeney's episode, and without even saying hello, she asked, "Are you OK?"

"Yes," I said. "I'm OK. Yes."

"You sure?" she said. "Because we have a connection, you know."

"I know," I said. I know.

From Lily Dale, I drive all the way back to Wyoming for my second year of graduate school. I end up befriending a young medium who is pursuing a master's degree in American Studies. Her thesis is about processing trauma in the afterlife, a project inspired by victims of a gruesome murder ten years earlier who'd started appearing to her. She had been living in Thermopolis, Wyoming, as a town-paper reporter, and had found herself at night, in libraries, in her bedroom, being visited by a woman and her three children, who had been shot by the woman's fifteen-year-old stepson just outside of town.

So she started doing research about domestic violence, mediumship, and healing, and took this to an academic context. Jess is incredibly happy-go-lucky, cheerful, peach-cheeked, ten years older than me but with the bright eyes and glossy brown hair of a much younger woman. She takes me dancing one night at the Buckhorn Bar '90s night, and then she tells me about being a medium the following week when she invites me to do a clearing with her at the Cooper House.

We sit in the big seminar room of a mansion that's been converted into the American Studies building. She's brought another woman along, also a medium, a jolly Catholic and employee of the university. We each sit against a different wall while Jess beats a hide-drum to raise energy—and then we are quiet, our eyes closed, and Jess starts speaking to a woman and two young children. That's who's there, she says. The other medium, alternatively, sees the teenaged Cooper House heir who died in the 1970s, and she gives him a hard time about all the acid he did. He is annoyed, she says, and angry. I see— what? My eyes are closed, and there is the lace-like hoop of a woman's skirt, two children darting around her. Jess tells them they're free to go, get, go on, no need to stay. And then we continue sitting in silence for a long time.

Afterward, we turn on the lights and gather at the seminar table usually used for classes, and the older medium brings out her crystal pendulum. "I don't think the nephew is ready to go," she says, and the pendulum starts swinging and swinging and swinging.

At the university, I meet a woman—a professor of social sciences— who grew up in and around Lily Dale, and while her parents weren't Spiritualists, they did casually attend Tuesday night "circles," like everyone in the area did, and they spoke openly about making spirit contact with dead relatives. When she thinks about it, she tells me, though she knew many practicing Spiritualists, she doesn't remember anyone explicitly stating that they were one.

She says that Lily Dale "attracts a group of people that's quite different, in that people are coming there from all over the world by choice, so it's a paradox in a lot of ways because you have this community of blue-collar folks—of which I'd count myself one—who are really shaped in a lot of ways by growing up in that area . . . I think there's a basic level of respect for the practices there, because people take it really, really seriously." She thinks about it and then compares it to the religious atmosphere of New Orleans: "You know what they say: It's 30 percent Baptist, 70 percent Catholic, and 100 percent Voodoo."

Maggie and Kate Fox start a movement, then abandon it, then take it back. Spiritualism makes an occasion to force the American people to shut up and listen to teenage girls talking onstage for the first time maybe ever. People continue talking to the dead, or they talk to the living, who tell them everything they need to know about what they'd want the dead to say. Spirits show up looking for resolution, so Jess writes letters to and visits a murderer in state prison who is now old and grizzled, seeing what she can do. Some women, between 1848 and now, make a lot of money, make a living, make a life, sitting in rooms or on stumps or in assembly halls, giving messages. Veracity has little to do with it.

The weird thing is that, at the end of the long, arduous year in Providence and three minutes before we packed up all of our worldly belongings and moved to Wyoming, Sweeney and I got married on the hottest day of my life. I had to run down the road barefoot from our rental house to the venue to make it in time, having just spent a spare twenty minutes scribbling a letter, sweating in my slip, on the back deck. At the inn, I found myself nearly bleeding through my dress. I needed a tampon. I did not have one. I said this very matter-of-factly, and my mom kind of looked at me, like, *Really?* and then began asking around.

Somewhere outside in the incredible heat was my bridegroom being made to wait in direct sunlight while I got my tampon, while our bridal party clustered at the back door, and while I cried as my brother, my stepfather, my soon-to-be-husband's aunt and uncle, friends we hadn't seen in months were ferried past me through a corridor. My dad took me gently by the arm and guided me into an empty hallway. "Where do you think the tears are coming from?" he asked. I looked out the window, trying to answer, and I saw two friends of Sweeney's I'm not even that close to wander up the drive, and I burst into tears all over again. "It's just that everyone is *here*—" I said, "that all these people are here together."

We'd brought all of these people together in some very brief vision of a more perfect society, though it lasted only for a second, in my mind, and then it was gone.

What my stepmother remembers most vividly from the ceremony were the vows. She said, years later, "We were shocked by the vows."

"The vows?" I asked, remembering mine, which had a reference to the woman in Proverbs who "laughs at the days to come" and to Woody Guthrie's "This Land Is Your Land."

"Yes, the vows," she said, "about the rib and all that. I mean, it was a wedding—where one asserts a new identity. So we were like, WHOA, OK then."

And I realized that she was talking about the scripture, not the vows. To kick off the pastor's homily, that radical feminist friend of mine, Amber, had read the part from Genesis about woman being made from man, Eve from Adam, the rib, and how it resulted in Adam writing the first poem of humankind.

The bridal party took whiskey shots under the trellis, at the altar, the shots poured into small Dixie cups that were distributed while my mother and stepmother played a flute duet.

Everyone in attendance was shocked for one reason or another. My friends and family from the West Coast thought it was the most traditional wedding they'd ever been to, but Sweeney's family and friends thought it was the weirdest, saying politely afterward, "Oh, it was so *you guys*." My friends didn't dare ask about the religiously structured ceremony, and it was so new-fangled, art-school Protestant that Sweeney's Irish Catholic family almost couldn't tell it was religious at all.

I was twenty-three years old. My own family members—who would have been perfectly happy if I'd never gotten married, or if I'd gotten married to three people, barefoot in someone's backyard— were politely tolerant. Our friends were excited for us, though they were also slightly overwhelmed by the whole thing, repeatedly saying things like "I'm happy for you, but I can't imagine getting married" or "I wouldn't do it."

Then we partied all night in the renovated train depot hotel we'd booked looking out over the Hudson, and then for the next two nights beyond that, three dozen friends, cousins, and comrades crammed into a house up the road we'd rented to share with them.

I saw something a few nights later. All our friends had finally left, and Sweeny and I were alone for the first time, and we slept hard. Then in the middle of the night I awoke and there was a bright green light, sort of the size and shape of a scarab, flying around the room. I lay and stared, trying to parse dream from sleep from waking. It was like a firefly's light, though it did not go out. Rather, it flew and flew all over the room for five minutes. Then darkness.

I figured Sweeney was asleep, but I whispered anyway: "Did you see that?"

And Sweeney said, "I did."

TRUE FACTS TOLD BY HER

Aimee Semple McPherson

I t's 1915, and Aimee Semple McPherson is living miserably as a homemaker in Providence, Rhode Island. The more obsessively she tries to master the tasks of an Edwardian housewife, the more violent her neurotic outbreaks are, until finally, after a protracted illness that results in a hysterectomy, or which results in near-death as she's being wheeled backward through swinging hospital doors in a creaking gurney, she submits to the voice of God—which had been whispering during all those hours of dusting and polishing for her to go preach. *Now will you go?*

And so she leaves, in the company of her mother and her two kids, travelling all over the East Coast, inviting the public into the roomy canvas revival tents to listen to her sermons, and to be moved to speak in tongues, to writhe on the floor, to receive God's healing power through her hands. She preaches to integrated audiences, holds court in Southern black towns, arranges for a local Mississippi newspaper to photograph her daughter getting baptized by a black minister. After a few years, she takes her roadshows west. She stuffs her kids and mother into a hulking Packard and starts driving. She is the first woman to cross the country without the accompaniment of a man, and she paints messages on the car doors: JESUS IS COMING SOON – GET READY or WHERE DO YOU WANT TO SPEND ETERNITY? By the time she arrives in Hollywood, she's a celebrity.

It's 1924, and as the stage lights dim in Angelus Temple, and the crowd roars following the end of an illustrated sermon—full cast, full orchestra—Aimee Semple McPherson dips behind the heavy gold curtain into the harsh lights backstage. The fluorescents bring her thick theatrical makeup and acetone-hardened hair into high relief and she begins pulling pins from her signature updo, one by one, gripping them between her teeth. She is dressed as a cop. She is dressed as a pilot. She is dressed as a beautiful milkmaid. A gauntlet of temple assistants flank her with brow towels and glasses of water, but she pushes through them, down the corridors, out the back entrance to a side street, where Charlie Chaplin sits in an idling car waiting for her to join him.

They sit in the backseat with the windows down while her throngs of congregants filter into the streets of Los Angeles' Echo Park. Aimee gently prods Charlie, as she always takes the opportunity to do, on the issue of his salvation, and when he waves her off, they move on to the true purpose of their meeting: He watched her illustrated sermon this evening and delivers to her now, upon request, a lengthy critique of the set and the choreography. McPherson nods, face drawn, scribbling notes on the back of an old issue of her magazine *Bridal Call*. After that, they laugh and trade tales from their strange weeks, two people famous and private, in the evening shadow of the first American megachurch.

* * *

It's the summer of 1926 and, for the first time in God knows how long, McPherson takes the day off. She and her secretary Emma Schaeffer pack a picnic for Venice Beach, bring the children, spread the gingham blanket, and then McPherson strips to her bright green swim clothes and shoots straight for the water. Her secretary dozes under an umbrella. When she awakes, Aimee has not returned to shore. The sun is setting. *Aimee!* How much time has passed? She spends the rest of the day combing the beach with police: *Aimee! Aimee!* but by nightfall McPherson is presumed to have drowned.

The coast guard searches for a body but comes up short. Some of McPherson's congregants take it upon themselves to continue the comb, and two of them die from exposure in the process. In the coming weeks, thousands of her followers will stand at the water's edge, holding candlelight vigils, singing hymns. Despite all that, the LA press almost immediately assumes it is a hoax. Ransom letters and reported sightings of McPherson and temple employee Kenneth Ormiston make their way up the California coast.

Five weeks later, McPherson staggers into a Mexican border town with an elaborate story about kidnapping, torture, and ransom at the hands of two bandits and one Mexicali Rose, who held her in an adobe shack in the desert, from which she escaped by her wits and with the help of a rusted soup can. Then she collapses.

She is rushed to a hospital in Douglas, Arizona, but no one she speaks to in Douglas believes her. She's dehydrated and sunburned and frizzy, as from an hour too long on a beach, and her clothes are clean, her shoes a little scuffed at best. Authorities are dispatched over the border immediately but are unable to find an adobe shack that fits her description. No suspects emerge. But it doesn't matter. Hospital photographs of a sleepy and suntanned McPherson tucked into hospital sheets splash across papers. There she is, surrounded by her mother and two children; there she is with her hair done up, reading the Bible in bed.

When she returns to LA, thirty thousand people are waiting for her at the train station.

A ngelus Temple opened its doors in 1923 as the headquarters of McPherson's new denomination, the International Church of the Foursquare Gospel. With its giant cream-colored dome, 180-degree mezzanine, and hulking Grecian pillars, Angelus commanded the landscape of Echo Park like some Californian Acropolis. The seating capacity was fifty-three hundred, and on a three-service day, it filled all three times. It was, upon breaking ground, the largest construction project in North America, and critics joked that it put the "cost" in Pentecost—but McPherson was just being realistic about her crowd-drawing powers. She'd spent the last several years holding standing-room-only revivals up and down the East Coast. She needed an enormous space. And that space needed twenty-five exits in order to prevent bottlenecking after services.

Inside that great coliseum of a building, McPherson preached, conducted faith-healing services, and produced morality plays in a voice at once husky, patristic, clipped, and musical. Sometimes she entered the sanctuary on a motorbike, once she chartered a plane to disseminate pamphlets for a Balboa Park revival, and once she administered a faith healing to a lion at the zoo. Her strategies were varied, and her public persona shifted, too. Earlier in her career, she wore her thick brown hair in a signature updo and a modest white servant's dress made of heavy muslin topped by a navy cape, but by the mid-1920s she was hot and stylish, with the glistening blond finger-curls of a flapper, high heels poking out from under form-fitting clerical robes emblazoned with a glittering cross, her arms spread as wide as a Marvel superhero trying to save the whole city.

Her congregation, at times running fifteen thousand strong, included old people, young people, brown, white, and black, poor and rich, and was equipped with a nursery, so even the newest of mothers could participate in the summoning of the Holy Ghost. Her services were among the most integrated spaces of 1920s and 1930s California, and it is said that she was the single most photographed person of her time.

This prewar period was marked by the nascent division of modernism and fundamentalism within the church—which is still very much the paradigm of religious discourse we live in today—and without meaning to, or maybe meaning to, McPherson embodied these divisions. She was at once a vocal social conservative, leading (for instance) powerful campaigns in a gorilla suit to require the instruction of Genesis in all California science classrooms, but she had also created one of the few American churches to ordain women, which was orchestrated through the temple's seminary program, LIFE Bible College. She was seen as both extremely hot and extremely maternal. She was against dancing, smoking, and movie-going, but in the months following her kidnapping and the ensuing court spectacle, the flappers were among her greatest allies. She was hardline on issues of sexual purity and marriage, though she was also a single mother of two—a sort of patron saint for any woman ever widowed, abandoned, or divorced, of which she had been all three.

In fact, McPherson's outreach to unwed mothers and pregnant teenagers was largely unparalleled by any religious organization at the time. As historian Matthew Avery Sutton writes in *Aimee Semple McPherson and the Resurrection of Christian America*, she claimed to be able to spot those desperate young women in the temple crowds: the flush of their cheeks, their sad, dark eyes. She'd find them afterward, let them cry in her arms. If she couldn't mediate reconciliation with their families (which, Sutton notes, on several occasions, she was personally able to do), the girls moved into the two-story church parsonage where McPherson lived. After the birth, McPherson would matchmake them with widows from the congregation who could take care of the infants while these new mothers became their own

breadwinners. Offstage, Sutton says, she also "helped women struggling with issues of rape, incest, and physical abuse." When the Big
Sister League of LA asked McPherson to speak at the opening of their
new women's shelter, she cemented her presence there by saying that
"there were some things a woman preacher could do better than a man
could," and that was that. Where just ten years earlier in Edwardian
America, a woman occupying similar celebrity might have reverted
to the old Victorian "cult of true womanhood" thing, McPherson instead offered an open door—a shrug, a wink. *Your guess is as good as
mine*, she seemed to say. There are just some things a woman preacher
can do better than a man.

Woman preacher or man preacher—what is a preacher? Why not
a minister or a pastor? "Pastor" comes from the Old French
pastur ("shepherd"), or the Latin *pastor* (same idea), which in
nineteenth-century American English becomes the person who "shep-
herds" a church community, inspired, of course, by Jesus' insistent
use of the metaphors of lamb and sheep. Beyond the pastures, "pastor"
enters the lexical register of the benevolent patriarch, leader, teacher,
facilitator, interpreter, but one who is ultimately non-hierarchal. The
pastor is one among the fellow congregants, a congregant themselves,
and only symbolic of God's interaction in the world. But preacher?
Latin's *predicare*, "to proclaim; to say," goes through a couple of iterations until we see its twelfth-century French use, *preachen*, meaning
"to give a sermon, to preach." "Preacher" enters American English in
a big way in nineteenth-century black, Southern, and Methodist theology, evoking a cleric who brings to the pulpit mysticism, zeal, passion, drama, prophecy—functioning more as medium than as teacher.
And so unlike a pastor—a lamb among lambs—the preacher is hierar-
chical, represents their church, and is separate from their congregants.
In the Latin Bible we see the word used in the context of ecstatically
proclaiming the "good news"—not to the congregation, but outward.
Preaching reaches out, above and beyond the choir.

McPherson's ministry was always outwardly oriented, despite the magnitude of her interiors. When she moved to LA and found the plot of land where her temple would eventually be built, according to biographer Daniel Mark Epstein, she approached the FOR SALE sign and scribbled upon it a building "in the shape of a megaphone." For those crowds of people huddled outside the temple who hadn't arrived in time to nab one of the fifty-three hundred seats, she'd installed loudspeakers facing the sidewalk. A year later, she bought a radio license and began broadcasting sermons, lectures, choral music, children's stories, and faith-healing services from a state-of-the-art studio on the top floor of the temple, so that the reach of her message was practically limitless.

But this was all strange, you have to understand. The Pentecostal movement was still new then, a somewhat quiet but charismatic fringe of the American Protestant church. Pentecostalism identifies itself as "the heir of a continuous tradition, from the initial Pentecost to now," that day that the apostles, Mary Magdalen chief among them, went into the streets and, possessed by the Holy Spirit, began beseeching passersby in tongues to accept Jesus the messiah and all of the other implications that go along with that: God is not who you thought He was; miracles occur every day; healing happens in the blink of an eye; try to speak and you will speak God's language; close your eyes and listen to God's voice, you can hear it; God will literally give you protection from rattlesnakes, from cyanide, from jagged rocks. And though, in the 1920s, women made up the bulk of Pentecostal missionaries, a woman cleric was rare. Plus home-radio sets were not yet commonplace, in LA or anywhere, and who'd ever even heard of a megachurch before?

Of course, McPherson's novelty often eclipsed her theology. While she was at the time perhaps the most visible American religious figure to date, historian Nathan Saunders notes that "The newspapers did not give credence to McPherson's words in the same way that they did those of [Harry] Fosdick and [Billy] Sunday," the other celebrity preachers of the time. "The early articles rarely reported the content of her sermons." Moreover, Sunday and Fosdick were often referred to in the press with the distinctions of "Rev." and "Dr." respectively, though neither held a degree. And McPherson, having received a variety of ordinations, was given only the title "Sister"—Sister Aimee. But she liked it that way.

It was through the radio, on those long drives in the Mountain West, that I first heard about Aimee Semple McPherson. I'd finally learned to drive, at twenty-four years old, and for the first time since I was a kid, I started listening to the radio. I was living in southeastern Wyoming, where signals were intermittent and journeys were long, so pop songs and the BBC World Service and the staticky boom of radio evangelists were close companions through the miles and miles of sagebrush prairie between one town and the next. One afternoon I caught the tail end of an interview with Kathy Lee Gifford, who'd just released a Broadway musical about McPherson called *Scandalous*. But McPherson was so famously in control of her own image that all attempts to retell her story are redundant. At midcareer, she produced her own autobiographical Broadway vaudeville act, which received mixed reviews and ran for only three weeks. If she couldn't do it, I don't know why anyone else thought they could.

Gifford's show flopped shortly after its debut. *Scandalous* was lost on its twenty-first-century public because they'd grown used to stories—much more grisly ones—of the fallen religious elite. And anyway, if secular audience members were familiar with McPherson at all, they already knew her as part of the cabinet of American curiosities, her sensational life story fixed for nearly a century as the woman whose neon name glowed twice the size of her denomination's on the front of her Echo Park temple, a charlatan who built a castle on the banks of Lake Elsinore, and who, one afternoon in 1926, after being missing for five weeks and presumed dead, wandered out of the Mexican desert in her Sunday best.

In Laramie I briefly found myself at a church that spent six weeks— that's six services—on Paul's letter to the Ephesians, wherein, in one part, he espouses that "wives submit to their husbands, as husbands submit to the church." (The following epistle, just by the way, addresses slaves and masters using a similar analogy. We did not address that one in Laramie, nor has it been addressed in any church I've ever been in.) This church congregated in a storefront to the side of a dusty thoroughfare at the edge of town. It fancied itself more open and cutting-edge than that old fire-and-brimstone variety and was well aware that many of its members had fled one mainline church or another. That was why they were going to take the time to unpack this difficult dictum. What if we read the text closely, over and over again, rather than revert to the same rote takeaway like in the past?

This could have been an interesting exercise in the new evangelical church plant movement (which, again, is the creation of new, highly localized, demographic-specific churches for, say, bohemian artists in Brooklyn or college students in Laramie, "planted" by larger church organizations), but I had seen it done so many times before—and it was the same this time. Six weeks of trying to find euphemisms for the word "submit" but which always came back to the same thing: In general, wives, listen to your husband. Your job is important, too, but God wants order, and this is the order He established, but here's a nicer way of saying it. Amen.

The last time I went to that church, in an experimental alternative to the sermon, the pastor installed six couples on the low carpeted stage to discuss how this "message" plays out in their marriages. One woman said she felt like the first mate on a ship where her husband is captain—and she's so thankful that he's a godly man. A different husband said that, during the years he was working full-time to support his family (as the scripture instructed), he was on the brink of insanity, but God gave him the strength to carry on. Another wife said that as a feminist she really doesn't know how to reconcile Paul's passage, and then she kind of shrugged and looked at the pastor.

The issue at this church was that they obviously did not know what to say about Paul's letter, other than the rote translation. They lacked the intellectual rigor of ecumenical continuity to truly bring new meaning to it. And by beating it like a dead horse over those slow six weeks, they made an already seemingly oppressive dictum even worse—oppressive *and* bland, as though it served only as a simple organizational rule to live by. If instead the pastor had just said the mystery of God compels you to submit to your husband, it would have been awful, though more intellectually honest, because that is, after all, what they were saying. And I would have walked out anyway, as I've walked out of so many other congregations before. (I thought of Elizabeth Clare Prophet, founder of the 1970s Church Universal and Triumphant and the ad hoc fallout shelter movement, who remembers sitting in church as an adult, crinkling her nose at the various pastors and how "Jesus would explain to me that they had not yet been given the full teaching.")

It was always the certainty of those church plants that frightened me, though I did appreciate their uncertain and ever-changing approach to the liturgy—one of the rare gifts of a lack of ecumenical continuity. At the church plant in Laramie, they approached the Eucharist in a deeply communal way, placing a fresh loaf of bread at the pulpit, presided over by no one, which each member approached— three or four people at a time, usually all strangers—and ripped off hunks, dipped them in wine, and said to each other up close, "The bread of life, the blood of Christ." And I remember there, as at other communion tables, the feeling of a breeze passing my cheek, and it always made me want to know what it would have been like to follow that feeling further, down the path of tongues.

* * *

As I began listening to the radio again, I remembered the media mavens of my childhood, overheard in the backseats of babysitters' cars or in darkened hallways adjacent to living rooms: Dr. Laura Schlessinger ripping her clients new ones with the moral strictness of Jewish law; Ann Coulter's fierce claims about the nation's irresponsible impoverished, the "bogus" science of evolution, and how "Jesus died for my sins, and that's that"; Tammy Faye Bakker's insistence that God wants you to prosper, and that any material lack is a consequence of some spiritual deficiency; Oprah's bottomless empathy and outrage, her smiling face on the cover of her self-titled magazine; and nationally syndicated radio personality Delilah, who, though Evangelical in spirit, neither moralizes nor condescends to her callers, and whose tagline is simply "Love someone." Like a sage older sister offering you a wine cooler and a prayer pamphlet, she consoles the broken hearts, the failed marriages, and the estranged daughters with just a few words about how her caller should forget the deadbeat man, the tyrannical father, and take comfort in knowing the embrace of a vague and generous God. And as proof, she offers you a song: Donna Lewis's "I Love You" or the Indigo Girls' "Closer to Fine." Unlike the others, Delilah never placed herself on a pedestal. Her three failed marriages and complicated adoptions of ten children were the currency of her vocation.

So I thought of her, and all of them who were all still there, on the radio or on TV, as I drove and drove all around Wyoming, back and forth to the Denver Airport and to the strip malls of Cheyenne and the thrift stores of Fort Collins and the ghost towns of Albany County and the trails of Vedauwoo National Park. There was a restaurant about twenty minutes from Laramie, standing solo in the barren stretch of the old Lincoln Highway where the smoking laws of the county didn't reach, and I'd go there to eat a burger and write. On my way I skipped through the stations and listened to news shows and voices of instruction.

I thought, too, of the great falls of the religious elite I'd witnessed in my own lifetime. As a child of the 1990s and early 2000s, it seemed that almost every single megachurch preacher and celebrity televangelist had been brought down by some kind of monetary or sexual scandal. The morally complicated life of megachurches and religious organizations is embedded in their very structure: With the blessing of the free market, they can grow with impunity, becoming—much to the chagrin of their Protestant ancestors—powerful religious oligarchies. Moreover, their tax-exempt status has been the pulsing green heart of many a scandal. American megachurches, and many faith-based media organizations, accumulate millions of dollars in revenue every year and are not required to make the same disclosures as, say, charities are on tax-exempt cash, resulting, sometimes, in astronomically rich leaders.

Jim Whittington of Fountain of Life ministries embezzled nearly a million dollars from an old lady; Marilyn Hickey's fundraisers, promising blessings from God, obtained money that was used for personal vacations and lavish homes. Then there's Jimmy Swaggart, who was repeatedly caught with prostitutes, after a life spent sputtering, red-faced, about the evils of sexual deviance. Even after his infamous televised sobbing confession, he was caught again—and again and, I think, again. Eddie Long was accused by at least five women and two men of intimidating them into sexual relationships with him. Ted Haggard, after years of vehement campaigning against same-sex marriage, was publicly outed for having a sexual relationship with a male masseur—and then there was the meth. In the fallout of the Rwandan Genocide, Pat Robertson, host of *The 700 Club*, rallied for donations to go toward his charity organization Operation Blessing International in neighboring Zaire, where, not long before, Robertson had allegedly settled a diamond-mining contract with then dictator Mobutu Sese Seko. According to employees from OBI, the planes meant for relief supplies were used to transport equipment to Robertson's mines.

And Paul Crouch, the man who started the Bakkers' host station, received massive amounts of undocumented cash as "donations" for the Trinity Broadcasting Network and was implicated in the Bakkers' eventual charges, which included every conceivable offense of American religious royalty—larceny, embezzlement, conspiracy, and rape—and finally ended in Jim Bakker's imprisonment. While Jim was in prison, he read the Bible the whole way through—admittedly for the first time—and conceded that his "prosperity gospel" was in fact not substantiated by scripture.

The thing about all of these people is that, for the most part, their transgressions would have simply been those of any excessively rich person, or in some cases the transgressions of someone disturbed in any class, but because they'd thrown themselves into the public sphere as conservative and condemning moral leaders, as preachers, as channelers, whose efforts self-reportedly sided with God, they'd purchased the privilege of such exposure, positioned themselves for monumental crashes.

While Aimee Semple McPherson did lay a sort of blueprint for the American church that grows exponentially, there are tremendous ways that she differs from her heirs: She ran a ministry that fed more people in LA during the Depression than any other organization; she ran programs and spaces to house the homeless and assisted women leaving the sex trade; for God's sake, she left trolley fare in a little lockbox under one of the temple's pillar panels for whoever needed it at any time.

I drove and drove around Wyoming, and I heard a rebroadcast of *On Being*, where Krista Tippett interviewed professor of religious and African American studies Anthea Butler on McPherson's legacy. Butler emphasizes that, above all, McPherson was running this giant ministry, operating a radio station, and building a megachurch during a time when the public didn't know they wanted it, needed it, or what it even was. There was no mold, no model, no system that was prebuilt for success or corruption. Those other mega-preachers later were cashing in on something they *knew* the world wanted. They knew their audience, their outlets, their tax codes. And their scandals eviscerated their authority, whereas McPherson's seemed to function as an inadvertent part of hers.

When Tippett pressed Butler about whether McPherson's scandals undermined her legacy, Butler sighed and said:

> If you think about the fact that you've done all this work, all this traveling, and you're taking care of two little kids, and your mother is always around nagging you—you can read the story of her disappearance as salacious or terrible, or you could read it as, you know, this is someone who hadn't had a break in *how* long? . . . I think that [assuming the scandals delegitimize her contribution] is an indictment against the rigor of religion, quite frankly . . . What becomes the issue is, how much are you supposed to give up of yourself to live for God? There's all these great songs, you know, like "I Surrender All" or "Put Your All at the Altar." People mean them. But no one bothers to think of a life like Aimee's . . . There's a point where you have to count the cost . . . Do you pull back when your family falls apart? . . . Or when you've been accused of running off with a married man? Do you pull back? Someone like Aimee says, "No, I will not pull back," and you pay a personal price.

It's 1925, and the temple lights are trained on Aimee Semple McPherson like kliegs. "It is very foolish to hesitate to trust God," she says in her warm, scratchy voice, sounding more like Bella Abzug than Tammy Faye Bakker. She recounts a news story of a man who slips from the Los Angeles palisades and, eyeing the sharp rocks below, spends ten minutes hanging from his fingertips, until finally, his fingers cramping, he says, "God, help me" and lets go.

"And he landed an inch and three-quarters from the rocks. *An inch and three-quarters!*" She thrusts her arm straight above her, the flared sleeves of her robe cascading to her elbow. She ticks off the miraculous visions of Ezekiel, the healings of Acts, the healings she has seen, that she has carried out with the power of the Holy Spirit: "I've seen tubercular bones, filled with pus and pockets, healed so that they leapt from their wheeling chairs, leapt from their crutches." And she's no Calvinist. Away with that "child of God" crap: "It is not enough to be born again. You need to grow in God . . . Don't be a baby. Grow up to be men and women, filled with the Holy Spirit!" Faith without works is dead—"Put your faith into action!" Without works, faith is like "a bird without a wing."

She grabs a girl. She grabs an old woman. She grabs a lion at the zoo. She lays her manicured hand on the leg, the eye, the heart. She enjoins the crowd for prayers, for cries. In Pentecostal fashion, she implores congregants to make noise: "Come on now—that's a Methodist 'amen.' I was raised Methodist, so no—let's hear a reee-allll HolyGhostPentecostal amen!" And the girl, the old woman, the lion—they all stand up.

It's the summer of 1926, and she's returned to LA after her hospitalization in Arizona. Almost immediately, she is charged with perjury. The story of her disappearance is a lurid, front-page media scandal: EVANGELIST's KIDNAP HOAX EXPOSED! Two witnesses accuse her of hiring them to fabricate evidence, and other witnesses prove that temple employee Kenneth Ormiston disappeared the same day McPherson did, that he checked into a variety of pretty little coastal hotels under false names and was later seen with McPherson in his Chrysler at a cottage in Carmel-by-the-Sea and on a cliffside picnic off of Highway 1. Meanwhile, no evidence of the kidnappers' existence surfaces. McPherson is subpoenaed and the press goes wild. She is outraged by the accusations and asks her congregation for forty-eight hours of fasting and prayer on her behalf, and during this time she is still preaching, is actually weaving the courtroom events into her sermons. She faints in public several times, is hospitalized for a nervous breakdown, and on one occasion is carried into court on an upholstered chair. But she arrives, always alert, at the pulpit on Sundays.

The prosecution builds their case primarily around the allegations of a single witness, who turns out to be a "lunatic," and the case is dismissed. McPherson sets off on a Vindication Tour, preceded by a lavish victory celebration at the temple. In *Vanishing Evangelist*, Lately Thomas describes the party as being so loud with cheers and hallelujahs that McPherson was unable to speak for the first fifteen minutes, after which she delivered a farewell message on "the Lord's conquest of his enemies, the ascendency of love over hate," as exemplified in her own triumph:

> The whole structure of this case against me was built like the Tower of Babel, rotten from the bottom. Each block, built one upon the other, reached just so high, and then, like the Tower of Babel, God looked down and confused the tongues of the builders. Each told a different story. One confused the other, and thus it has ended, leaving standing only the true facts told by me.

In this statement, Aimee Semple McPherson aligns herself with the Old Testament God, a priest of the Lord, a preacher, a channeler. When she sets off on the train that will take her from city to city, where she will spread news of her innocence, she shakes hands with everybody and blows kisses and throws flowers and candy to a crowd of thousands.

But then there were other things to follow: a botched marriage and divorce; she accepts donations from the KKK and then admonishes them; her accountants accuse her of cooking the books. Having once lived in a small house next door to the temple, McPherson returns from the Vindication Tour with plans to build a Byzantine stucco mansion at Lake Elsinore in an attempt to get away from the limelight. The mansion, when realized, is full of latticed ceilings, furniture inlaid with mother-of-pearl, mirrored alcoves, palatial bedrooms, and underground passages. And it's while she is living there that she and her mother, her unwavering wing-woman for decades, get twin facelifts and break into a fistfight, after which they'd never speak again; and it is where McPherson's own daughter, having come of age, sues the Foursquare church's attorney for slander and gives up her position as heir.

But the church would go on, and the radio would go on, and Aimee would go on, continuing to travel, continuing to save souls, scandalous Evangelist or not.

It's 1932, and she's standing before a dark curtain on a Hearst Metrotone News soundstage. Her hair glistens in blond finger curls against the fluffy bright white fur trimming of an open jacket. Under that is a multicolored striped top with a V-neck—and she knows this outfit will come at a cost, that she has changed her style. She is about to take a voyage to the Holy Land but has been invited to say a bit about Prohibition before her departure.

Her eyes almost never look at the camera; they are skating around the ceiling. She tells the parable of the great lecturer, the preacher, who is a hypocrite, and she begins to girlishly fiddle with her shawl. "He said, 'Dump all your booze in the river . . . now let us go drink from the river.'" She laughs. "And with that one bit, he did away with it all!" But she's looking down now, looking away from the camera as she says, faster, stumbling through her words, "And that's the way perhaps with us over here in America, we teach it but so often those who make the laws do not quite live up to them . . ." At this, she literally looks straight down, down at her feet. And then without even a beat of time, she finishes with, "I wish you could all have the joy of going with us this Easter tide to the Holy Land where we shall visit on Easter Day the tomb of our risen Lord!" Then it goes black.

After Sweeney and I left Emmaus Road, we popped into a Lutheran Church, the liberal Evangelical Lutheran Church in America synod, whose services are almost as liturgically conservative as Catholics but are helmed by slightly more touchy-feely Scandinavians. The ELCA split off from the more conservative synods in the 1970s when they started ordaining women, and those fissures furthered when, in 2009, the ELCA officially started to carry out gay marriages.

The day we went to Trinity Lutheran, the church's intern, Seth—a strapping blond Nordic man our age—gave a sermon on the problematic shame of divorce within Christian churches. Afterward, there was an Oktoberfest luncheon in the rectory, and Seth and his wife Jen approached us with a six pack of unmarked beers they'd recently brewed at home, and we shared them over pasta salad and potatoes. The majority of the congregation was elderly. Jen was a nurse at the local hospital, and Seth was completing his yearlong internship for seminary in Iowa. He and Sweeney made plans to get together and study Greek later that week.

And they did get together, week after week, translating Greek and then Latin and then Hebrew. Sweeney, who was teaching World Literature at the University of Wyoming and at a nuclear missile base in Cheyenne, and who'd by that point received two fine arts degrees in poetry, was already shifting tracks and applying to PhD programs in theology. Seth and Jen became good friends of ours in the coming months. We'd sit on their deck during the brief season of Wyoming warmth, or at pubs during the many moons of deep High Plains freeze, or snowshoeing up Sheep Mountain, and talk about our lives, but also a lot about the church, too. Sometimes I'd get home late on a Saturday night and find Seth and Sweeney chain-smoking and playing poker in our study over a case of Old Milwaukee, and Seth would have to pull himself away because he had to preach come sunup.

But we did not agree on everything. While Seth was proud to be a part of the inclusive ELCA, he had stayed up late that night in 2009 to hear the ecumenical council's determination on the sanctification of gay marriage and found himself disappointed with both sides of the debate—he thought the arguments weren't theological enough, but more pragmatic. Strengthening institutions like gay marriage strengthens trust and stability within society, yes. Liberal humanism can say whatever it wants, but Seth thought liberal Christianity has to use the religion, its understanding of God and the scriptures, and not liberal humanism, to justify its attitudes toward gay marriage. We debated this often, and once, over burgers at the Crowbar, he offered Peter's vision in Acts 10 as something the 2009 council could have used to uphold gay marriage and, in using, might have forced the Missouri synod to consider its own position: Peter is taking a rest on a long journey, and he goes up to his gentile host's roof to pray. Smells waft upward from the gentile's kitchen, and amid his prayer he gets hungry, and then Heaven opens up "like a large sheet being let down to earth by its four corners. It contained all kinds of four-footed animals, as well as reptiles and birds. Then a voice told him, 'Get up, Peter. Kill and eat.'" *No, way*, Peter said, *I'm not supposed to eat those things, and especially not with gentiles.* But the voice spoke to him a second time, saying, "Do not call anything impure that God has made clean." Do not call anything unclean that God has made pure. I think what is meant, or what Seth thought it meant, was: Here is God, a long time ago, saying it's time to overturn those laws, the *mitzvot*, about shellfish and sex and everything else, upon the arrival of the messiah. Jesus is going to break all the old laws, and you must follow his lead. And Seth and many other churches and clerics have been spending the last thousand years trying to figure out how far that overturning actually reaches. To me, it seems it must go pretty fucking far—otherwise, what's the point of a messiah?

Aimee Semple McPherson also found herself in a culture war and, whether consciously or not, she elided both sides. Her biggest goal was to bring people into the kingdom of God, to save souls, to "win" them by whatever means necessary. In a way, she offered resistance to reconcile paradox. Because in the Pentecostal tradition, God is still speaking, which is to say, change is always possible and imminent. That she didn't want to concede to a camp of modernism or fundamentalism says to me that she recognized the divine possibilities that might be foreclosed on if she did. To force her into a box is to miss the whole point. She said:

> If we want to be a soul winner, we will have to be a middle-of-the roader, glory to Jesus. Especially when we come into a citywide revival campaign, lots of us have our own ideas, theories, particular side line of doctrine. If you want to win souls in the greatest, widest sense of the word, drop everything for a little while, just fix your eyes upon Jesus, the crucified Lamb of God, bleeding, dying, hanging on the tree, saying, "Come unto Me all the ends of the earth and be ye saved."

I met an old man named Ron one evening in the back room of Laramie's Roughed Up Duck. The "room" was little more than clapboard and a corrugated tin roof, and during the long months of below-zero weather, it held a hot woodstove. You could smoke there. (I cannot conceal the ways in which the spaces I spend my time are organized around access to smoking.) Ron overheard me telling someone about Aimee Semple McPherson's purported drowning and he said, "I've just never been able to imagine how it would feel to drown." He crinkled a smile and continued as naturally as if we'd been talking all night. He told me that, once, while fur trapping in Northern Minnesota, he almost died, not from drowning but of hypothermia. He told the whole story: his broken compass, the three-mile walk home, up to the point when that glorious and lethal warmth washed over him. He paused and said, "Now that's a goddamned good way to go."

I asked him how he ended up in Wyoming, and he said, in tone and timing fit for radio, "Well, let me tell you a little about myself." He told me about his marriage to a beautiful woman named Claire, how they'd owned a little bar in Kansas for a while and then moved out to California to help a friend build houses, until Claire got cancer and her parents, too, and she asked to go home to Wyoming. "I buried all three of them," he said. He then told me a story about when he enlisted in Vietnam, his older brother got jealous and enlisted, too, but then died in a car accident in Minnesota the day before he shipped out. "Just like that, my older brother, gone in a flash." He talked about being in helicopters in Vietnam. He talked about an old girlfriend named Rose who drove her car into a tree. Before he left, he said, "But I'm a toughie. I'm a toughie. I've got a good friend. His name is Jesus."

I saw Ron time and time again in the back room of the Roughed Up Duck over the next couple of years, and the stories were always the same—whether he told them to me or some girl sitting next to me. The stories were so scripted, so paced, so well timed, he'd clearly told them to a million girls in a million bars, just like this, and every time I heard him say, "Well, let me tell you a little bit about myself . . . ," this thought came rushing through my mind: *You're telling the wrong stories. We're telling the wrong stories.* What did this mean? And who's telling the story? These stories defined his life: constellated, hardened, the only visible stepping stones that led to the present moment in the back room of the Roughed Up Duck.

And now I have told you the same story about Aimee Semple McPherson that everyone has told before. I'm telling the wrong story. *Where do you want to spend eternity?* What if what's interesting about McPherson are not the lurid scandals but the real and quite regular person, the strange bird who existed in that interstitial silence, who gave her life away, who stopped at nothing to win souls? What if Aimee Semple McPherson wasn't the woman who emerged one afternoon from the Mexican desert or who died of a barbiturate overdose on revival tour or who was beautiful or widowed or a charlatan, but rather the woman who left out the back door with Charlie Chaplin, or the woman who set out on the road with her mother and children in tow, one hand on the wheel and the other riding waves out the open window?

It's not a matter of pretending she was normal; she was not. I can't dismiss the spectacle as simply the public's failure to notice her "real" feats—the spectacle was her currency, it was part of the real, and it was deliberate. It was true *and* staged, and the sheer force of her conviction made her virtually indestructible.

Have you ever felt indestructible? That ringing freedom from inhibitions, when perhaps you're sitting next to an open passenger window against the roaring highway wind, feeling, if only for a moment, that you've figured everything out? How do you behave? You touch the cheeks of your adoring fans and throw your head back laughing. You wear an angel's gown over high-heeled shoes and a bedazzled cross bigger than the one above the pulpit. You preach in Hollywood, in the segregated South, from the boot of your big black car while you're tearing across the country. You open your towering lakeside mansion to every pregnant girl in Los Angeles who asks, because you're "everybody's sister."

And two, three times a night you sweat under stadium lights and bellow the gospel truth to the music of a hundred brass instruments and the cries of your devotees. You help anyone who asks. You feed them bread through the Depression, pose for more photos than any movie star, and of course your private life is made strange by all of this. You get facelifts. You go to China. You become a pill head. You punch your mother in the nose. You start your own radio station without any programming prepared. You stage your own death to spend a week with the man you love. You don't think it through. You don't have to.

HEAVENLY MOTHER WILL BELIEVE YOU

Eliza Snow

The Salt Lake City Temple Square grounds are crowded with tourists. I step into the North Visitors' Center, where a bird's-eye diorama of first-century Jerusalem dominates the foyer. The diorama is behind glass, and a wide-eyed blond woman surrounded by her six towheaded children gesticulates over it, describing Jesus riding into the city on a donkey.

"A donkey!" two boys squinch their noises, giggling.

"Oh, yes," she says, and she traces the path where his followers had lain out palm fronds like a red carpet, much to the Pharisees' chagrin.

I trail behind them into the next room, an atrium of paintings depicting Jesus' miracles or Old Testament prophets predicting them: Jesus feeding the masses at Galilee; Isaiah prophesying the Virgin birth; Jesus healing the leper; Ezekiel's desert vision of the Messiah's four faces; Jesus surprising Mary Magdalene outside his tomb—there he is, with his arms out, like, *Mary, "oh, ye of little faith,"* you've been *punk'd; I'm alive!* It's high divine comedy, the resurrection. When I look up, the family is gone. I scan the room for evidence of anything other than mainline Christiandom but come up short, except for the three sets of missionaries, with their laminated nametags and identical uniforms, idling in pairs at the information desk.

It isn't until I ascend a spiral ramp to the second floor that the Mormon cosmology begins to reveal itself. A gleaming twelve-foot Byzantine Jesus stands at the landing, surrounded by a 360-degree painting of the solar system in saturated blues and purples. Visitors encircle the statue on benches, snapping photos or whispering among themselves. Here is a Christ no Calvin or Luther could have conceived of. A risen Lord who presides not only over the earth but over the universe, who calls forth a new set of questions about the nature of our existence and the scope of His domain, especially in regard to other planets.

The first place where Mormon theology departs from mainline Christianity is in its interpretation of the first line of Genesis: "In the beginning, God created heaven and earth," for which the original Hebrew uses the plural form of "god": *Elohim*. Catholics interpret this plurality as the trinity—Father, Son, Holy Ghost—but Mormons read this as evidence of multiple gods presiding over other parts of the universe. But our Heavenly Father, to whom we owe worship, is also referred to as Elohim, and he is the literal parent of Jesus, and the literal parent of all human spirits on Earth. As Latter-Day Saints founder Joseph Smith said, even "God the Father had a Father." Smith taught that before earthly time, God was a man on another planet, who ascended into Heaven and created the Celestial Kingdom where every single soul that would ever exist on Earth was born. So Smith professed a theology whereby married men, sealed in eternity to their families, could one day assume godhead in the afterlife. (But Mormons think about this probably as often as Presbyterians parse out the trinity when they pray: *Am I talking to God, Jesus, or the Holy Ghost? Whatever, please accept my thanks, please help me.*)

The rest of the second floor is devoted to more wall-to-wall paintings depicting other Old Testament parables and the minor miracles of the New. Around a bend, I find life-size figures of Adam and Eve, coifed and wearing tunics, against a pastel Eden. Here, too, I begin to see differences: They're confident and healthy; there is no apple or serpent in sight. Eve is not the bearer of the Fall, nor the temptress, but rather the woman who gave us the opportunity to be fully human.

Flanking each gallery are movie theaters screening two films on repeat: in one, the passion story, and in the other, the narrative of the Book of Mormon, the lost testimony. I sidle in as quietly as I can, only to find that I am completely alone in the two-hundred-seat theater. I sit in the back row anyway. The film dramatizes the story of how, amid great persecution, the lost tribes of Israel journeyed to North America six hundred years before the crucifixion; upon their arrival they battled the natives for untold generations until the lost tribes were almost extinct. During the three-day journey from Hell to Heaven following his crucifixion, Jesus visited the remaining Israelites in America and delivered his final dictum, which was inscribed onto golden tablets by the prophet Moroni and discovered by Joseph Smith in the woods outside of Palmyra, New York, approximately one thousand years later.

It's the basement of the North Visitors' Center, which I almost miss, that explicitly depicts the religious history unique to Mormons. That it's in the basement—the site of secrets or storage, that which we'd prefer to keep out of sight—calls into question the idea of assimilation, the merits of revealing theology in degrees if you're used to nonbelievers calling you a cult. In the middle of the room is a pyramid structure of the Book of Mormon in all eighty-three languages it's been translated into, and toward the back are small video stations where visitors can watch various addresses given by current and former presidents of the church, the living prophets, on any number of topics, from parenting to politics to gender parity.

Along the wall are a series of exhibits. Beginning with the Old Testament prophets, I work my way through Job, Isaiah, Elijah, Daniel, Peter, Paul, and then Joseph Smith. I look up and see Sweeney across the room, legs akimbo and face tilted upward, like the gallant Adam I saw upstairs. He's standing in front of a smaller quartet of exhibits, the forgotten prophets who happened in between: Nephi, Lehi, Alma, Moroni. The New Testament ends, and the Book of Mormon fills in the gaps: God *continued* to create prophets, and continues to today.

It was 1845. It was night. Eliza Roxcy Snow sat on a little upturned barrel trying to write. They were fewer in numbers by then, many having given up and stayed in Illinois or returned east. She'd left her family in Ohio, long back—it wasn't even a disagreement or anything; they'd converted, too, but they just hadn't been willing to keep moving. They had property, other children, all of that. So Eliza Snow went west with the Latter-Day Saints, over the Mississippi River into Missouri, where they'd been battered and run out, then deeper into the heartland, to Nauvoo, Illinois. By then she was considered old, and she was barren.

Something had happened to her during the Mormon War in Missouri about which no one spoke but everyone knew. Joseph Smith had approached her in a little stand of buckeyes and proposed to her a plural marriage, to make her a "mother in Israel," if not on Earth. She moved into his home. Then two years later he was lynched, and now they were on the move again, in wagons. She tried to keep her focus on the Celestial Plan, what Smith had whispered to her in the moonlight, under the trees. He was up on some new planet, tending and tilling for their eventual arrival, all the wives and children. She pressed the graphite to the paper again, trying to understand a celestial organization that could take her as she was, a God who could understand what it felt like to be a woman on Earth at that moment. And then something new happened:

> *I had learned to call thee Father,*
> *Thru thy Spirit from on high,*
> *But, until the key of knowledge*
> *Was restored, I knew not why.*
> *In the heav'ns are parents single?*
> *No, the thought makes reason stare!*
> *Truth is reason; truth eternal*
> *Tells me I've a mother there.*

A Heavenly Mother. Women weren't supposed to—*aren't* supposed to—be able to receive revelation, and so the church has never acknowledged the poem "O My Father" to have been divinely inspired. Rather, the church's narrative focuses more on Snow's selflessness, how she sought to comfort the Saints with poetry during the worst of their persecution by reinforcing the religion's full scope: that their souls were literally conceived in Heaven by God, where they existed in a pre-birth state as a family in the Celestial Kingdom.

> *For a wise and glorious purpose*
> *Thou hast placed me here on earth*
> *And withheld the recollection*
> *Of my former friends and birth*

So the church accepts this premise, braids it into doctrine, says nothing. "O My Father" is adapted into the official hymnal. Later, when Snow starts performing blessings, no one says a thing. She gets to Zion. She enters into a plural marriage with Brigham Young. She starts the Women's Relief Society. She runs that town.

We know now that Eliza had likely been raped not long before she wrote "O My Father," during the war. But it took two hundred years before historian Andrea Radke-Moss said this out loud, from a conference lectern at Brigham Young University, after an agonized unveiling of some old primary documents. Mormon women from all over the world clung to this news: women abused and assaulted and silenced. Eliza Snow, like the Heavenly Mother, might know the pain of continuing to live in that body, a body violated and made invisible. Weirdly, my first association is musician and activist Kathleen Hanna in the documentary *The Punk Singer*: She's standing on her deck, squinting into the sun, saying, "When a man tells the truth, it's the truth. And when as a woman I go to tell the truth, I feel I have to negotiate the way I'll be perceived. I feel like there's always the suspicion around a woman's truth—the idea that she's exaggerating." Concerning her own experiences with abuse, and how it led to the formation of the riot grrrl movement, Hanna says, "I wouldn't want to tell anybody the whole entire story because it sounded crazy. It sounded just, like, too big of a can of worms. Like, who would believe me? And then I was like, *other women would believe me.*"

Sweeney and I are at the Salt Lake City temple grounds with my father and stepmother. It's summertime, and it's hot. My dad and Tessa were going to drive out to Wyoming to stay with us but decided that the trip would be too much; they suggested we meet them in Utah. So we drove across the Continental Divide, not so far off course from the Mormon Trail.

This same summer, Latter-Day Saints human rights lawyer Kate Kelly will found Ordain Women, an organization seeking gender equality in the Mormon church. OW, among other things, is compelling the prophets to pray for the ordination of women in the priesthood: to allow them to administer the sacrament, blessings, and baptisms, as well as to assume seats of authority within the annual priesthood sessions. The hope for ordination is primary here, but it's more symptom than goal to OW's larger mission: to intervene in what they see as a failure in the church's imagination, a failure that has stymied women's full participation and potential as Latter-Day Saints. OW is not claiming revelation; they are asking the First Presidency, the church's highest governing office, for the right to try to seek it—and, in a somewhat more complicated move, they are compelling the First Presidency to seek revelation on their behalf. They do not identify as rebels. Their mission statement asserts that the "fundamental tenets of Mormonism support gender equality: God is male and female, father and mother, and all of us can progress to be like them someday. Priesthood, we are taught, is essential to this process." The last time there was an onslaught of people proposing feminist prophecy in the Mormon church was in 1993, when six members were excommunicated for, among other things, publishing at length about the importance of the Mother in Heaven.

But today I am only dimly aware of this. Sweeney, my dad, Tessa, and I are at the temple grounds only as happenstance tourists.

After I find Sweeney in the basement of the North Visitors' Center, the four of us reconnect on the central walkway and decide to step across the street for a cigarette—a luxury my parents partake in only when they're with us. Tessa smokes a clove.

I ask everyone what they think so far. I turn on a small digital recorder.

"I don't know yet," Sweeney says.

Tessa pipes up. "I find the architecture really focused and imaginative and purposeful. It's quite enviable, really, because as a musician I'm used to seeing squashed-down committee rot. This is very intentional and quite amazing, actually. Looking at everything, from the staging to the fact that there was all this rehearsal space in the convention center, the sense of color and proportion. There have been no compromises."

My dad spews a bit of smoke. "What she said."

"Also," Tessa says, "when you look at the choice of flora that they use on the externals and the internals of the architecture—it's a really carefully chosen English pastoral version of what plants are supposed to be. In no way do you have native plants around here, or rough, unruly plants."

"Yeah," I say. "No feisty fighter plants. Which is interesting because I feel like desert plants would actually be emblematic of the Mormon experience."

Tessa nods. "Yes, but this is the afterlife."

I nod.

My dad finally speaks. "Actually, this place creeps me out—"

Tessa: "What he said."

My dad: "—where you've got one religion, one intention, and everyone follows along. And so yes, you can pour all your resources into realizing one unified, you know, vision or manifestation, like that conference center, but it doesn't reflect any independent thought, either. So it's admirable and creepy."

"Why do you think there are beehives everywhere?" I ask.

Tessa responds instantly. "I think it's all being part of the hive, being in service. Yes."

Women pass us by, wearing T-shirts under their tank tops, on their way to the grounds. It seems we are the only people smoking cigarettes for a thousand miles, and I'm embarrassed.

A couple days earlier, Sweeney and I had gone to one of the two bars in Provo, a city of one hundred thousand people. (For perspective, we had just been in Walden, Colorado, a town of six hundred people and eight bars). At the Provo bar, we were served in thirty-two-ounce glasses because all the beer is 4 percent alcohol content. We were visiting our friend Hallie, who was working for the Utah Forest Service that summer and renting a room just down the street from Brigham Young University and the missionary training center headquarters. Hallie had taken us to the bar, where the clientele was like a cartoon of "bar" types: everyone had tattoos, facial piercings, biker beards, and late-stage alcoholism. She looked at us as we walked in, like, *Right?* Instead of coffee shops, there were ice cream parlors everywhere. We slept in hammocks on her porch that night, and talked with her roommates, all ex-Mormons who had all completed their missions at twenty, twenty-one years old, and then promptly left the church. Anyway, I can't remember if this is true or not, but I felt like I could see Salt Lake from that porch, shining, yellow as sulfur, far below.

Eliza Snow grew up in a progressive Reformed Baptist family in Mantua, Ohio, and, like her brothers, received a full intellectual education. She started publishing poems in periodicals at seventeen years old, and even as a child, according to Brigham Young professor Maureen Beecher, had composed her homework in verse. On Independence Day of 1826, she was tapped by a prominent newspaper to write the elegies for John Adams and Thomas Jefferson, both of whom had died within hours of one another. From there she became a minor name of letters, a wunderkind.

Meanwhile, it was the Second Great Awakening. Americans went to revivals as a form of entertainment, often al fresco. You went to get your heart moved, to have demons cast out, to feel the real, material presence of the Holy Spirit, and to have a conversion experience—even if you already belonged to a church. Religion was hot. The part of New York where Joseph Smith grew up was called the "burned over" district because it was considered to have been torched by revival, and he was part of that moment. And somewhere in the wilds of Ohio, Eliza Snow was awaiting her own conversion experience.

Snow's parents actually helped establish one of Mantua's Baptist congregations, and also, later on, participated in its split, entertaining various itinerant preachers and doctrines for a number of years, until the Latter-Day Saints were invited to their church one day in 1831 to give their spiel, just a year after Joseph Smith had dug up the golden tablets. But Snow was notably the last of her relatives to join the Saints.

Snow said of her upbringing, "Although my parents adhered to the Baptist creed, they extended to their children the right, and afforded us every opportunity we desired, to examine all creeds—to hear and judge—to 'prove all things.'" Snow, too, was actively engaged in the theological conversations of her parents and community. She even wrote in her journals prior to her Mormon conversion about studying the "ancient prophets" and attending LDS mission meetings and discussions, and being especially convinced by individuals' testimonies and the reasoning behind a belief in the continuation of prophecy. Still, she carried on in removed consideration for four years before asking for a baptism.

All of this is to say: Snow's conversion was deliberate, and its story helps to show that she took great pains to familiarize herself with Mormon doctrine and theology—and she refused to concede to it until she felt that she fully understood.

When she wrote "O My Father" on that wagon train, they were heading west to Zion. They were finally somewhat out of American society's reach, and the Ute Indians didn't take issue with the faith's new reading of the Crucifixion. She entered into a plural marriage with prophet Brigham Young and became a presidentess. She saw to the needs of widows, the sick and elderly, and organized the education of wives in domestic industry: how to can, pickle, save grain, reconstitute rags, purify water. Her op-eds on family welfare, domestic industry, theology, and politics were featured often in the *Women's Exponent*, as were her poems. Later she labored for women's suffrage, too, but she was not a feminist, and she was not fond of what her contemporaries were up to back east.

Snow wasn't against the idea of equal rights per se—she just wasn't focused on things happening in real time. For her, equal rights for women was eschatological. In her 1976 paper "Eliza R. Snow and the Woman Question," LDS research historian Jill Mulvay Derr clarifies that for Snow, female empowerment could happen only within the proper bounds of hierarchy provided by the divinely sanctioned priesthood. Derr concludes that Snow saw her role, and the role she inspired other Mormon women to fulfill, as that of a "steward" to their godly husbands, and that she believed the passage to liberation could only happen by fulfilling their mandate as helpmeet, abolishing the "curse of Eve."

In an 1852 address to the Women's Relief Society, Snow—critiquing the rebelliousness of the eastern suffragists—says:

> It was through disobedience that woman came into her present position, and it is only by obedience, honoring God in all the institutions He has revealed to us, that we can come out from under that curse, regain the position originally occupied by Eve, and attain a fullness of exaltation in the presence of God.

And what was Eve's original position, in the LDS tradition? It is starkly different than all other Abrahamic readings. Eve was equal partner to Adam, co-creator with God, noble and mighty, "Mother of All Living," and she understood the necessity of the Fall: that in order to multiply, in order to have children and populate the Heavenly Kingdom, in order to experience spiritual ascension, she had to become mortal. So, after a deep emotional, intellectual, and spiritual deliberation, she selflessly partook of the Tree of Knowledge. She was a hero.

Thinking of Eve, Snow (according to Derr) "did not ignore the woman question, but rather attempted to synthesize an assortment of Mormon doctrines into a neat package that would provide for the eternal expansion of women's roles"—and by "the eternal," she means the celestial realm.

But it actually happened. Snow drastically enlarged women's lives in Utah in many of the same ways as her eastern contemporaries—except not by protest, but by being so fine an orator, so close to the core of the empire, that she was able to give agency to women while still satisfying her role as a mouthpiece for men. The rhetorician of Zion.

She was sincere, don't get me wrong—a true believer. I don't mean that her revelations and piety were disingenuous. Rather, she must have had great faith and loyalty to the kingdom to have known both so well that she could usher in seismic changes in their own language. Snow introduced socially controversial charges by using theological reasoning—that women should be allowed to perform blessings and devote their lives to vocations, and that a Heavenly Mother resides alongside the Heavenly Father—without ever being seen publicly as anything but the ideal of Mormon womanhood.

Missionaries roam the Temple Square grounds, offering to answer questions and give tours. I decline a few times but finally accept one from Sister Alvine, a young woman around my age from Cameroon. Our first stop is the old tabernacle. She asks me to sit in the pews while she assumes her position behind the pulpit. Dropping a penny and then a pin upon the lectern, she demonstrates the astounding acoustics. Then she plays a recording of "O My Father" so that I might get a full taste of what choral music sounded like during the century and a half when the hall was used for annual church conferences.

She walks back to me along the central aisle and exclaims what an amazing feat it was for the pioneers to have built this space out in the desert where "there was no one." Of course, there wasn't "no one"; there were all the tribes of the southwest deserts, like the Ute

Indians. She runs her hand along one of the columns that hold up the mezzanine, which are constructed from pine painted to look like marble ("Could you have guessed?" she asks) and continues to speak of the great, beautiful Utah desert—the desolate, lonely gift of a place—which she considers now with a visceral affection, as though she herself had been among the pioneers.

The connection to the landscape of Zion is a significant part of LDS inheritance, even for an ex-Catholic émigré from Cameroon. The openness of the desert, perhaps, made possible a certain kind of theological reflection, a reordering of the American man's relationship to the earth. I think of essayist Gretel Ehrlich's description in *The Solace of Open Spaces* of the expanses of the American West as having a "spiritual equivalent" and being able to "heal what is burdensome and divided in us . . . Space represents sanity, not a life purified, dull, or 'spaced out' but one that might accommodate intelligently any idea or situation." The Saints found terror, but also freedom from persecution, at the shores of that improbable lake, not much more than a mirage.

Standing now in the tabernacle with Sister Alvine, I wonder what her feelings are about the fact that just twenty years earlier, women weren't allowed to be missionaries, let alone what's going on with Ordain Women. But when she smiles, all I ask is, "Do you know the work of Eliza Snow? I think she wrote that hymn." She smiles at me but shakes her head. Then she clasps her hands together. "Shall we go to the Main Visitors' Center?" She leads us across another big green lawn. While we walk, she asks if I have any questions, and I have a lot, but all I come up with is whether Latter-Day Saints believe in the Trinity, which I already know the answer to. (They don't.) "You know, some people think we baptize corpses, dead bodies," she laughs. (They don't.)

Inside the next building, she offers us our own copy of the Book of Mormon and her missionary calling card before leading us to a model cross-section of the temple, which looks like an elaborate dollhouse. The temple itself—huge and castle-like and gleaming white—sits just outside the window. Only those in good standing with the church, the most pure of heart, the sanctified, are allowed inside, and it is where all the most important ceremonies are carried out: marriages, baptisms, sealings—Sister Alvine describes the belief about celestial families, how in order to spend eternity on your heavenly planet with your loved ones, you must be sealed. My stepmother, who has held it together until now, screws up her face. "But what if your family sucks and you don't want to spend eternity with them?"

"Oh," Sister Alvine says, "it's not required. Just if you want to, like a marriage."

To picture it is ridiculous, all of us together: me, my mom, Aaron, my sister Charlie, my stepbrother Noel, Leo, my dad, Tessa, my stepparents' extended families, from whom they are almost entirely estranged, all our pets over the years—everyone, alone on a planet, tending a garden, like the Little Prince on asteroid B-612 with a rake, a tree, a single flower. I know that's not right, that we'd be gods—or maybe just the husbands would be gods, I'm not sure. Surely Mormons have weird families, too. But there is something about the idea that strikes me.

I remember suddenly the feeling I had when my father-in-law Dan told me about the family escape plan. It was years ago—I'd probably been with Sweeney for just a few months at that point. We were sitting at Michael's Pub in Pleasantville, New York, and Dan said, "Have I told you about the escape plan? I think it's time to tell her." He looked at Sweeney, then his daughter, then his other son. "Here it is: If there's ever a natural disaster, or another September eleventh–type event in New York, in the city, no matter where we all are, we all have to try to gather at thirty-seven Sutton Place—" that was Sweeney's mother's house, which Dan had moved out of years ago after the divorce and which, through a contentious settlement, they were in the middle of selling, mostly by Dan's insistence. I knew that; he knew that I knew that; but that's where we had to meet, all of us, "even Grandma Rodway. Then we'll make our way up the Taconic Parkway to Jo Jo's Pizza. So if someone can't make it to thirty-seven Sutton Place, then they should just go straight to Jo Jo's, by whatever means, ninety miles north. There will be water there, pizza, a goat farm, other animals." From there we could begin to eke out a plan for the end of the world.

Now, whether or not heading up a major highway out of the nation's biggest city is a very sophisticated plan is debatable. I doubt any other family would choose Jo Jo's in particular, but there would be millions and millions of people heading up that thruway. And then—what? Was this a mass shooting, a flood, the apocalypse? In Dan's scenarios—and he brought up the escape plan with me over and over for years—it always seemed to be all of the above. And in a way he, and therefore we, greatly relished in these plans to survive the end, about where we would go from there—Maine, Cape May, the ocean.

I have never known anyone to fantasize about the apocalypse as much as Dan. There's a heroism in it, that's part of it—he's a lawyer, and he loves saving people. I don't mean to imply that those two things are inalterably linked, but for him they are. If you're in trouble—booked in jail, having a mental health crisis, stuck on the side of the highway in Ohio, or just scared and sad—he will drive over valleys and rivers to get to you. His kids inherited his fierce sense of family loyalty, too, a mythology so powerful that it had been made true. But preparing for end times also springs from his conservative politics, ever battling that "house of cards" liberal administration, the "shredding" of the constitution, the end of America. When I first met him, he told me he used to be Republican but was now an anarchist, although his was an anarchism that mimicked the Tea Party, which of course didn't exist yet.

As the years went on, we'd fight bitterly about politics, about human rights, white privilege, racism, cresting one night as protests formed in Ferguson, Missouri, following the murder of Michael Brown.

"What would you have done if the military started driving tanks into Pleasantville?" I demanded.

"I'd pack up my family and go!"

"Well, you should be so lucky that you had enough capital to do that!"

"Do you blame me for raising my family in Pleasantville, for making money?"

The next time I saw him, Sweeney was having a panic attack and so Dan had left work early, come to our house, and then called his other kids to come, too, and we sat in our little living room, laughing, talking about the darkness, and he said that we must always, always do this for each other.

He is always saving people. That's his thing. And when he told me about the escape plan, I felt saved, I felt accounted for, very squarely and haphazardly accounted for, whether it was a good plan or not. I was going to be counted on the last day. They were going to be waiting for me at Jo Jo's. It felt like what I imagine a sealing might. He had vision. Jo Jo's was the afterlife.

In 1867, as the president-elect of the Women's Relief Society, Snow announced, "We will do as we are directed by the Priesthood—" winking, if not to anyone in particular, then to herself, "—to do good, to bring into requisition every capacity we possess for doing good." But the scholar Maureen Beecher notes that when Snow's Relief Society initiatives were thwarted, she often commanded that the disapproving priesthood leader should be "reasoned" with. Moreover, in that same address, Snow calls her fellow Mormon women "stewards" to the priesthood, "relieving their masters of certain tasks." Just a few minutes in, and we are in murky terrain; she is already making agents of the women. "Do not run to him with every trifle," and, "If anything, we should relieve the Bishops rather than adding to their multitudinous labors." In saying both of these things, Snow was able to make a case satisfying enough to the priesthood for women to continue their spiritual, social, and professional work with relative independence. This was the sort of public reasoning she used, over and over again, to justify that women should be trained in medicine, business, accounting, and journalism, and allowed (though not officially ordained) to perform blessings.

In 1870, during the height of accusations that Mormon women were "enslaved" by, among other things, plural marriage, Snow asks the women of Zion, "Do you know of any place on the face of the earth where woman has more liberty, and where she enjoys such high and glorious privileges, as she does here as a Latter-Day Saint?" Derr insists that Snow's exhortations were not "mere rhetoric," primarily because the mid-1800s had in fact ushered in a massive expansion of the female sphere in Utah, since they lived in a society at that moment that was egalitarian by necessity, including, that very year, the right to vote.

But fifteen years in, the Women's Relief Society was making the priesthood wary. What did they do, exactly? Organize child care, demonstrate food-saving practices, start hospitals, build granaries, publish a newspaper, sure, but what *else*?

In 1880, the priesthood—bishops, husbands, whomever—called for an accounting. Snow invited them to give final remarks at the Relief Society's annual conference, in order for, in her own words, "the stronger to follow the weak that if anything needs correcting, it can be corrected." The minutes from the conference report that, among other similar elucidations, "Sister Eliza explained that she had been given the mission to *assist* the priesthood [in organizing Relief Societies]." As the men, their arms waving frantically in explanation, emphasized that the women's roles were to remain distinct from the male sphere, that they were "set apart" for special work, Snow nodded, her mouth trained in a serious listener's frown. That's right, she said, taking the stage back, women need to "serve and uphold [your] husbands and brothers like the devout and steadfast Miriam in upholding the hands of Moses."

Miriam? I look her up: She was an Old Testament prophetess. Does anyone in the room register this? She was Moses' heroic sister who sang a song for the Jews as the Red Sea collapsed on the Egyptian army. She was given the words and the melody by God, picked up an instrument and told others to do the same, and then led them, with music and dance, into the utterly unsafe desert. Set apart, you see, for special work. In the camps described in Exodus, Miriam and her other brother Aaron seethe: "Was it only to Moses that God spoke? Did He not speak to us as well?" God intervenes here, corrects Miriam. Yes, he did speak to her, and to Aaron, but Moses has been chosen to lead, all right? So God punishes her, and Aaron too, for their complaints. Miriam gets zapped with illness and Moses has to ask God to please just let her be, so he does. It was like that back then, with God.

I don't know what happens to Miriam after that; she disappears in the landscape of Jewish patriarchs. But Eliza Snow could have invoked anyone as a model that day at the conference, she could have said Sarah or Mary or many other women whose lives and meanings have been pilfered by patriarchy and appropriated—but she said Miriam, the complicated prophetess. And no one in the room but her seemed to know.

Back at the temple, we're leaving, driving away. Tessa remarks that the most moving parts of the visit for her were the depictions of the plants and animals, especially the twelve golden oxen upholding the baptismal font in the temple basement, which of course we did not see in person, we saw it in a miniature model of the temple's interior. Tessa is saying she believes in the mystical power of things on Earth, social contracts, earthly empathy and ethics. She keeps reiterating, as we drive through the endlessly undulating brown mountains, that she can't understand why anyone believes in this shit, or that she has no patience—"I just have no patience. I believe in animals, that's my religion. You know?" I mean, I do know, in a way, and I don't— because it actually seems really important to me that one should try to understand why people believe the shit they do, and I feel like my position on this should be obvious to Tessa by now. Bewilderingly, my dad, a small feather hanging from his earring, says nothing. Sweeney is driving, and he drives like a go-cart racer, and everyone is nervous but me.

In 2014, Kate Kelly, the founder of Ordain Women, was excommunicated for apostasy.

I listened to an episode about it on the podcast *Mormon Stories* a couple of months later. *Mormon Stories* gives voice to the experiences of progressive or post-Mormons; the host himself, John Dehlin, is an observant Latter-Day Saint, though he also has been excommunicated for his public acceptance of homosexuality. In this episode, Dehlin interviews Kelly at length. She is quick and funny and articulate about her formation in the church, her devotion to the theology, even the contested historicity of the Book of Mormon—she doesn't really care because divine inspiration works in strange ways.

Dehlin asks her about the accusations, saying that it was not the content of her request with Ordain Women, but the tone that had pinned her as apostate. Kelly laughs, says that of course the accusation revealed more about the church than her: "When they say tone was the problem, I agree that it was a problem for them. The tone was effective . . . It was respectable, because we spoke the language of Mormons, because I said 'I am a returned missionary, I was married in the temple, I went to BYU, and I believe that women should be ordained.'"

She says that while women's ordination is one of her concerns, what she thinks the church is most rattled by are her ideas about how revelation takes place: "I believe revelation is participatory."

She jokes about how the church now believes she'll be cast into the outer darkness when she dies—though she is not worried. She discusses an upcoming Ordain Women action, a worldwide fast for gender justice in all religions. She is confident that her excommunication portends greater changes to come. "I'm not sure when, but someday a young Mormon girl will say I'm a sellout." She laughs. Then she adds, "And I'll be happy!"

In the few years after this interview, Kelly goes to Kenya, works for women's rights in Somalia, maintains her board seat for Ordain Women, gets a divorce, and moves back to Salt Lake City to work as a strategic advocate and policy counsel for Planned Parenthood. In 2016, she appears on a live audience taping of *Mormon Stories* once more. She looks absolutely vibrant, sitting onstage with the host. She wears a stylish sleeveless dress and dark-rimmed glasses, smiling. She shares a bit about her feelings about transitioning out of the church, the clean break it allowed her because the church revealed itself to be "fundamentally misogynistic" and because she knows she did the right thing. She shares about trying alcohol for the first time, talks about her divorce, and laughs about how she's fulfilling all of the things Mormons warn about. "You see, you see . . . That's what happens to apostates. And I work at Planned Parenthood now, so I'm, like, at the bottom of the slippery slope." She laughs and laughs, and the audience laughs, too.

She talks a lot, then, about reproductive rights, about what Planned Parenthood Utah does and is up to, and about how important sexual education is within the church and outside of it, and she talks frankly and passionately about how important a woman's right to choose is—no exceptions. And I watch this video, brimming with joy, because I think I'm about to see a theological defense of abortion, a theological defense of women's rights.

A woman from the audience asks Kelly how her belief in the Heavenly Mother informs the work she does now, and Kelly takes a while to answer. She's kind of deflated now, but also incredulous, like, *I don't have time for this kind of thing anymore, I just don't have any patience.* She says finally, sharply—"It wasn't empowering at all because no one talked about her." I'm waiting, as I always am, for a religious feminist to say that the moral framework of Christianity fundamentally compels her to support women, to dismantle the patriarchy as Christ did, or whatever, just to do the thing that the Religious Right does and say something like, "I just know that I am fulfilling God's will, and anyone who disagrees is a heretic." Instead she says, "Does the woman down the street have enough to eat? Can women control their own destinies? Those are the things that matter to me. And so I actually don't think about God that much at all." She presses her lips together, looks directly at the questioner, and nods.

But I guess this is the thing—is that God? That *is* God. That is thinking about God. That is a life in service. That is everything Jesus/ God was talking about. And once you're doing it, once you're *actually* doing it, you're like, whatever, middle fingers up—God, no God, I'm gonna make sure that lady has enough to eat, and that that other lady can control her destiny.

So why does Kelly remain in Ordain Women? She's doing it for her niece, she says, and for all the LDS girls like her niece. But her participation will not last long, cannot last long, if she has no stake. If she is only a secular savior, then her arguments will lose meaning for everyone, mostly her. What do you do, as a leftist feminist, in any church? You stay in the shitty place where you'll never win because the systems by which it operates are so fundamentally patriarchal that there is no way out, save a revolution. So you do your amazing work and forget God. Who can blame her? She's like, *Ah, what am I going to do, battle around for decades with these old-man "prophets" with dementia about fuck-all? Nah.*

So what do women do? They break away and make their own church. That happens. Or they stay and wait for eternity in faith that things will change, but things don't really change, not much. Or they become secular.

I say all this to Sweeney, and he says, "Dorothy Day stayed," and I say, "Yeah, but she basically started another religion," and he says, "She would be offended to hear you say that."

In recent years, the list of requests from Ordain Women have deescalated in scope. Rather than full ordination, they've gotten more specific: They want to be official witnesses at baptisms (a role reserved for males), sit with young Mormon women during their private worthiness interviews with local male leaders, serve as witnesses at marriages and sealings (again, a duty assigned to males), and hold their own babies while male priesthood holders perform naming blessings. Much of their work takes place on the internet, or standing plaintively outside of priesthood meetings waiting to be invited inside. In 2015, they released a series of photos of women performing the various tasks of their request, so that the Mormon public might be able to see what it would look like, literally, so that people could begin to imagine it. To have revelation.

THIS BUILDING IS YOURS

The Takeover

T oward the end of 1970, a pack of young women sailed down 1st and 2nd Avenues on bicycles, the freezing wind at their cheeks, sneakers mashing pedals. They looked as formidable as the Women's Army from Lizzie Borden's *Born in Flames* or a matriarchal *Mad Max*. They were scouring the streets of Manhattan for a headquarters.

On the last day of the year, more women, crowds of them, set out into the snowy night, through drifts so thick it muted their laughter, led only by candles and streetlamps. When they arrived at the building they'd chosen, they didn't worry whether or not the police in the 9th Precinct across the street could see them.

They climbed through the windows of 330 5th Street.

When they were all in, they cheered and smiled in the dark, ducking under beams and over glass. Some of them made out in the shadows; some began sealing the windows from the cold. Maybe they passed around bottles of wine and shared stories in the moonlight, huddled in their sleeping bags for warmth.

By morning, they'd secured the fort: the Fifth Street Women's Building.

During the following days, they made a world inside. They jerry-rigged some lighting and laid out afghans and rugs and strung floral sheets from the rafters. They opened their doors to women in need. They held workshops, parties, and feasts. They fought among themselves. Some of them hooked up in the icy stairwells, fully clothed in sheepskin jackets and wool socks.

Every afternoon, the police across the street picked their teeth and caught what images they could through cracks in the black-curtained windows: a child's plastic tricycle, the corner of a table set for twenty, an arm gesturing in a consciousness-raising circle, paper snowflakes strewn across the floor.

Twelve days later, the cops stormed the building. One month after that, it was bulldozed. Today, a dozen Dodge Chargers sit where the building once was. The site is now a parking lot for the 9th Precinct.

Or, at least for a long time, this was the story I told myself.

I was twenty-two years old on the hundredth anniversary of International Women's Day in 2011, and I was feeling pretty blue. I was in the last months of college and my baby sister Charlie was in some trouble with the law. I was sitting at my computer arranging for last-minute travel home to Oregon to help her out when I got an email from a professor with the subject line "pictures to cheer u up."

It was a link to a *Huffington Post* slideshow that actress and activist Marlo Thomas had put together, chronicling her involvement in the Equal Rights Amendment campaigns. "It was like a pipe had burst, and our homes could no longer hold us," wrote Thomas. "So we took to the street. And we marched. And we lobbied our legislators. And we made speeches. And we were being heard." The images in the slideshow were of Thomas herself, and Bella Abzug in her big hats, and Betty Friedan in old age, and Gloria Steinem and Flo Kennedy and Shirley Chisholm, all of these women hanging out at apartments, circling the capital, linking arms, laughing.

The images gave me pause. I was born in 1988, an American girl, white and middle-class, the beneficiary, in one way or another, of civil rights secured by second-wave feminism: birth control, abortion, gay rights, Title IX, "girl power." As a child I was given Marlo Thomas's book *Free to Be . . . a Family*, an attempt by my parents to salve the wounds of divorce. And while she'd always held a special place in my heart, Thomas was among a group of activists whom my generation has seemingly dismissed for their sentimentality, for their middle-class-centrism, for their inability to create a feminist rhetoric comprehensive enough to include women of color, working-class women, women in developing nations, queer women. I knew this. But I couldn't stop looking at the slideshow.

I flew home the next day to see my sister. She was under house arrest. I sat around for a few days while my parents whispered "How did it come to this?" at our tiny kitchen table and while my sister sat stonily in the basement watching reruns of *Ugly Betty*. I was frustrated that no one really wanted to talk about our underlying family dysfunction. So, on the last day of my trip, I climbed the apple tree in our backyard and sat there, sullen, smoking cigarettes, waiting for something to happen. Eventually, my sister lugged herself out of the basement and climbed up into the tree with me, risking setting off the alarm from her security anklet. We sat and stared out at the foggy valley, unsure of what to do next. And all the while, I kept thinking about the women in the slideshow, their care for each other, and how I wished I was there rather than here.

Was it that they looked like they were having fun? That they were out in the world together? That it was an incredibly public, or at least visual, display of solidarity? Or was it just nostalgia for a moment when feminism seemed coherent? Was I just envious of their clothing? I'd come of age in the individualistic American third-wave feminism, each girl a lone wolf who could be anything she wished, wear anything she liked, and who took for granted—or was at least told—that her needs would be met, that the world had changed to meet them. But I was beginning to feel like I'd missed some important part of the story.

I started reading more about the Fifth Street Women's Building when I returned to New York from Oregon, skimming *Feminists Who Changed America, 1963–1975*. There was an entry for the author June Arnold, which linked her to a takeover of the building on New Year's Eve 1970 but provided no other details. And then I found links to Arnold's out-of-print novel *The Cook and the Carpenter*, and it was from there that I cobbled together a story of what might have happened during those twelve days.

In 1970, New York was bordering on bankruptcy. Some 25 percent of all properties in Manhattan were abandoned. The system was eroding from the inside out. Families squatted in buildings that had been left to decay or burn. City Hall was in the process of clearing slums and replacing them with middle-income housing that was unaffordable for those who had been displaced. Most people on public assistance were women with children, and the city was failing to protect their jobs or provide daycare or health services.

At the same time, Gloria Steinem was testifying in favor of the Equal Rights Amendment. Flo Kennedy was forming the Feminist Party, nominating Shirley Chisholm for president. *Roe v. Wade* had just reached the U.S. Supreme Court. It was the eve of radical feminism, lesbian feminism. The women of the Fifth Street action were not the same feminists who were in Marlo Thomas's slideshow, but they shared a common ethic.

For a long time, I couldn't find any details about the exact location of the building. I couldn't find much of anything. I walked the length of 5th Street, snapping pictures with a disposable camera of every abandoned lot between Broadway and Avenue D, feeling like a veteran (as Joan Didion once wrote) of a guerilla war I had never fully understood.

It wasn't until I found an old leaflet in the digital Lesbian Poetry Archive with a crude ink drawing of an almost castle-like building (WOMEN THIS BUILDING IS YOURS! scrawled in the center) that I noticed an address etched above the door. I sifted through the photos I'd taken during my pilgrimage down 5th Street and found a parking lot full of Crown Victorias.

I'd found what I was looking for: a concrete site onto which I could project fantasies.

I decided to tell myself the story again. I invited a few friends over to my apartment in Bed-Stuy, which we then systematically wrecked—knocked over furniture, scattered trash, hung sheets— and, dressed in pantsuits and patchwork, with fists raised in triumph, photographed a simulation of a break-in through the ventilation shaft. There's a photo of us creeping through a giant pile of refuse from a recent renovation, and another of us strong-arming our way over a metal railing. The final photo in the series is of us sitting cross-legged on the floor of the building we've just "taken over," encircling a single candle.

I called it the 1971 Sistergate Takeover and presented it as a fictional museum entry in a gallery show the following week. In a corner next to the panels of photos and "historical" placards, I built a covered fort with blankets and pillows, into which I installed a shelf stocked with original editions of books like *Sisterhood Is Powerful*, *SCUM Manifesto*, and *The Dialectic of Sex*. I thought that somehow, by sitting in that fort with other people and looking at these books and just talking, I might figure out what my longing was all about. One woman compared my project to a nerdy indie-music obsession with analog equipment, a sort of vain aesthetic fetish. Another woman sat with me, for a long time, in fact. We drank beer in the fort long after the gallery had emptied out, and at the end, she said, "*This* was the Sistergate Takeover."

I looked at her. She was a friend of mine who had just finished writing a poetry manuscript about a lavish penthouse she stumbled upon in a dream. The poems narrate her experiences inside the penthouse while she practiced lucid dreaming for over a year.

Maybe any time a woman reimagines indoor space is a political act. Maybe any time women make something together is a political act. Maybe any time two or more women stay up all night somewhere they're not supposed to be is a political act.

But it wasn't enough. I wanted to tell the story again. A while later, I found myself teaching a women's studies course called "Bad Girls in Music, Art & Literature" at my old college in Brooklyn, and it was then that I decided to track down the women who were involved in the Fifth Street Takeover.

Reeni Goldin, one of the women who rode their bicycles through the Lower East Side in 1970, told me that she met June Arnold while thumbing through a card catalog at the West Side Women's Center. As Goldin puts it, June looked over her shoulder and said, "'Hey, we're interested in the same things!' And we just started talking about it. We started saying, you know what we should really do—we should get a building. We should start a women's center." June was wealthy, in her forties, and Goldin was working-class, almost twenty years her junior, but she says, "We both had the same vision."

Together with two other women, Jane Lurie and Buffy Yasin, they procured a list from City Hall of every abandoned public building on record. They scoured the Lower East Side and eventually decided on a dilapidated old welfare office and women's shelter, four stories high, full of junkies and winos to whom they suggested that "they ought to move out," because next week they were going to be taking it over.

They gathered others and started making lists of materials they needed: padlocks, heavy-duty plastic, staple guns. "And then we put out leaflets saying that we were going to have an action, a women's action, and to bring water, warm clothing, sleeping bags, food—but we're not telling you where we're going."

On New Year's Eve, in the middle of the night, two hundred women met at Washington Square Church. Liza Cowan was there as a young journalist for WBAI Radio, and in graduate school a number of years later she wrote a paper analyzing the action: "The Fifth Street Women's Building Takeover: A Feminist Urban Action, January 1971." When I spoke to her on the phone, she remembered being moved by a particular snapshot. "It's the pews, the women gathered there in the pews, chatting and listening to each other."

At midnight, they set out.

"We had a parade through the streets of Lower Manhattan," Goldin says. "It was snowing. And everyone thought we were drunken New Year's Eve revelers. And we were singing and chanting, and we took a very circuitous route to the building, unlocked it, and climbed in through the window."

When they were all in, they cheered. "And *then* we told the women what we were doing: We're starting a women's center!"

In her memoir *America's Child: A Woman's Journey Through the Radical Sixties*, Susan Sherman, another Fifth Street organizer, remembers that one of the first things they did when they broke into 330 5th Street was "change the name on the portable heater June and Reeni had brought. The 'M' in Mister Heater was painted over with an 'S' and it became 'Sister Heater,' our official mascot." Goldin also remembers being warmed that first night by the "propane heater—no, it was a kerosene heater. We slept there," she says, "in sleeping bags, next to Sister Heater."

But in the morning, there was a lot of work to be done. "We set up tables," Goldin says. "Probably hunks of wood and bricks, where we had books, and we had food. We cooked food in there!" They filled old toilets with garbage bags and kitty litter. They brought in professional electricians and oil-burner technicians. "There was this one woman, she was like the town bag lady, and she had six coats on and her push-cart, and she was living with us," Goldin says. "We took care of her."

They started a food co-op, a clothing swap, a "crash pad," martial arts classes, twenty-four-hour child care; they started a feminist school, a lesbian rights center, a health clinic, a drug rehab center, a book exchange. "It sounds sorta big," Goldin says. "But it was really like one person said, 'Oh, I can teach that,' and then three women came." Every morning, according to Liza Cowan, some of the women went all the way up to Hunts Point for fresh produce and arrived home with a larder.

"I mean, the building was decrepit," Cowan says. "I remember thinking, how the hell are they ever going to make this into a hospitable environment? But I was impressed . . . They were doing construction, working on wiring . . . and I'd never even heard of a food co-op before that! I had no idea how people even got produce into the city."

Every day, the women negotiated bit by bit with City Hall: They said they would restore this unused building to safety code; they said they'd already made it less of a public hazard than it was before. They'd establish a community center. They'd make it a resource for women all over the city, forever. And they sought expert help. Goldin laughs when she remembers activist and television host Ronnie Eldridge coming by: "And we're like on folding chairs. And the place is a dump."

For a while, it seemed like the city was seriously considering their requests. But the terms being proposed started to betray the women's values. At one point, Goldin remembers the city saying "OK, OK, we'll let you have the building, and we'll give you funding, but you have to take in welfare women." Becoming part of that system was never the plan, Goldin says.

> I had a friend who worked for the welfare department and she had to go into these women's houses and count their socks and see how many shirts and underwear they had, and if they had too many, they were docked. It was really intrusive, invasive. And that's what they would have wanted us to do. And we were like, "We're not counting anybody's socks, are you kidding me? We're not gonna be their jailer."

The women kept countering the city's proposals until, as Goldin puts it, "They got mad at us. So they arrested us all . . . and called the cops right across the street."

Susan Sherman still lives around the corner from the parking lot where the Fifth Street Women's Building once stood. She was tasked, that fateful New Year's Eve, with being a lookout, and she remembers the deep, freezing silence of the snow while the women filed through the window. She met me at Café Mocha on the afternoon before my twenty-seventh birthday, carrying an elaborately carved Mexican cane and an embroidered burlap satchel.

She recalled the differing ideologies in the group, and the challenges of a democratized decision-making process. She remembered inviting Flo Kennedy, the famous civil rights lawyer and a friend of hers, to come help with negotiations. But Kennedy's suggestions were dismissed; the group was wary of old patriarchal hierarchies. "And oh my God," Sherman says, "I'll never forget [Flo] saying, 'I have memorized the face of every woman in this room and not one of you had better ever, and I mean *ever*, ask for my help again.'"

Sherman remembers there being several symbolic arrests at the front doors of the building on January 12th; those were the ones photographed in the papers. She says a number of others wanted to have this rally in the parking lot next door. "I warned them not to. I'd done actions like these before. It was a cul-de-sac," she says. "They were trapped."

She was right. Once the press left, a violent melee ensued in the lot.

"This was 1971," Goldin reminds me. "The cops didn't expect women to stand up for themselves. They certainly didn't expect them to fight back." One woman smashed her handbag into the back of a cop's head. Another, who happened to be the Lower East Side handball champion, was grabbed by four cops, one per limb, and Goldin remembers that "she kept contracting her body, and then spreading out, contracting and spreading out." It took twelve cops to get her into the paddy wagon.

"A couple of us got back in the building—we had the keys to the padlocks!—so we were standing up on the third floor screaming, 'Women united! We'll never be defeated!' And the cops were like, 'What the fuck are you doing up there?! We got you outta there!'"

About forty women were arrested.

Most were ultimately released with $25 tickets. And over the following weeks, a bunch of them crashed at Goldin's apartment, an "old-law" tenement with bathrooms in the hallway and a claw-foot tub in the kitchen. "It was a cramped place, but we had like twelve women there most of the time," she said. It wasn't until those days following the end of the takeover that Goldin came out as a lesbian.

She laughs, thinking about it. "Probably out of the five hundred women [who were involved], four hundred and seventy were lesbians. But I wasn't out yet when this thing started. I was, like, a slow learner."

And then, ten days after the arrests, the Fifth Street Women's Building was razed.

When I ask Goldin why the building takeover was the right action for that moment, she says, "We were taking the structure of 'the man,' if you will, and using it for our needs." Later, she adds, "It was the best time to be alive, the best time to be a lesbian. There was nothing you couldn't do. You just came up with these ideas and you just did 'em. And you weren't alone. There were hundreds and thousands of women who would come along with you."

There were other takeovers, too, that decade—many. There was the takeover of the Cambridge, Massachusetts, building that resulted in a Women's Center that still exists today. There was a takeover of the Statue of Liberty, and of the East Asian Studies Hall at the University of Kansas. There were Manhattan takeovers by rapidly growing Puerto Rican communities, like the 11th Street Homesteaders, and by the crust-punks of ABC No Rio; and many of the residential buildings in Bed-Stuy, where I staged my takeover reenactment, were settled under the Urban Homesteading Act, which the Fifth Street action, and others like it, helped to fuel.

It was an exciting time, and complicated, too. As in many social movements, people got left behind—poor people, rural people, people of color. But I still feel the need to see what might be useful, even life-giving, about second-wave feminism, despite its faults— faults of which we, in the third or fourth wave, are not absolved. In part, it's the second wave's ability to create a body politic, and its articulation of the nature of patriarchy as not individual men, or "men," but as a series of corrosive systems in which both women and men exist, that is still incredibly potent. But there's something else, too: the inventiveness of their actions, that visible display of solidarity, one that took place on the streets, that was visceral in addition to ideological. At that moment, as had happened before, feminism became a spiritual journey of presence and transcendence both, when religion had failed to offer any substantive recourse.

In *Men Explain Things to Me*, essayist and activist Rebecca Solnit talks a lot about direct-action activism. She writes:

> Walking in the streets can be a form of social engagement, even
> of political action when we walk in concert, as we do in uprisings,

demonstrations, and revolutions, but it can also be a means of inducing reverie, subjectivity, and imagination, a sort of duet between the prompts and interrupts of the outer world, and the flow of images and desires (and fears) within.

The Fifth Street Women's Building modeled that duet, prompted by and also interrupting a world failing to care for women— especially poor women, women of color, and queer women. And the action is as symbolic as it is physical. They cut their legs on glass as they climbed through the broken windows, and the next morning there was a building to announce that the women, at least the women of New York, were not going to be ignored. They evoked the subjective and the collective. Their revolution was reverie.

When I first met up with Susan Sherman for coffee on the Lower East Side, she asked, "So why are you interested in the takeover?"

"Well," I said. "Well, I've just always loved the story."

I had a dream the night before I met Sherman. I woke up in my old apartment in Bed-Stuy, only to find that she had been living next door to me all along. She invited me into her building, which was very tall, hollow, with a cool concrete interior. Platforms were suspended by wire going all the way up to the ceiling, each about ten feet apart. And on each platform was a bed where a woman, each one an artist, precariously slept, alongside a little studio space. All the women were in their seventies and eighties, naked, rising out of bed at my arrival to say hello. In the dream, I worried for them because their bodies were so fragile, so old, and they had to maneuver these flimsy ladders to get around. But when I said something about my worry, they looked at me like, *Well, get over it, this is just how it is. We've had to make it work.*

THE BLACKOUT

The Prodigal Son

I inherited a cassette tape a while back that I turned and turned in my hands for years before ever pressing play. The cream-and-orange Norelco label boasts a LIFETIME GUARANTEE and MADE IN HOLLAND, during a time when such common household items like dinner plates and toothbrushes and cassette tapes were made in relatively small batches by people who went home at night. In runny blue ink, Side A says STANLEY SHIRK ON THE DEPRESSION" and Side B says "STANLEY SHIRK ON THE BLACK OUT. The former is a Q&A with my grandfather conducted by my seventeen-year-old dad at the behest of a high school history teacher. The latter is a bewildering hour-long recording of an afternoon when my father came home and found Stanley sitting at the table in their burned-down kitchen, unable to recall the events of the last five months.

"What happened?" Stanley asks, gesturing to the charred kitchen. "Who's been taking care of the cats?" he says, as one of his wife's

Abyssinians slinks through the room. "Who's been taking care of *us*? Do we have enough money? Where have we been eating? Where's Harriet? Where have *you* been?"

The recording, as I said, is an hour long. Every few minutes, Stanley's mind seems to reset and, incredulous, he asks the same set of questions again. My father patiently answers twice, three times, twelve times. *The kitchen burned down last month because someone left the stove on. You've been taking care of the cats. We've been taking care of ourselves. We've been eating at Marvin's Dinette. Harriet is at Bryn Mawr studying for her PhD. I've been at school. I've been right here.*

My father begins to develop a kind of inverted Socratic method. For instance, by the fifth round or so, he's gotten Stanley to put a deposit slip in his pocket so that every time the questions loop back to a frantic "But do we have enough money?" my father simply asks him to pull it out for proof. Stanley pauses between each wave of amnesia and says, "I'm just in a complete fog," to which my father psychologizes with shades of difference each time. He offers that Stanley has been depressed in Harriet's absence, that he resents being left to care for her show cats, that he's bored and simply "switched off." Toward the middle of the recording—either because it becomes clear to him at that moment, or because he's been trying to make this point the whole time—my father explains that Stanley is not *in* a fog but has just come out of one.

In a way, the story of my dad's life is on that tape. His strained relationship with his father, the spoils of his evil stepmother, the manner in which he'd conduct himself at American Federation of Musicians board meetings for three decades. He sounds exactly the same at seventeen as he does at fifty-seven: the measured, guiding voice of a seasoned parent, annunciating slowly, almost patronizing but ultimately soothing.

While my dad carries on like a wise old man, the funny thing is that the kitchen fire Stanley keeps asking about was started because my idiot-kid dad had tried to deep-fry a carrot a month earlier and left the burner on. (He never told anyone about this, except for my mother's mother, my grandma Gale, whom he loved, years later.) He does not take responsibility on the tape. The burned kitchen in this moment is just one detail among many that Stanley cannot wrap his head around. So my dad continues to try to reconstruct his memory: *Remember, Harriet has left for the year so that she can become an English teacher. We've been taking care of her creepy cats, remember? One even recently died of heart murmur and we tried to hide it from Harriet, but a fellow Cat Fancier caught wind and got us in trouble, remember?* Several years earlier, his stepmother had decided to start raising cats for the show circuit, and before long there were dozens of reddish, reptilian, inbred felines yowling around their house, which were either sold up the river or presented by Harriet herself at expo centers, lit to the nines with halogen bulbs, the wrinkly hands of older ladies pinching the bloated bodies of Persians and hairless Siamese as they examined them for various prizes.

But I didn't know any of this—not the tape, nor Stanley, nor the cruelty of his stepmother—when my dad took me to that Cat Fanciers Society expo as part of my ninth birthday outing (which ended with seeing *Mystery Men* in theaters). The trip to the expo center was a weird offer, but I loved cats and so I accepted. We trailed through rows and rows of caged felines extending their forepaws in desperation. I was bewildered that there would be no opportunities to pet and hold them, and so I quickly lost interest. As we were getting ready to leave, my dad looked over his shoulder and said, "Sorry—I thought I saw Harriet."

He didn't say another word about it, but I know now that this was around the time he'd found out that Stanley had died without funeral or function, in Denton, Texas, a year earlier. My dad and his half-siblings had hired a PI to track Stanley down after he and Harriet—thirty years his junior—disappeared without a trace from their home in Boise. Stanley was eighty-nine. Dementia was setting in. Even before she absconded with him, Harriet had moved him out of their shared home into a little apartment downtown, alone, where he would wander from kitchen to living room to bathroom and did not remember who my father was the last time he'd flown to Boise for a visit.

What does it mean to black out, when you use it as a verb? I guess to forget, or to have forgotten (past tense), or, in essence, to have lost access to your memory, short or long term. It's an experience of amnesia—if such a thing can be experienced—caused by forces beyond your control. Although, that's not true: It can be caused by blood-saturated benzos, blood-alcohol content, low blood sugar, the sight of blood, or anything that leads to fainting, which is basically just the constriction of blood flow to the brain. Doesn't it mean, perhaps, to intentionally "block" out, too? People questioned under pressure have been known to say, "I don't know—I blacked that out." Or do they say "blocked," as in "I blocked that out," and is that different?

And what about the noun? One of the earliest noun usages was the theatrical *blackout*, describing the darkened or darkening stage, while actors and set pieces rearrange themselves frantically, or have reached intermission, or have come to the end. A drunken blackout after the fact is a noun, as is a benzo blackout, as is the blackout in the wake of a car accident or a fistfight or a rage so total that things "go black." When there's an electrical failure in a city's grid, or when city light is intentionally extinguished during wartime, we sit in our dark homes with candles, waiting. Then there's a media blackout, which comes in one of two ways: The powers that be enforce a blackout of dangerous or "objectionable" information passing through certain channels (television, radio, the internet), or the inverse, when a political group refuses to communicate with the powers that be.

What happens during a blackout, any of these types? We are safe. We are in danger. We feel serene because we are oblivious or we feel fear because we become self-conscious of the absence of knowledge. We look at the redacted parts of a document and there is no way of knowing what lies beneath those bars. What do we feel? Longing, itching, an insatiable, even irrational need to see, to know.

Family trees, like all historical documents, are full of blackouts, gaps, omissions. The stories of victors—men, fathers, and sons—are usually clear, but less or little is known of the women. Who gets blacked out? (I think the answer is obvious.) Yet in my family, all of the genealogists are women. They have been the ones to fastidiously save the letters, photos, civic records, and birth certificates, who have recorded the family histories, and to make sure those records get into the hands of the next generation.

I am often the casual beneficiary of this labor: For instance, the cream-and-orange tape. But also Stanley and my Grammy Evelyn's love letters, organized by date, a romance that no one had particularly warm feelings about, except presumably them at the time, and they are both dead and did not like each other anymore by the mid-1960s. I sift through the love letters but am more interested in what might be more like a hate letter shuffled into the mix. The letter is dated May 1970, and it's from Stanley to my Grammy, then his ex-wife, berating her for requesting to change my father's visitation schedule that summer for the purpose of a big camping trip. "Again," he says toward the end, "I feel it is in the best interests of Kenneth's welfare and development, both physical and emotional, to adhere to the schedule which was of your own choice." It is a clipped, type-written letter, full of the subtly brutal rhetoric of divorce court. "I am not sure you are fully cognizant of the fact that Kenneth is in my care, that he is my full responsibility, that Newberg is his home. Only harm to Kenneth's emotional equilibrium can come from your designs to 'upset the apple cart.'"

Folded into that letter is one written by my fourteen-year-old dad, also addressed to his mother: "I suppose you have gotten his letter now, or you will soon. When I had a talk with him about it, it was clear you didn't make clear to him what you planned to do or what dates so that he would know why you needed me earlier . . . So you will probably find his letter a bit disagreeable." Then without skipping a beat, without starting a new paragraph, he continues: "Looking over your list, I can tell you what I have on hand: sleeping bag, sox, undies, PJs, all shoes, all writing stuff, tarp, rain gear, all shirts, pants, jacket, gloves, and hat." And finally, "Do you think I'll need any books or *Mad Magazines* or stuff like that?"

This is a more or less random artifact in the scheme of things, but it made me terribly sad, and so it sticks. It's strange to think now about my dad and I having divorced parents in common. My own parents' divorce was unremarkable to me as a child and has worn on me only in retrospect. I was so young when they split up, so I had no attachment to, no real memory, even, of their relationship, their marriage, so I found nothing objectionable about its ending. Now I can appreciate that the shifting back and forth was hard, but at the time I had no other reference point by which to judge the quality of my experience. I just remember going back and forth and the strange dull ache, like a bruise, every time my brother and I landed at the new house, when there'd be a period of adjustment, feeling alien briefly in one of my homes, then finally settling in, only to leave again.

I realize now that my dad experienced this, too: the silences and the terse letters, the pick-ups and drop-offs in the carports of parents' homes. In the same box where I found the letters, I also found a series of photos taken of my dad on his high school graduation day. He's grinning dutifully into the camera, a flap of golden hair falling beneath his cap. Neither of his parents would go near each other after the ceremony. I don't know who took the photos, but in each, my dad fades further and darker into the background, as though the photographer is gradually drawing away himself, and in the final one, my dad is small, fragile-looking, his smile faded.

The day my dad left Newberg, Oregon, for college, he swore he'd never come back. As he finished packing his bags, he listened to the yowling and scratching of the Abyssinian cats echoing from every room. Harriet approached his bedroom and sneered at him from the doorjamb: "We'll be glad to have the extra space when you're gone." My dad did not respond but looked out the window to where his father was puttering around in the vegetable garden with a watering can, as deaf then as he'd always been to the shitty things Harriet said. My dad is too patristic to have said something back to her like, "Well, I'll be glad to go"; he ignored the comment, carefully loaded his bass trombone into its giant case, and drove himself to college.

The day my brother left home, he was picked up from our house in a small gold car dispatched by the local army base. He had just turned nineteen, or he was about to. Grandma Gale took the train down from Seattle for his big sendoff, and so she, my mom, my sister, Aaron, and I spent the afternoon snapping photos with a disposable Fuji on the back deck. We took two rolls of film, each of us smiling against the bright damp green of the garden, directly into the sharp light of the sun. It was one of those booming spring Portland days, the first after the eight-month rainy season. (When the photos developed, we found that our faces had been contorted and blacked out by shadow in every single frame.) Then Aaron got into the army car and was taken to a hotel near the Portland airport, where he'd sleep before going off to complete eight weeks of boot camp in Columbus, Georgia.

Aaron's entrance into the military was strange on many levels. We are a peace-loving people, highly educated, a family filled with educators and artists. We had never heard Aaron talk about the army until the day he enlisted. And though no one was thinking this at the time, eight generations earlier, in 1732, some peasant Anabaptists, from whom we were directly descended, had sailed across the Atlantic and set up home in Lancaster County, Pennsylvania, so that, among other things, they could stand in resistance to military warfare.

Our father's family springs from these early Anabaptists, who are distinguished by their firm and wild belief in adult baptism. In the tumultuous throes of the Reformation, "Anabaptist" was actually used as a pejorative term, a fifteenth-century ribbing, meaning "one who baptizes again," casting the belief as silly and excessive by disapproving Catholics and Protestants, groups of whom shunned, terrorized, and at some points actually burned Mennonites alive. While mainline Mennonites today, which is most Mennonites, assimilated into modern life like most other Christian sects, Old Order Mennonites—our particular inheritance—still wear cape dresses and plain clothes and live a self-identified "countercultural" lifestyle: communal, agrarian, off the grid. They believe in a literal interpretation of the Sermon on the Mount: no taking up of arms, no violence against enemies, no oath-taking (including their soon-to-be new country's pledge). Early proponents of the separation of church and state, they agree to passively obey government, though they're never to hold political office or rank.

And so, sometime in 1732, my ninth great-grandfather, Ulrich Scherk—and his wife; what was her name?—fled Switzerland with nine children in tow and settled in Lancaster County, Pennsylvania. He didn't live long enough to witness the American Revolution, which happened a good forty years after he built their house and the first Mennonite cemetery in North America. The community grew, house-churches formed, farms became solvent. Can you imagine it? This man and woman, wrangling toddlers and teenagers across the Atlantic, believing that whatever mysterious and difficult life lay on the other side was worth leaving a land they'd already fled to in exile, to practice this radical belief that baptism should be sought only by believing adults.

It went on like this in Lancaster County for a long time. Then one day, my great-grandfather Christian, Stanley's father, broke the spell. He decided to leave. Of course, I have no idea how this went. The Old Order Mennonites believe that using any sort of "labor-saving" technology risks replacing or disrupting the reliance on family and community, and maybe one clear morning Christian bolted upright in his straw-mat bed in a cold sweat, unable to deny the capitalistic roar of the encroaching twentieth century, and couldn't for the life of him see the use in ignoring the changing world. He had spotted once, by accident, an early automobile prototype rolling through town, and he must have seen the commensurate realities: the brewing of a world war, the technological advances, the screech and groan and oil of these rumbling beasts. What more could you do but go to the city?

He was the first to leave after five generations of unbroken Old Order Mennonite life in Lancaster County. He fled for the godless Philadelphia to become (again: *gasp!*) a Methodist minister. He drove a car and bought a house and used electricity and probably never saw his family again. The Methodist church was a leading liberal church at the time, and it had been among the most active in abolitionist causes forty years earlier, and early to ordain women and black men, eschewing the elitism of seminary. Preachers were trained quickly, usually within churches themselves, and then sent out across the land to spread the word. But Christian would stay in the city.

And choosing the city foreclosed the past to his ascendants: You can never go back. My dad has always had the demeanor of a man who's never been called into action, never been used for the thing he was supposed to be used for. He grew up in Portland's upper-class West Hills and the bucolic suburbs of Newburg, he played music and became a musician union officer, and all of that was fine, but these were never felt deeply as homelands or passions. There was a Roz

Chast comic on our refrigerator for a long time titled "At the Corner of Irate and Insane," featuring four people, each with thought bubbles above their heads bemoaning the four basic life gripes. We'd stand around and choose which one we identified with: "Enraged at inability to fly," "Mad because she's not Bob Dylan," "Angry because 'The Wizard of Oz' was fiction," and "Furious because it isn't the 18th century." My father's selection was the final one, and we would joke, though we were mostly serious, that he was born to be a Mennonite farmer.

I've only been to Old Order Mennonite country once, and it was by accident. Four friends and I took a road trip from New York City to Madison, Wisconsin. We all spent the first night on a living room floor in Philadelphia, and by noon the next day we were broken-down on the shoulder of a small highway in Shippensburg, Pennsylvania. As the AAA contractor towed us into town, we saw the horse-drawn buggies with their weather-resistant cabins and turn signals, men dressed in plain dark cotton clothes, women in bonnets. Sitting in front of a motel next door to the mechanic, we ate cold red kidney beans out of a can while the tow-truck guy told us, "Yep, yer transmission's definitely dead, and the shop's not open till Monday." So half of the group hitchhiked to Harrisburg to rent a car, and the rest of us kicked around a patch of grass behind the motel, rolling cigarettes from an enormous can of Drum. A man living in the motel came out to greet us. He asked if we were the Manson family. He told us about his life and who he was, though I remember only the parts where he described all the nice Old Order he knew and all the mean ones. There were apparently a lot. It was a damp gray day. He kept saying, "Oh, yeah, so-and-so—he's an ASShole."

Had no one ever left the fold in Lancaster County, would we all have emerged from Shirk loins anyway, spent our days planting beans and shoveling chicken shit, fathers and sons plowing side by side, mothers and daughters fastening our bonnets and silver-buttoned frocks, sitting around a big wooden table by candlelight telling stories after the sun went down? Maybe. But maybe my brother would have come in from the fields one day and burned down the barn anyway.

When I think of my relationship with my brother, I think of the years he was a teenager and I was an adolescent, even though this overlap was brief. I remember those years much more vividly than the years of taunting and rivalry.

These memories orbit around the time of his sixteenth birthday, when he inherited an old 1986 hatchback Subaru from my grandparents. It was ugly, with a rusted maroon paint job, faux-fur seat covers that changed color when I ran my hand up and down the back, and a broken fender. Different parts of the car would start to rattle when you hit sixty, and at seventy, the whole dashboard would shake. Every thirty miles he had to stop so the car wouldn't overheat. It was perfect.

It was around the time he first got the car that we became what felt to me like friends—I remember the first time it was just him and me on the highway. We were lagging a few miles behind our parents. I had this fantasy that he'd take a different exit than they did and we'd ride off into the sunny distance: Fuck this town, fuck this scene. But we stayed about a mile behind them the whole way. Aaron ranted about drivers and an ex-girlfriend and our stepfather. He hissed and spat and spoke with a frightening edge in his voice that had been developing over the last few months. When another car would pull in front of him, he'd hit the steering wheel and yell "Goddammit!" at the top of his lungs.

I was terrified, but I smiled nervously and loved that it was just me and my brother in his gross little car. The two of us against the world.

Or maybe just him against the world.

He worked nights washing dishes at an Italian restaurant. I'd hear his car rattle up the driveway around midnight and I'd count the steps up to the door where his key would click in the lock. He'd knock on my door—"Are you awake?"—and I'd snap on the lamp, and he'd lay on my small rug, staring up at the ceiling, and we'd talk late into the night.

Then Aaron and his car were out of sight. He wasn't home much and no one investigated further until the end of the following summer. I had just turned thirteen when they found all the drugs in his backseat.

Shortly thereafter, he drove me to the bleachers perched over the baseball diamond at our old elementary school in order to explain why he was in trouble with our parents. He shook a cigarette out of its pack and lit it. For the first and only time in his life, he said, "I'm sorry I was such an asshole to you when we were younger. I don't know why I was." It was almost like those moments when an old man with dementia surfaces suddenly after weeks, or months, or longer of meandering across four-lane highways in search of his childhood home, of not recognizing his wife or his children, and says, "I'm so sorry this is happening."

The day my father's father left home in Philadelphia, he was nineteen or so, too, and he walked out on the last fight he'd ever have with his father—there would be no more of that. Stanley went to college in New Jersey, met a girl, started a dairy farm, and taught shop at a local high school. Later he left again, left his first wife and his two kids. He was middle-aged by then. He flew out to Portland, Oregon, in the early 1950s for his new job as chief engineer for the Oregon Museum of Science and Industry, soon after which he met my grandmother Evelyn, a spunky divorcée and mother of four who lived in a rambling house in the West Hills. At their wedding, a silver "S" was embossed proudly onto their napkins and drink coasters, and for a brief time they lived in marital bliss, surprised a year later to discover that, against the odds of middle-aged biology, they were pregnant with my dad.

By the time my father tracked Stanley down in Denton, Texas, in the late 1990s, all that was left was a death certificate. He'd been dead for a year—died just two weeks short of his ninety-first birthday in a ticky-tacky house at the dead end of a long subdivision road. I look at the address now on Google Earth. The property is obscured by lush thickets and separated from the highways by a bottle-blue reservoir. There was Stanley, all alone, staring out an east-facing window from a plaid-upholstered chair worn threadbare from sitting, watching the breeze ripple across the water, waiting for Harriet to come home from work, which didn't happen much those days. He wondered if he had children. He thought for a second—yes, he did. And like a headlight passing quickly across a wall in the dark, there were the stray details from the last summer he'd spent with his eldest, a teenager roaring down a steep street on a skateboard, and later dodging the draft. He thought about his youngest, with the fair soft hair of a baby, those black-framed glasses, his lip quivering that day in divorce court when he had to decide which parent to live with. And there was that short-sleeved sweater he'd bought him for Christmas, only to forbid him from ever wearing it because it was either too hot or too cold. *Why had I been such an asshole about that?*

He was cold. She didn't come home.

The death certificate says that the immediate cause of death was gangrene of the lower extremities. The underlying conditions included an abdominal aortic aneurysm and heart disease. I have no idea how often Harriet was with him—infrequently enough for the gangrene to have taken over so completely, to have seeped into his body? What did she think when she walked in, his head fallen to the side and white-lipped?

She packed up what remained of his life and took it to the dump, his body to the crematory, his ashes to a funeral home that no relative would ever visit, would never even know existed, as far as she knew.

Stanley's father Christian died in Florida, a retired minister who approved of nothing his son had ever undertaken, whose children he'd never bothered to meet. And Christian's father, Joseph Shirk, a Mennonite minister, died long before that, on the land he'd worked for nearly all eighty-three years of his life. He was buried in the Old Order Mennonite cemetery that Ulrich had built when he first arrived, when the first of his kin began to die, and where all of his descendants until Christian lay in repose, whose bodies will eventually dissolve into the damp earth until all that remains is a corner of granite that looks like someone, at some point or another, intended for it to be there.

Once, several months after graduating from high school, Aaron didn't come home from his night shift at the Beaumont Market. My parents wandered like zombies around the house, phoning his friends, making sure the clocks were all accurately set. As far as I knew, he'd been spending the better part of his free time dropping acid and driving around with his eyes closed. "Hey, check this out," he'd say, taking his hands off the wheel and laughing. Just a week before, he'd taken me out to egg my ex-boyfriend's house and then hadn't said a word to me the entire ride home. I spent the twenty-four hours of his disappearance cross-legged on my bed, hoping that the time had finally come when he'd hopped in his car and gone for broke, vanishing into the Mountain West or Munich for a life that might satisfy his cravings for mayhem, like a vigilante. Instead, he stumbled up onto the porch the following night and told us he'd enlisted in the military.

A few months later, we flew out to Georgia to see him graduate from basic training in Fort Benning. We found him mute and glassy-eyed.

My parents asked him gentle questions and took him out to dinners, to see the National Civil War Naval Museum and *Pirates of the Caribbean*. All the photos from that trip were double-exposures—I've never seen anything like it: My brother's vacant stare superimposed over my sister sitting on the waiting bench in a restaurant; my brother swimming in the motel's 1970s swimming pool with a close-up of my sister hamming it up in front of the lens; my mom smiling with the corners of her mouth downturned, her arm around my brother, whose mouth is in a straight shiny line, exposed on top of me, fourteen years old, impatiently standing outside a café, hiding my stomach with my crossed arms.

We flew back to Portland and he flew to San Antonio to complete a year of vocational training. A month later, a sergeant phoned to let us know he'd been missing for forty-eight hours. My mother checked and found out that his bank account had been emptied.

And then we waited.

I sat in the sunny backyards of my best friends, draining Slurpees and running through sprinklers and smoking weed for the first time, thinking it was only my timing that had been off, that now was the hour—the kind of drama Aaron would have waited for—when he would make his grand exit to the desert, to a life of adventure or crime. It was the only kind of life I could imagine him living.

But four days later he pulled up in front of our house in a white Mazda he'd purchased on the long drive west. I heard my mother say, catatonic, "There he is." He stepped out of the car in the pressed trousers and button-down he'd fled the base wearing, a smile spread tightly across his face. He sat silently on our back deck for a week, chain-smoking, and then the army flew him back to Texas.

When he'd completed his training in San Antonio—after they'd readmitted him with a brief psych evaluation—he came back to Portland to serve weekends at Fort Vancouver and do whatever else he wanted with the rest of his time. Upon his arrival, my stepfather forced us around him in a big group hug, and then for weeks he wandered around the house, yelling and speaking in interminable strings of words, his eyes unfocused.

One afternoon around that time, I was sitting on the back porch with my mother and stepfather discussing the terms of a continued punishment. I was fifteen going on sixteen, and I was in trouble for drinking and smoking pot. A lazy crescent of sunlight fell between us on the table. A breeze shifted through our maple, disturbing nothing on the deck. The oilcloth covering the table gleamed under the sun.

"Don't think of this as punishment," my stepfather mused, smiling.

"We just want to keep you safe," my mother said.

From our spot on the deck, I could see through Aaron's bedroom window. He was staring at the wall, expressionless, the blue wash of television bouncing off his face.

The following month, he rented a dingy yellow house with two friends. And then three months later, his work called my mom to ask where he was. He'd skipped his last two shifts. A couple of days went by—a frenzied search. Finally, Aaron called. He needed my mother to take him to the hospital. He'd woken up in a crawl space in his garage. Two of his fingers were missing.

He convalesced in our spare room. A week later he was arrested for arson and armed robbery.

I called my dad the day after Aaron was arrested. He was in New York on a business trip, and I was crying, and he remembers me saying, "What an asshole. He's going to bankrupt the family." What a weird thing to say. I do not remember saying it.

Then I found myself in the office of a high-profile lawyer being asked if I could account for anything strange about Aaron's behavior before the psychotic break. I told every story I could think of, starting as close to the beginning as possible of what I thought my brother's story was. Though, more and more, the stories I was telling about

Aaron did not seem to match the stories that the rest of my family was telling, and in the same way, I was beginning to notice that the stories I told about my family in general were increasingly different from the ones they told about themselves. Had I blacked out or had they? I was sixteen and furious that nothing was matching up. I was not invited back to speak with the lawyer after that, and I scarcely saw Aaron again, just a handful of times, until he was released from the Oregon State Hospital seven years later.

I could probably write something much simpler or more straightforward about my brother, whose absence had such a profound effect on me—but then I'm left thinking of his feelings about my own relative absence from his life, all my years away from Oregon, which have never been questioned. And then what of my present-day brother, who is now doing so well: an art school graduate, a game designer, a photographer? And what of present-day me, making excuses for myself? How can I write accurately about him when all I have is my own narrow experience as a lens, when there is still so much I don't know? Straightforward telling implies accuracy, finality, and I don't want to have the last word on any of it.

If stories are the bread of life, it seems that in a family, stories are often forces of either communion or division, and rarely anything in between. So when there is no common ground, when there is fragment, when there is blackout, I zoom out: If our stories don't match, then there must be a larger story, expansive enough to contain and make sense of the seemingly disparate parts, perhaps the story of a lineage of difficult fathers and difficult sons, of difficult departures and difficult severances, of difficult exiles in a difficult country, of illness and absence. And if there are still contrasting narratives about even our eighteenth-century ancestors, then I zoom out further still, to a story wherein literally everyone is implicated, like the parable of the prodigal son.

I have watched Aaron walk across the fields toward home a thousand times, and each time they say, "Bring him the best coat and the fattest calf," and each time he goes away again. *The son says, "Father, give me my share of the estate." So he divided his property between them. Not long after that, the younger son got together all he had, set off for a distant country and there squandered his wealth in wild living.* He'd come home with his head bleeding; he'd go to Germany and come back more withdrawn; he'd walk up our steps saying he'd joined the army; he'd walk up our steps having just gone AWOL for a week; he'd walk up our steps in his fatigues, saying, "I burnt the motherfucker down and now I'm going to shoot the mayor." He'd go away, do drugs, disappear, wander in the cold, come back. *He brought shame and suffering on his family.* In fifteen minutes, with the help of a young thrill-seeking man, Aaron burned down the small yellow house he'd been renting for only three weeks. His friends, he knew, were unable to fathom his mastermind; he called them lowlifes, lemmings, said he could start a cult if he wanted to, and he was probably right—forge checks, sell drugs, jump from windows.

When they caught him, he poured a glass of orange juice over his head. When they tried to stop him, he bought a car and left. *Years passed and he didn't return.* Well, he did return once, when he left Texas in the white Mazda he'd bought with all of his savings. *So he went and hired himself out to one of the citizens of that country, who sent him to his fields to feed the pigs,* and when the prodigal son reached the pig pen, he found himself salivating over their trough. *Fuck,* he thought. *What am I doing?* He practiced an apology speech before the swine and then *he set off and went to his father.* Pushing ninety in that white Mazda, Aaron was setting off, but not to his father.

Many things could have happened, and maybe did happen, but we will never know because of the blackouts, the blackouts, the blackouts. During the proceedings that would land him in the state psychiatric hospital, he talked about these long periods of blackouts. Now the tape is rolling: *What day is it? Who's been taking care of the cats? Who's been taking care of us?* He is either in a complete fog or he is just coming out of one. In the parable, his father is waiting at the farm. He sees his son from across the pastures and smiles as he approaches. Without missing a beat, the father takes him in his arms. He says, *Bring him the best coat and kill our fattest calf. We are going to feast to his return.* The painfully over-achieving siblings are, of course, livid. *"Look! All these years I've been slaving for you and never disobeyed your orders. Yet you never gave me even a young goat so I could celebrate with my friends."* The father smiles, shakes his head, like, *Don't you understand?* This guy was lost, and now he's found!

The funny thing about the prodigal son is that he says to his father, *I have sinned before you and heaven,* but the reader knows he is posturing a little, if not a lot. And the father knows this too, and he doesn't care. Also, if you hadn't figured it out yet, the father is God and we are all the prodigal son: going away and coming back for redemption, going away again and again and again and coming back with pitiful, hilarious excuses. The father simply leads the son home, across the fields. Nothing has changed. Did the prodigal son mean what he said? Did he go on to do it all again? Does it matter? The point of the parable is that it does not.

SHADOW AND SUBSTANCE

Sojourner Truth

By the time Sojourner Truth arrived in Florence, Massachusetts, she had been through hell and back. She was forty-six years old and she had come north to join the Northampton Association for Education and Industry on the bank of the Mill River, to live among freedom fighters and make silk in protest of slavery. She would figure the rest out as she went. It was 1843, and she had been bought and sold as a slave three times, then released unto the scattershot mill towns of Ulster County. She had successfully sued for the freedom of her son; defected from a doomsday church in Kingston; scraped by as a domestic laborer in New York City; escaped a cult leader in Westchester county; walked across Long Island and Connecticut, preaching the gospel and giving testimony at camp meetings with little more than a bindle stick; and she had just—that past Pentecost—changed her name from Isabella Baumfree to Sojourner Truth. It was time for a big change, though the size and shape of such change was constantly growing. She had a calling. Her name was the first step. Women were going to be at the moral frontlines, she knew that much. At those camp meetings, there had been mostly women, white women, and Truth knew that God worked more violently and strangely than they could ever know by themselves.

The Northampton Association of Education and Industry was a cooperatively owned and operated silk factory in Western Massachusetts. (They also dabbled in beet sugar.) Every laborer owned a share of the company, and their output was modest if not ideological during the century of cotton and cane. The whole outfit was a rangy collection of properties stitched together by the Mill River, including a four-story factory, a sawmill, a dam and waterpower site, and a variety of outbuildings and slipshod dwellings. There were certainly lots of utopian social-justice collectives at the time, but historian Christopher Clark asserts that the NAEI was unique in that the fusion of abolitionism and equal rights for women were the bedrock of its existence, unlike others that may have included those pursuits as aspects of, though not central to, their mission. For NAEI, the justification was theological. Even their promotional materials espoused that the organization was founded "upon principles . . . the best calculated to fulfill the designs of God in placing man in this life." Truth remembers her time there as providing her with an "equality of feeling," "liberty of thought and speech," and "largeness of soul"—a sense of self and agency.

At night, they ate communal meals and often hosted guests, especially, when they could, esteemed public intellectuals in the realms of their social justice mission. Truth and Frederick Douglass met for the first time at NAEI, and historian Nell Irvin Painter notes in "Representing Truth: Sojourner Truth's Knowing and Becoming Known" that Douglass, in his letters about Truth, distinguishes himself from her by casting her as "salt of the earth" (as opposed to his own "refinement"). Then there are anecdotes in *The History of Florence* about

Truth ridiculing him openly, poking holes in his arguments. She had a dry sense of humor. "Three thirds of the people are wrong," NAEI member Frances Judd recalls her saying, maybe over dinner. Someone points out to her that that means everyone, and she says, well, shit, "I am sorry, as I hoped there were a few left."

Truth was born in the Catskills region of New York in 1797. Even in her sprawling autobiography, there is much she refuses to disclose, things she saw during those thirty years in slavery. Among the few things she's willing to describe: a baby thrown to its death against a parlor wall, and a young man she loved tortured until he promised to stay away from her. She knows that her audience—mostly white progressives, whom James Baldwin later calls his "innocent countrymen" in his essay "My Dungeon Shook"—could not even begin to understand the rest. She says as much in her book, though it comes to us in the third person; *The Narrative of Sojourner Truth* was written down by her friend Olive Gilbert at Truth's dictation.

> Were she to tell all that happened to her as a slave—all that she knows is "God's truth"—it would seem to others, especially the uninitiated, so unaccountable, so unreasonable, and what is usually called so unnatural, (though it may be questioned whether people do not always act naturally,) they would not easily believe it. "Why, no!" she says, "they'd call me a liar! they would, indeed! and I do not wish to say anything to destroy my own character for veracity, though what I say is strictly true."

Because she was illiterate, there were always others doing the writing for her, like Olive or, later, the stenographers at her talks. Truth even acquiesced to an interview with Harriet Beecher Stowe, which turned into the ridiculous feature "African Sybil" published in *The Atlantic*, wherein Truth is depicted as "simple, quaint, unlearned," speaking in Southern dialect and tidy parables invented almost out of whole cloth. When she found out about it, Truth dictated a letter to the editor saying, essentially, uh, I'm American, not African, and I never call anyone "Honey." This tension is at the center of Painter's *Sojourner Truth: A Life, a Symbol*: that Truth is "known for words she did not say" or that we are not sure she said.

Everything we know about Truth, at least us laypeople and school-children—the "Ain't I a Woman" speech in Akron, the bared breast in Indiana, the meeting with Abe Lincoln—happened in the years after her time at the NAEI. The NAEI seems to be where she gathered her powers, where her theology and sense of purpose crystalized. Truth and Gilbert worked together on *The Narrative* for a good year or so while Truth labored as a laundress alongside the Mill River. At the time, she did not predict that the book, as well as the professional tintypes she would go on to make, would end up being the literal currency that would allow her to eventually go off on her own, buy a house, and book public speaking events about abolition, women's rights, and the Holy Spirit's role in it all. She just went on working with her friend by lamplight on this long book in a clean cool room at the back of the mills, listening to the rush of the waterfall as it crashed, endlessly, through the dam.

There's a memorial for Truth on the corner of Pine and Park Streets in Florence, Massachusetts. The committee that erected the memorial first gathered in 1993 in response to news of the Rodney King beating that had happened some three thousand miles away. Now was the hour to respond. What would their intervention into the history of American racism look like, and how should it appear in their particular community? It took almost ten years before they raised enough funds for a statue and for Florence to cough up a small bit of land for it to sit on, and even though no one from the Rodney King riots on the other side of the country knows it's here—hell, no one from *this* town seems to know—it is an intervention. The committee cast Truth in bronze in a little traffic circle, taller than any man, with plaques about how she helped make silk to challenge the slave production of cotton, and how she said that Jesus came from a woman and God—"Man had nothing to do with it," so I guess, yes, that is something like truth and reconciliation.

She's tall. Her hands are strong, copper-colored, vivid, showing veins. There are flowers everywhere, lilies, a rest home next door that appears to be for elderly vets, but what do I know. There's an old guy in olive drab sitting on a folding chair, looking at me. I'm sitting here, on the bench in the memorial's little garden, imagining her walking from Long Island to Connecticut, preaching—and my grandma is dying.

I get a call from my cousin Galen while I'm in a strip-mall parking lot with a Chinese restaurant, the Pine Street Café, a laundromat, Sam's Deli. He is crying. A Pakistani woman serves me in a convenience store. She has no idea what I mean when I ask if I can leave my car in the lot while I go look at the memorial. What memorial?

I listen to my mom's voicemail: "Oh, honey . . . Should you come out to Seattle?" She wants things to be simple; she wants to protect my time at my writing residency. "Absolutely *not*. Unless you want to."

I take a walking tour using my phone. Florence is dusty and empty today. Nearly vacant old mills, beautiful old homes, little original Colonials with modest details crowding around the river. Some are restored, others are slouching. Part of the old silk mill now holds Innovative Mental Health Services and cooperatively owned sustainable energy development. My phone map tells me that these particular buildings were run by a guy who employed fugitive slaves. The main silk mill where Truth laundered and worked as an equal among white men now holds an art collective and a record store. Two bored twenty-somethings sit on a threadbare sofa on the loading dock. I get only as far as site No. 3 on my walking tour: the steep falls that powered the NAEI's mills. I stand behind a fence attached to a small power plant and look down into the river. I'm shocked to find it's full of people: teenagers on floaties, homeless dudes drinking beer, an old, very skinny man with a full beard, tanned from exposure, apparently hallucinating and jabbing his arms in front of him.

I walk in the hot sun, through brush and dog shit to the messy banks, and change into my swimsuit underneath my dress. A guy my age with a cigarette hanging from his mouth offers me a floaty that looks like a pizza slice, but I decline, eyeing my backpack holding my computer. I wait until he's out of sight, until there's no one around, and then I jump straight into the cold water—it stinks, sort of like mildew, but it feels good. I float on my back. The smokestack on Sojourner's old mill across the street casts a late-afternoon shadow.

I'm thinking of my grandma—skin and bones, skin and bones, even when I saw her in May. She is scared, she is fighting, I am doing the elementary backstroke: chicken, airplane, soldier. I have asked Sojourner to come meet her, save her, help her, or some woman from beyond with a lot of strength, who's a mother, who knows not to be afraid. Or not a mother—I think she could use Flannery, too, at this time, since she's the one who brought her to me (or the other way around, who knows?). *Are we still friends?* She's saying this to a sulking me, a long time ago, holding my hand by the turtle pond at the zoo.

I'm sitting on smooth moonrock now at the base of the falls where it is sweeter and cleaner and greener. I swim in the dark punchbowl and brace myself on a rockslide for a rest. Sitting in the shadow of the old mills where they made silk and sugar beets to combat the tyranny of cane and cotton. It was faith in action, and it only lasted a few years, but so what? Did they swim here? Were there as many trees then as there are now? Is this truth and reconciliation? How do you represent the palimpsest of a life, in a life, at its end?

It's not that Truth and my grandma have anything in common; it's just that these things are happening at the same time. It occurs to me that Emily Dickinson's garden is nearby, somewhere off near Amherst, where there are daisies, foxglove, ephedra, plums, lilies, artichokes, peace roses—

My grandma's peace roses. My cousin Galen and I stayed with her in May for five days. I'd wake up to her moaning, screaming, cursing, and when I'd race downstairs she'd be sitting silently, hooked up to her new oxygen machine, pointing with her new walker at a package of cheese she'd dropped. "Dammit—can you, can you *get that* for me. *Jeez*." One of these times in the early morning, she asked in her new pained way if I could go outside and cut two of the roses from the bush growing over the driveway. There they were, awash in the most beautiful colors, like tie-dye, cultivated for the sixty years they'd lived at that house. I cut them and put them in a jelly jar on the kitchen table, and over the next few days she would smell them and smile, turn the glass. Then she asked me to pick a giant asparagus from the garden, and an artichoke, and we boiled them at breakfast in a single pot and ate them with butter and salt. And then I left for the airport. That was the last time I saw her.

I park behind an old church converted into a Veterans of Foreign Wars center. No one seems to know that there's a life-sized statue of Sojourner Truth down the road, or why I might be wandering the quiet, hot streets of Florence on this summer day.

I walk to Truth's old house. It's empty. The stone path up to the front porch has been scratched away, leaving just loose dirt. The ceiling of the sitting porch is still painted light blue, the way they sometimes did in the nineteenth century to mimic the sky. The house is a plain white Folk Victorian–style building, looking a bit rickety, with spindly posts and jigsaw eves. Leaves in the gutter. There is an orange sign in the bottom-floor window announcing a building permit.

She bought this house the same year she gave the "Ain't I a Woman" speech in Akron, in 1851. She eventually sold it and bought two more, one after the other, each in Michigan. She died in a house she owned, surrounded by her daughters, whom she'd found by then or who had found her, I'm not sure.

After she was freed, in 1827, her family already forcibly scattered, her parents separated by slavery and dead, her children out of reach, she lived in the country and then the city. She won two landmark court cases—one for her son who had been illegally sold from New York into the still-ongoing Alabama slave trade, and another where an employer had accused her of poisoning her family. She tried to reconnect with her kids and get them gainful employment, got her son sent off on a longshoreman outfit and then never saw him again. For years, she quested after a spiritual home: She was a part of the African Methodist church in Kingston, and then the Millerites—don't even get her started. She thought seriously of donning those white robes with them and standing on the hill, waiting for morning to bring Christ's one-thousand-year reign. Later she lived in Matthias Kingdom, a Westchester County commune, which was helmed, like most (all?) of them, by a predatory asshole posing as the Messiah, and she had to flee.

In the *Narrative*, it says:

She left the city on the morning of the 1st of June, 1843, crossing over to Brooklyn, L. I.; and taking the rising sun for her only compass and guide, she "remembered Lot's wife," and hoping to avoid her fate, she resolved not to look back till she felt sure the wicked city from which she was fleeing was left too far behind to be visible in the distance; and when she first ventured to look back, she could just discern the blue cloud of smoke that hung over it, and she thanked the Lord that she was thus far removed from what seemed to her a second Sodom . . . Her mission was not merely to travel east, but to "lecture," as she designated it; "testifying of the hope that was in her"—exhorting the people to embrace Jesus, and refrain from sin, the nature and origin of which she explained to them in accordance with her own most curious and original views. Through her life, and all its chequered changes, she has ever clung fast to her first permanent impressions on religious subjects.

Truth believed that the Holy Spirit was the "premier means of enlightenment" and that biblical literacy "stills the voices in one's head," so she was, in a way, against interpretation. What she called for was an encounter—an encounter with her, an encounter with the living God, an encounter with text. You show up. You listen. You figure out the rest as you go.

Women, who were the majority of the attendees of these revivals and camp meetings that Truth spoke at, they would listen to her testimony, all that she'd suffered and all that God meant to her for it, and how she feared for her children's lives and salvation, how her whole family had been shredded. The white women would dab their eyes—yes, we love God like you, we love our families like you, we are one. But the thing is, no one really knew what she was talking about. The tears at the camp meeting full of white women, offers Professor Naomi Greyser in *Affective Geographies: Sojourner Truth's Narrative, Feminism and the Ethical Bind of Sentimentalism*, "suggested they regard Truth as affirming their understanding of family rather than complicating it by bringing up the issue of slavery."

It is not enough to feel like you know. You don't.

Still driving all around the Berkshires. Grandpa on the phone says, "We've got a really sick grandma over here." He tells me to hold on and then I listen to him hobble with his two canes to the front porch. "I don't want to wake her. She's just fallen to sleep. I've been holding her hand for the last two hours, waiting for her to nod off. She's got a million things going through her head—and she's so sensitive to her environment, she wants to know what's going on at all times: 'Who is that?' 'What are you moving around?' 'What's going on over there?' But she's also thinking, 'Why is this happening?' 'Why is God doing this to me?' or whatever is up there." He stumbles over this one. "She's on her last legs. She'll go into hospice soon probably, which could last twenty-four hours or twenty-four days. Or maybe she'll come out of it. But I've just been sitting with her, holding her hand, holding her hand. She droops her head, but then Robin comes through to clean something or ask a question and I have to say, 'I need you to stay away right now!'" Then he says, though he said it twice already, "Your mom is out getting the medicine from the pharmacy, but Obama's in town today with his entourage, so I bet she's backed up on the Aqueduct."

I am sitting in another parking lot, in another town just on the other side of the Massachusetts border. It's so hard thinking of her there now. I was just with her. Wasn't I? I made her a terrible grilled cheese sandwich, where the cheese wasn't melted enough, and a pasta sauce with summer sausage—it was all wrong. She was in pain and she slept so much with her eye mask on during the day and the oxygen up her nose, but then she'd wake up at night to watch movies that Galen had brought (Charlie Chaplin shorts, *Twin Peaks, After Hours*) or, later on, *The Daily Show*, and we would laugh and talk about how much we missed Jon Stewart. I had always felt so close to her, but during that trip I understood I had never asked enough questions, and now it was too late.

I get back in the car and keep driving.

My mom finally calls and I pull over in a McDonald's parking lot off of I-90. She says, as always, that she is fine; things are "sur-prisingly OK," she's "takin' it easy," taking care of herself, making sure grandma is comfortable, "that's the most important thing." We talk around and about things, just updates. She is tired. Then I start crying again, sad to have lost so much time with my grandma these past several years since leaving home.

"Shouldn't I come out to Seattle?" I say. "I mean *you* got to be with your Grandma Lulu when she died!"

"NO," she says. "No, I did *not* get to be with my grandmother when she died."

"What?" I gasp. "What, sorry, I'm so sorry."

"I was on my way to Eugene," she says, "on a bus. I had just seen her at the hospital. She was fine. And then when I got to Eugene your dad called me and said she died, and I said, 'What? No. That's impossible.' And then I caught a bus going back. And when I got there, ya know, everyone was like, 'You should go over to her house and go through her stuff—it'll help.' And I was like, 'NO, I do NOT want to do that.' And then they started saying, 'You should play music at the funeral!' And I was like, 'I am not doing that, I can't'—but somehow I did."

I asked her what she played.

"Let's see . . . I played some really pretty Debussy . . . Oh, yes, and 'Danny Boy.' *Jesus*, 'Danny Boy.' I don't know how I kept it together through that one."

I'm wandering around the grass behind the McDonald's, trying to keep my crying down. Oh, we've lost so much time—it could've been different.

"Yes, and then—and then!—maybe I haven't told you this. A little while later I went to a concert with Carmi, and the performer ended by playing 'Danny Boy,' and as soon as it started I burst into tears, just like a volcano, it was so unexpected, it was pouring out of me, like waves, like I had no control. Waves and waves. It was incredible—I still remember that feeling."

I buy a disgusting chicken sandwich from McDonald's.

Later, I'm sitting on a hill overlooking Harvey Mountain. The sun is going down and the fireflies are filling the fields. I came here to write about Sojourner Truth, but the minute I got here, my grandma started dying.

She has effectively been a shut-in now for several years, though no one quite talks about it that way, not even me. She has always had her jeweled glasses, her lamp, her fresh *New Yorker*, her festering wounds on her feet. And for every issue of the *New Yorker*, she complains about 75 percent of the content—the terrible poetry, the inscrutably twee fiction—with very occasional triumphs and pleasures, but she reads every week anyway, and we always agree about the brilliant Emily Nussbaum. "That's because," my grandma would say, "like all great critics, she is not just writing about TV. She is writing about everything." When I was in college, she'd ask me to send her my work and she'd always say (thanks, Grandma) that it was "better than most of that shit in the *New Yorker!*" And she would ask for more. We'd write letters, lists of book recommendations, chronicles of meals and seasonal flora—"The magnolia in the backyard is finally blooming. Made a tasty stew." Whenever I visited her in Seattle from wherever I was living, we'd sit down and she'd extract, with the greatest delight, every story about myself to date. But, otherwise, for those years I'd been away, her life had become the windows in the kitchen and the living room, the television and the book.

She wasn't always like this. My whole childhood, until I was a teenager, we walked and took the bus everywhere. And we used to go to the zoo most of all, in Seattle, Portland, wherever we were and wherever there was a zoo. Her zoo thing started in the late 1980s to battle some life-threatening depression and anxiety, which she never talked about and I never asked about.

I remember one time at the Washington Park Zoo in Portland, which is now called something else, we were in the gift shop and she refused to buy me a toy, or maybe she was horrified by my toy choice, and I ran out of the store and sat on the fountain by the fake turtles until she came and found me. I'm sure she was scared, but she wasn't mad, and she sat down and was warm and said she wouldn't tell my mom and stepdad, and that we were friends, that we'd always be friends. "Are we still friends?" And then she laughed with her mouth closed. She went on to ask me this as a joke for literally twenty years, every time I saw her: *Are we still friends?*

One of the last times we ever went to a zoo together, I was fifteen, and I had just gotten in trouble for drinking and smoking pot. In the parking lot, a condom, a bright pink condom, fell out of my purse onto the pavement. I picked it up and blushed. And she said, "What was *that?*" and laughed. Later we walked by the orangutans, and Melati, her closest orangutan friend, gave us the finger. She and Melati had been staring at each other through the habitat glass, nose to nose, for almost a decade at that point, but it had been several months since she'd last visited, so the finger made sense. "Did you see that?" My grandma chuckled, and then mimed the primate.

The very last time she went to the zoo, it took three years to convince her. I wasn't there for it, but my mother and my sister Charlie said that when they shuttled her to the visitor center, a young male attendant reported that she was going to have to be put on a list to get a wheelchair, to which she muttered back audibly, "I'll put *you* on a fuckin' list." But five minutes later, she was giggling with her mouth closed, like, *Joke's on you. I'm fine.*

We did everything together for the years that I remember— she always came for Grandparents' Day, took me garage-saling and to the zoo, made me fancy lunches, read me books, slept in my bed while I slept on the floor, and when she snored I'd yell "GRANDMA!" and she'd stop for a moment. We bickered all the time, about everything. She'd provoke me, or I'd feel dramatically wounded by something she'd said, or she'd cut me off, or I'd get whiny, and we would have a real balls-to-the-wall snap—but they were energizing. I remember once, when I was eight or nine, a nurse in a hospital (we were visiting her friend) looked at me in horror and said, "You shouldn't talk to your grandma that way!" and my grandma thought that was hilarious. For years after she'd follow *Are we still friends?* with *You shouldn't talk to your grandmother that way!* And then laughter.

A few days after my brother was arrested—so I must have just turned sixteen—my grandmother was sitting on the back porch. I got home from school, wearing these tight jeans and a floral top that laced up in the back like a bustier. I looked pudgy and depressed, and she took a photo of me squinting at her, my fingers in my hair, and another with my face pressed into the crook of my arm, both of us sitting at a table with a takeout box and a glass of juice on it.

She gave me a small amused smile and said, "Listen—it's so loud out here." We listened. The trees were full of all kinds of birds, screaming. They were in the giant cherry trees just over the fence and the chestnut overhead. "I am always amazed how loud it gets," she said.

I often took the train up to visit her by myself—starting when? Fifth grade? I'd take the Cascade line, ride business class, and get a free box lunch. And then we'd do the usual: go to the zoo, go to a movie, go to the book store, do crosswords, eat Indian food, maybe go shopping at the Catholic charity thrift store, watch *Mad TV*, go to the Science Center or to the Pea Patch to garden. I did this almost every summer until I turned eighteen and moved away to college.

And then I remember just a couple of years ago I visited her in Seattle and she said something strange. She was sitting at her pew—an old pew pulled up to the kitchen table and the window overlooking the garden, which has been her seat since time immemorial—and she said, "You wanted to get away from all of this," obliquely referring to my family, offering an explanation for why I'd gone to college in New York all those years back.

I said, "No, no, that's not what I had in mind at all—I really wanted to go to Pratt."

And she said, "But you wanted to get away, too. You needed to."

But then, this decade of not leaving the house, of inaction, of a fuller life not lived. And why don't I have a mythology for her, the

AND YOUR DAUGHTERS SHALL PROPHESY

way I do for my grandfather? My grandfather is the man who wanders unencumbered, but my grandmother the hippie witch—a neighborhood kid in the 1960s called her that, and it stuck—is still and always a mother, a grandmother to me.

I am sitting on that hill overlooking Harvey Mountain, going through all of this in my head, and on the phone now my stepbrother Noel says, "Ya know, that pity thing, that's OK because it's part of how you grieve, but it doesn't do any good for her." He added, "You know what they say: You gotta know the name of your devil."

I wonder if she ever did. I wonder if I do. It's a terrifying thing, to think that the dragon is lurking there, and you either can't or won't see it, and you don't know which.

There were a lot of black women preaching truth to power in the nineteenth century, more than will ever be named. Jarena Lee, Zilpha Elaw, Julia Foote, Florence Randolph, Harriet Jacobs: women who literally ministered on foot, women, in some cases, who had escaped slavery, walking hundreds of miles to preach. Lee and Jacobs wrote books about slavery, about sexual and physical abuse, and about conversion and talking to God: God is coming, repent, all ye sinners—God loves you and God is full of wrath and Christ will come again. And God loves us, we who are women and are black. When Truth writes her *Narrative*, she offers something similar, and she eventually figures out how she could make a living off of its distribution.

In 1851, in Akron, she comes out to say that if we are to overturn any system, any world, black women need to be included in the category of "woman," a category around which there is much anxiety at that time—the whole "cult of true womanhood" thing: pious, pure, domestic, submissive, white. Someone calls Truth's name off a piece of cardstock and she bundles her Quaker-style skirts together and walks onto the stage.

Well, children, where there is so much racket there must be something out of kilter. I think that 'twixt the negroes of the South and the women at the North, all talking about rights, the white men will be in a fix pretty soon. But what's all this here talking about?

That man over there says that women need to be helped into carriages, and lifted over ditches, and to have the best place everywhere. Nobody ever helps me into carriages, or over mud-puddles, or gives me any best place! And ain't I a woman? Look at me! Look at my arm! I have ploughed and planted, and gathered into barns, and no man could head me! And ain't I a woman? I could work as much and eat as much as a man—when I could get it—and bear the lash as well! And ain't I a woman? I have borne thirteen children, and seen most all sold off to slavery, and when I cried out with my mother's grief, none but Jesus heard me! And ain't I a woman?

Then they talk about this thing in the head; what's this they call it? [*member of audience whispers "Intellect"*] That's it, honey. What's that got to do with women's rights or negroes' rights? If my cup won't hold but a pint, and yours holds a quart, wouldn't you be mean not to let me have my little half measure full?

Then that little man in black there, he says women can't have as much rights as men, 'cause Christ wasn't a woman! Where did your Christ come from? Where did your Christ come from? From God and a woman! Man had nothing to do with Him.

If the first woman God ever made was strong enough to turn the world upside-down all alone, these women together ought to be able to turn it back, and get it right-side up again! And now they is asking to do it, the men better let them.

Obliged to you for hearing me, and now old Sojourner ain't got nothing more to say.

It's amazing, right? On many levels. In 1851: Your essentialism is suffocating every social justice movement. The rights of all disenfranchised are bound together. My life has been profoundly different from yours, and I am telling you, nonetheless, I am a woman. If you don't believe me, if you can't understand, we're not going to be able to get it "right-side up again." And also, Christ was made by God and a woman—"man had nothing to do with Him."

But is that even her voice? (Here I am, too, putting words in her mouth.) There are two versions of this speech, both transcribed by white people—this one, by Frances Dana Barker Gage, being the most widely referenced and perhaps the most obviously doctored, published twelve years after the convention in *The History of Women's Suffrage*. Historian Nell Irvin Painter famously reveals this to us much later: Truth spoke with a Dutch accent—a Dutch New Yorker's accent, in fact—and she would have said "aren't," if anything, and she did not have thirteen children, she had five. That the stenographer recorded her speech patterns, her rhetoric, her syntax, in such a way as to uphold the dominant narrative of what a black American woman might sound like in 1851, and not what Truth actually sounded like, seems likely to Painter. I think of Truth responding to Stowe's feature in *The Atlantic*: "I don't call people 'Honey.'"

Yet something extraordinary is happening here. She wasn't asking that black women be considered pious, pure, and domestic angels like the aspirational middle-class Victorian white women—she was poking holes in the whole concept of womanhood as it existed at the time.

Sojourner Truth said such an obvious thing, but something that had seldom or never been said before: *Where did your Christ come from? From God and a woman. Man had nothing to do with it.*

Then, sometime after Akron, she hires a photographer to take her portrait. Painter describes her style of dress in these photographs, the *cartes des visites*, as Quaker-style antislavery garb, distinguishing herself as a part of the resistance. At lectures, she starts selling these photos like trading cards, alongside copies of *Narrative*. "Selling the shadow to support the substance" she calls it, and these words are literally printed on the photos. The substance being her message, the shadow being the image of herself.

When I think of her, I think of how much she had to go through. She passed from one religious cult to another, enduring massive amounts of physical, sexual, and psychic abuse from men, women, congregants; then she ends up in this silk plant run by socialists, and it is there that she is able to bring four of her daughters, it is there that she begins to compose—out loud, on the page, whatever —"Ain't I a Woman" (or "Aren't I a Woman"). She was shifting the paradigm.

Another way of saying it:

After running from a thousand crazy, misogynistic religious movements helmed by men—Matthias, Miller, her fucking slave master—and after all but one of her children were sold away from her and into slavery, and after having been physically, sexually, and psychically abused by everyone who'd ever exercised any power over her—*she becomes Sojourner Truth.*

Today I find myself reading about Yvonne Delk, the first African American woman to be ordained by the United Church of Christ. There's a sort of spiritual CV online, an essay and self-styled Q&A narrating her path toward ordination. I first find Delk and her essay while developing a list of the most famous twenty-first-century black American women ministers and preachers, because I realize I don't know who they are. (Malcolm X once said that "the most segregated hour in American life is high noon on Sunday," and that is still true.) But first, how many institutions ordain women today? Not many: the Episcopal Church, Evangelical Lutheran Church in America, Presbyterian Church of the USA, United Methodist Church, Pentecostal Church of God, Assemblies of God, African Methodist Episcopal, Disciples of Christ, United Church of Christ (Delk's denomination), and Christian Science, still, of course. In more than half of the institutions that do this, the first to seek ordination were black women.

In her essay, Delk draws on Truth for strength, in an invocation, to do what she needs to in the UCC. She calls herself a daughter of the biblical Hannah and Sojourner Truth. Her occupation is, in her own words, a Justice Ministry: battling misogyny, racism, classism, the things the church was always tasked with. The colonizers and slave holders, the religious powerbrokers and patriarchs, they never knew what was coming. She describes the day of her ordination in 1978, surrounded by an all-male clergy with anointing hands, when she asked God for help in this journey. "As I knelt before that altar, I was part of a circle of women who had heard their names called and had stepped out of the shadows of racism and sexism to say, 'Here I am, God; use me' . . ." She says that she was on a journey toward "an unimagined future." She says, "Let's not worry about whether the world or our churches are ready for truth, because truth makes room for itself."

The day before I flew out to Seattle to see my grandmother for the last time, Sweeney's grandmother was diagnosed with stage-4 lung cancer. I sat on my grandma's couch and told her this, and she sort of smiled, a small empathetic smile, though her dentures were falling out and she'd lost so much weight. And the next day she said, "You know, after you told me that, I had a dream that *I* had cancer." She put her hand on mine and laughed with her mouth closed.

Later in conversation, another one of my cousins, who was currently living in my grandparents' spare room, said to her, "Sometimes I still feel like my eight-year-old self," and she looked at him, her eyes popping like an owl's, and said, "*I'm* sixteen."

I worried that she wasn't happy to see me that last time, the way she had been in the past. That was hard. I wondered, was our connection gone? Was it because I made her that terrible grilled cheese sandwich that sent her into a kind of spiral of depression? Of course, she was in excruciating pain and probably very scared, but all of this, in my narcissism, I took entirely personally.

All I want to say to her now is that I love her. She taught me to love books and reading and movies; she taught me to laugh, at just about anything, at any time; she taught me to love finding things at garage sales. Grandma, you were warm and protective, you were willing to fight with me without ever shutting down; you were fun and loving, but even now I am not sure that I ever really knew you, and that's hard. You loved your children, even in those later years when you began to snap and lash out and withdraw. You had good politics. You were welcoming, you asked lots of questions, you read my writing, you taught me to love that I wrote; you donated livestock in my name every Christmas for fifteen years. You were wise and discerning and hip, and even if you didn't say it, you got stuff no one else got. You had the mind of a writer; you saw the world as a complex system of psychologies, relationships, tragedies, and tensions, all of which were inevitable, but which you could see, catalog, smile at, laugh at. You could see how it was all working.

You remember the day America dropped the bomb on Hiroshima. You remember the day your Japanese neighbors were forced out of their house and never seen again. The particular details of your life came to me rarely, but you encouraged the particular from me.

Truth and reconciliation. There has to be truth and reconciliation. I am only just now beginning to understand what that means.

She died while I was on speakerphone. Everyone—aunts, uncles, cousins, parents—was gathered in the living room; I could hear their voices. My sister was crying on the other line, saying that grandma only had an hour left. Then my mom's voice: "OK, Nan is here—the chaplain. She's going to say a blessing now." A chaplain? For my family? Nan gathered everyone around for a prayer:

"Dear Lord"—*something something*—"Gale, a beloved daughter, wife, mother, grandmother—" For some reason it made me jump out of my skin, those words being more like stations in life, none of which were her whole self. She was a beloved person, a beloved woman, an amazing thinker and wit, all of those things, but those four words the chaplain said, they were stations, and they were so imprisoning in so many ways, and it was going too fast now. ". . . who was a source of support and love for her family . . ." Then I heard Robin interject—"And challenge! She challenged us, too, right guys?!" And we were like, *Right, right.* Nan's voice wavers, continues: ". . . Please bless the fruits of the marriage between George and Gale, and bring peace to her survivors . . ." Then she opened the floor to us, to add anything we wanted, and we all burst out, started telling all these inappropriate stories, talking about Black Pine Lake and how Grandpa drove her crazy and how snarky she was, how she and I fought while she taught me how to fly a kite at Seaside, how much we bickered but how wonderful it was. Her saying "I'm going to put *you* on a fuckin' list," and Melati, too, her old friend the orangutan—"old buddies," Grandpa kept saying. Grandma was nonverbal at this point, but her eyes were still open. Then the poor chaplain interrupted us, "I don't want to offend you, but we should bring some closure here." So she recited the Lord's Prayer and everyone said amen, probably had never said it before in their lives, and then the chaplain was gone and ten minutes later Gale Adair died.

Sojourner Truth leaves the Northampton Association for Education and Industry in 1846, and she gets help to buy her house. She pays for a photographer to take her portrait and she sells it at camp meetings, with her book, each photo captioned: "I sell the shadow to support the substance." She wears plain clothes to show that she means business, that, if anything, she is like the Quakers, not the women in bustles and crinoline crying at camp meetings. She starts to get famous, get read, get heard. She meets the president, Abe Lincoln, and in one version he is deferential to her, and she even gets the last laugh ("I've heard a lot about you," he says, to which she responds, "So have I"), but in another version he is dismissive, barely acknowledges her, treats her like a child. She rejects the definition of what it means to be a woman because that definition doesn't include her. Somehow she sets this kind of thinking in motion: a resistance of which we are still the heirs. The legal stations of female life—daughter, mother, wife—were not ever granted to her, and if those stations cannot include her then it is those stations, that understanding, that must be lacking, because ain't she a woman?

She is invited to speak at the Women's Rights conference in Akron, Ohio, in 1851, and either we know exactly what she said or we don't at all, but what we do know is that she climbed the plywood steps in her heavy skirts and got onstage, and at that moment (I think of Frank O'Hara's elegy to Billie Holiday), everyone and I stopped breathing.

WITCHERY

Marie Laveau

I t was one, two, three in the morning, sometime in the 1860s. The St. John's Eve ceremony had just ended, a ceremony that Marie Laveau had been presiding over for some thirty years. Tar barrels burned along the lakeshore, lit up like Christmas, though it was a warm wet night just after the summer solstice. Laveau's followers had come to wash their hands in the waters of Lake Pontchartrain, present offerings, sing, dance, let the spirits take over their bodies to gorge on cake and liquor, and in turn provide them with refreshment and healing for the new year. The ceremony had lasted for hours, and now Laveau looked out at her tired crowd—free women of color, slave men, white women, white slaveholding men—gathering their things to head back to the Marigny. The wind was kicking up offshore, and she thought that this was as good as any ceremony to be her last. This was the night she would give herself over to the hurricane.

It's a good story, and one version of many. In *Mules and Men,* Zora Neale Hurston writes that as the wind and rain started to rage, Laveau "resisted rescue, saying that she wished to die at the lake . . . she perhaps felt that, being old, her end was near. She preferred to exit with nature itself playing its most magnificent music, rather than die rotting in bed."

Herbert Asbury, too, wrote of that night around the same time as Hurston, reporting that it was Laveau's cabin, not her body, that sunk into that great, huge lake, and that "she protested that the Voudou gods wanted her to die in the lake, and was only pulled from the water against her will."

In Carolyn Morrow Long's biography of Laveau, *A New Orleans Voudou Priestess,* she assembles a bunch of these stories. Another source claims that a few of Laveau's followers found her washed ashore the next day, after which she spent seven years wasting away in bed. Yet another claims that *she* found Laveau floating creekside, days later, and nursed her back to health with coffee and herbs, after which Laveau returned to her duties as priestess. Still others insist that Laveau did in fact die the night of the storm, and that any account of Marie Laveau after the 1860s was actually her daughter acting as priestess in her name. The newspapers, both local ones and *The New York Times,* report that she died in her bed in 1881, having returned to the church, surrounded by saints pinned to the walls.

Some of these stories are from the press, and some are based on interviews from the Louisiana Writers' Project, conducted in the 1930s by writers like Zora Neale Hurston, and some are later semi-novelized in Robert Tallant's *Voodoo in New Orleans,* then re-novelized in Francine Prose's *Marie Laveau,* and then later televisionized in *American Horror Story,* and even at this very moment are being reinvented and retold in front of Laveau's tomb (where she may or may not be buried) in one of three simultaneous tours of the

St. Louis Cemetery No. 1—until the story of Marie Laveau's life has become a perpetual feedback loop.

Marie Laveau was a "Voodoo Queen," a Voudou priestess, a conjurer, a mambo, and according to biographer Martha Ward, the ostensible founder of American Voudou. She was born sometime around 1794 to a free mother of color and a mixed-race Haitian father. She had seven children, though that number sometimes shifts to fifteen—like Sojourner Truth's fictional thirteen—and of the seven, only two survived to adulthood, one of whom was her daughter, Marie II, who certainly operated later under her mother's name, though to what extent we have little way of knowing.

As Long says, by the end of the nineteenth century,

> most of the elements of the Laveau Legend were firmly established: the extraordinary beauty of the Voudou queen, her wealthy white planter father and her lovely mulatto mother, her profession as a hairdresser, her marriage to the carpenter Jacques Paris and his subsequent disappearance, her second marriage to Christophe Glapion, their fifteen children, her special friendship with Pere Antoine, her repudiation of Voudou and return to the church, and the idea that she was nearly 100 years old at the time of her death.

But her entire thesis is that barely any of this is verifiable, and in many cases it's downright wrong.

What do you do when the record is so thin? When all you have are civic records, financial transactions, marriage licenses, baptisms, interviews with very old people? During Laveau's lifetime, there are only three direct mentions in the press (or thereabouts) of her being a Voudou priestess or related to Voudou at all. She herself, like many nineteenth-century American women of color who were descended from slaves, left no written record and is presumed to have been illiterate.

Then there's the fact that black American women were—*are*—the object of so many corrosive rhetorics, perpetually caught in the damning, flattening, racist binary paradox of the white gaze: magical or evil, simple or calculated, hypermasculine or sexualized feminine. So much of what we know about Laveau has been filtered through that shitty cheesecloth, too.

What do you do when there's no record?

Slavery, suppression, erasure of culture, religion, relatives, entire family lines. You no longer work in linear narratives. Or you do, but only by imagining unbroken lines of connection wherever they've never explicitly been debunked. You have to.

Voudou has always been a religion of the erased and undocumented. The information comes in other forms: through the spirits, through the ceremonies.

In 1999 the contemporary New Orleans Voudou priestess Sallie Ann Glassman oversaw the St. John's Eve ceremony, Marie's ceremony, and she announced in an interview with the *Times-Picayune* that the spirit of Marie Laveau had come to her the evening before, presenting herself anew, mother and daughter merged into one. When the reporter asked Glassman what Marie was like, she said, "Marie doesn't like people who stand back at a distance and are judgmental," adding that she "does not like newspaper reporters much either." In Glassman's book, Laveau is acknowledged as "the historical Iwa of New Orleans": the deity, the patron saint.

I thought I was never going to make it to New Orleans. My summer had been sunk in work and caretaking. My grandmother died. Sweeney's grandmother found out she was dying the week I flew to Seattle to sit with mine for the last time. My father-in-law was sick, had almost died, was administered last rites three times, but had lived. I was at my stepbrother Noel's house in Portland after a long visit to home. His grandmother had died just a few months before.

I had just enough money in the bank for a train ticket, and I walked into Noel's guest bedroom and saw Robert Tallant's *Voodoo in New Orleans* on the shelf.

"You want it?" he said. "Take it."

And I did take it: as a sign, or permission, to go.

Noel made us breakfast on a skillet—eggs, sausage, home fries—and while he cooked we talked about our family. He had been estranged from my stepfather, his father, since the day after my wedding four years earlier. Noel was twenty when our parents married. Noel is black, with two white parents, a white stepmother, white stepsiblings, in the whitest city in America. We grew up together in one way or another, during profoundly different life stages, though he had always occupied the position of protector. The night my brother torched his house, Noel sat on our porch till dawn, and I had listened from my bedroom, which was right next to the front door, to the fumble, to Aaron's strange, crooked laughter, as Noel caught him in his arms. I walked outside and found Aaron, immobilized in his army fatigues. "I burnt the motherfucker down and now I'm going to shoot the mayor!" he shouted. Noel held him there until the cops had formed a circle around our house.

As a child, when I or anyone in our family drove in a car with Noel, we were often pulled over. The first time a cop pushed him to the sidewalk and frisked him, Noel was fifteen years old and walking home. When he and my stepdad Leo escaped from a gang of skinheads who had surrounded their car at a gas station, the cops they finally flagged down said there was nothing they could do. And during times when Leo couldn't stop yelling, at me or my mom or God, Noel would come and take him away for an hour, a day, a week, till he cooled down. And now it had been four years since they had spoken.

So I stood there in the doorway while he fried things on the skillet, talking about all the missed opportunities in our family, all the gaps, and by the time I was trying to swallow my first bite of breakfast, I was crying. Noel looking at me, his face softened by pain for my pain, tolerant with the question, for the hundredth time: *When are you going to accept things as they are?* That terrible sensation of hot eggs and a stuffed nose and trying to swallow. "I will never not be sad," I kept saying, and later he hugged me goodbye and said, "Stay sane, sista."

And then, just like that, I was heading toward a train they call *The City of New Orleans.*

Marie's great-grandmother might have been born in Senegal, a Wolof trafficked to the American South in the mid-eighteenth century. She was separated from her children, who also bore children into slavery, some to white men, to slaveholders, some to Creole or mixed or slaves or freed slaves, though one by one, over many decades, each had purchased their freedom. By the time Laveau's mother was born, her great-grandmother was a property owner, and Marie herself was born free. She might have learned rootwork and conjure from her mother or her grandmother. Biographer Martha Ward speculates in *Voodoo Queen* that, like most New Orleanian children of color, Marie learned Christian theology from the Ursuline nuns—an order of well-to-do French sisters who operated in relative independence from the church and "built a community of Catholic mothers and a convent where women of every race, class, and nationality could find refuge and support."

Twenty years went by, maybe more. Marie became a Voudou priestess. People traveled to her, from far and wide. She was pregnant, gave birth, raised children—amazing on its own, all of it. She sat on her porch, filed her nails, gave haircuts, cast out demons, thwarted domestic violence, repaired relationships, healed the fissures of slavery. She sat vigil in prisons with inmates on death row, helping them build altars, helping them get free in some cases—in this life or the next. She cured countless people of yellow fever. There she is, dabbing the forehead of some wan-faced patient, or sitting in the parlor of a rich white woman, casting spells, resolving infirmities, her clients sitting pretty, pawing at her lap as she braided their hair. Then she'd host ceremonies in Congo Square, around the corner from her house.

Ward says that Laveau "bore witness to her relationship to God and the spirit world each time she recited the Apostles' Creed, at each Mass she attended, every time she danced in Congo Square—*I believe in one God. . . and in all things seen and unseen . . . and in all things visible and invisible*," a hybrid that seemed a natural extension of her Catholic education, all that tongue-speaking on Pentecost and resurrecting and Holy Spirit possession. At some point, it was Marie and her daughter, both, interchangeable, leading the Congo Square ceremonies. Ward paints a picture:

> When the two priestesses danced in Congo Square and at other places in New Orleans, they shouted—*Voudou, Voudou*. Through the sacred word, a widespread African name for spirit or deity, they invited or invoked the spirits to enter their bodies, to be incarnated in them. After 1820 local newspapers used the word to describe the social group—a cult of primitive superstition, idolatrous rites, and snake worship, they insisted. Regardless of the low value placed on the religion by members of the press, practitioners, then as now, tell us that the word Voudou in all its spellings translates best as "those who serve the spirits."

Some of her family hailed from the most brutal factions of the Atlantic slave trade in the Caribbean, and had survived. But then to be out of that by one generation, somewhat safely integrated into New Orleans public life, a black businesswoman with white clients—how did she reconcile that? Then there's the evidence of her and her husband's own slave ownership, which Ward speculates in *Voodoo Queen* were transactions based on the slaves' eventual freedom. There is evidence that some of the purchases came with a permanent condition of the slaves' eventual enfranchisement, even in the event of another sale. Marie "did what she had to do," Ward says, "what she knew how to do, to fulfill Voodoo's obligation, to earn Voodoo's greatest gift. When the Great Serpent sang to Marie Laveau in Congo Square and insinuated himself into shapes that only conjure and poetry can, she submitted to the drums, and her songs echoed his voice—*There is life after slavery. There is freedom before death.*"

But Long, in *A New Orleans Voudou Priestess*, contests this certainty. She looked closely at all those financial records, too. She found no hard evidence that Laveau and her husband ever freed their slaves, or purchased slaves expressly for liberation purposes. In fact, there is only hard evidence, only records, that they profited.

I have been on the train now for two full days—the *Empire Builder*. They'd advertised Wi-Fi but did not actually provide it. I am, to my surprise, able to sleep at night. I have my own row with those wide footrests. I am wearing my grandmother's shirt, a green crinkled rayon thing, giant on me, held together by only three buttons so it's basically see-through at most angles, but I don't care. I am also wearing three of her necklaces—two with amber beads and one of blue clay—which I have barely taken off since her memorial party in Seattle a couple of weeks back. We'd thrown a huge party in her honor and cleaned out their house for the first time in twenty years. Entire rooms came alive under those layers of boxes and dust and old bicycle parts, and my brother had scrubbed outdoor furniture to be placed under the plum tree in the backyard, and my cousin and I set up a TV in the living room playing old camping home movies from the 1960s on a loop, showing, at times, my grandma in long braids stooped over a Coleman stove, frying up flapjacks or fish. It was a perfect beautiful May day, clear as a bell, and I cling to that beautiful afternoon, full of family members and old friends, sitting in the tower with my brother watching the sunset over Mt. Rainer, smoking cigarettes, talking about the game he's designing. The rest of the trip, down in Portland, had been hard, strained, stretched: a grief that would not lift, a family dynamic that would not change, Sweeney's mind off with his father recovering from a horrible stroke, and me, walking through a city I no longer recognized.

While we were there, the famous television psychic Miss Cleo died. I woke up on the second floor of the Victorian brick we were rooming in and saw the news on my phone. She was young, early fifties, heart disease. I remembered her commercials in the 1990s: a blue background and her orange *tignon*, her laughing Caribbean patois, saying, "Call me now for your free readin'," to have your future divined. There were fade-out clips of her talking on the phone, pulling cards, the disembodied voice of a soft-spoken woman on the other line getting news about her love life.

Within a few years, the company she worked for was sued for fraud several different times. Miss Cleo, whose real name was Youree Dell Harris, was the poster child for the company, and so for the scandal, too, although she was never fined or imprisoned, contrary to popular belief. She retreated from the public eye, down to South Florida, and she continued to have clients and to be a spiritual counselor. Four years later, she came out as a lesbian in an interview. She'd waited so long because being a lesbian had been taboo in her Jamaican household growing up (and beyond that household too, of course, of course). She even started her own podcast, and she still identified as an Obeah—a West Indies shaman. She remained a spiritual counselor all those years, someone who lived quietly and advised.

I think about Miss Cleo as I head down south. I am worn out. I sit in the observation car at night and look out at the darkness and try to read, try to write. I meet a guy who makes his own jerky, has three kids, is on his way to Montana to help his brother drive all of his adopted kids back to Oregon for a family reunion. My passenger car smells like a toilet, so I steer clear for as long as possible. I subsist off of instant oatmeal and instant coffee and baby carrots and Jif peanut butter. I feel hopelessly distant from my family, or like I am without hope for change. What a strange conclusion to draw, considering that my brother, against all odds, has his own apartment, a fine arts degree, a workout regimen, and my sister has her whole life ahead of her. And Noel, Noel is making a good life, full of hope.

I get off in Chicago and eat a weird hot dog, drink some coffee, smoke, cry on the phone to Sweeney.

On the next leg of the trip, on the *City of New Orleans*, my seatmate, a young man, asks what I'm going to New Orleans for. I assume he's from there so am cagey in my response. But it turns out he's on his way there for the first time too, to tend an urban garden in the Ninth Ward and to learn how to become a beekeeper. When he gets up from his seat I notice an envelope with his name on it, stamped with a return address for Church of the Brethren, so when he comes back, I start asking all these questions, trying to get to the bottom of this religious beekeeping thing. Now he's the one who's cagey, trying to read me, but I finally get him to say that he's connected to this urban gardening organization via Church of the Brethren, and they, well, they come from Germany, out of the reformation. (I often ask people impossibly nuanced questions about the religions they grew up in and don't think about in nuanced ways, like, "Well, so do they have a call to confession during service? How often do they serve the Eucharist?")

"Anabaptists!" I say. "Like the Mennonites," those people who baptized adults and got burned for it. They went to Switzerland, then to America, and now there's none in Germany.

The Brethren, he tells me, started the Peace Corps, AmeriCorps, other benevolent organizations. The boy had just completed a training for this service work where they'd taught him about "warm climate culture" and "cold climate culture." Had I heard of this?

His parents run a mission on the Navajo reservation in New Mexico—"I am the classic preacher's son," he says—and run a church, yes, where his mother and stepfather serve as co-pastors, and they also run a literacy center, a computer lab, a thrift store, a fresh-water well. He is telling me how the Navajo cosmology moves in a spiral, representing both individual lives and the life the world. Their houses are built in this spiral, he says, and the spiral functions so that the old and the new are constantly made to intermingle, must be subjected to constant change though always in proximity to the center, the origin. I am not explaining it well. He explained it much better, and he was only eighteen. But Leslie Marmon Silko talks about this in her novel *Ceremony*, I remember.

I write in my notebook: "Look up the earmarked pages in *Ceremony*."

That night I sleep in the observation car—or I try to. And the next thing I know it is gray dawn, and glowing before me are hot pink neon letters: MEMPHIS.

When I return to my seat, we are speeding through Mississippi. The train is emptying. Then, after Hammond, we sail over a long causeway, across the wide endless bayou, which reminds me a lot of the Wyoming prairie. The sky is gray-blue and so is the water, and every once in a while we pass through these scraggly ravaged swamp forests, by a houseboat, a floating shack.

The first miles into New Orleans are all warehouses and semi-trucks and freeway, and a shadow crosses the New Mexico boy's face. "So far, this just looks like any other city," he says.

When we arrive, he slings his guitar over his shoulder and I wish him good luck.

My taxi driver at the train station is Egyptian American, born and raised in New Orleans, and he talks darkly about Katrina like it was yesterday. I can see out the window, through cracks in the side streets, the old architecture, the short houses, Creole houses, some beautiful latticed balconies. My heart is pounding. I am not sure why

I'm here. He drops me off at a small shotgun house across from a gutted car wash that is now just a cement slab full of middle-aged dudes drinking malt liquor and blasting music.

I check into my Airbnb and close the shades and get under the covers and sleep.

When I wake up, it's getting dark, and I set off into the Marigny—the hub of public life for free people of color in the nineteenth century. I buy a pint of Abita Brewing Company's Purple Haze at a bar and listen to a jug band. I walk to the address of Marie Laveau's old house on St. Anne and find a pretty mint-colored single-story building with gingerbread eves—it looks Victorian, which should have been my first clue. In the dark, I read a plaque stating that this building was constructed in 1909, after Laveau's death. I notice, then, the Marie Laveau Apartments next door, with a sign bearing snakes blooming from a witchy cauldron.

The lamps are flickering, and I walk to the Louis Armstrong arch, lit up like Broadway, back and forth along streets named Love and Hope and, yes, Desire. The neighborhood is quiet and oddly empty. I buy a fried oyster sandwich, another Abita. I continue walking for two, three miles, until it is very dark, my heart pounding, hurting. I can barely speak, on the phone, to the waiters. When I do speak, it is as though I am miles away from myself.

New Orleans did not develop in parallel with the rest of the United States. When the Louisiana Purchase took place in 1803, things had already changed a lot during the years of French and Spanish rule: According to Long, in 1769, 7.1 percent of the New Orleans population were free people of African descent, and by 1805, 33.5 percent were free people of color.

New Orleans was frightening to Anglo-Americans when they started to arrive around then. Here was this place that had a complex caste system: white people, mixed-race people, free people of color, slaves, slaves with light skin, slaves in the city, slaves who lived in their own homes and ran their own businesses. Caught in the competing colonial forces of French and Spanish rule, this place had at one time abolished ties to the trans-Atlantic slave trade and then, later, reinstated their part in it. Then, of course, there was religious mixing—Yoruba and Haitian Voudou and Catholicism and more—and none of it was kept separate, nor secret. Free people of color married white people, white men had public partnerships and common-law marriages with free women of color, not to mention white men, married men, rapists, who openly fathered slaves, sometimes purchasing their freedom and their homes and the livelihoods of their children. New Orleans had a complicated system of laws by which wealth and property could be protected and kept by women of color and their children, and of course a slew of laws that undermined those laws, and so on. White men married black women, brown women married brown men, black women owned slaves, and all of the children of New Orleans were mixed—were, after 1803, Americans. And all of this religious, cultural, and moral ambiguity showing Americans what America had always been like, would always be like.

The New Orleans Voudou gatherings and ceremonies reflected this: You could find white men, free women of color, white women, slaves both men and women of all colors, and they were all there together in the rooms and temples and lakeshores, though some services required higher fees, and Marie Laveau presided over all kinds—and as Anglo anxiety encroached, these ceremonies would more and more frequently get busted by the cops, and the newspaper men would write shrieking reports, horrified because they were bewildered, though less by the content of the ceremony and more that all of these people were together.

At St. Louis Cathedral, Marie Laveau's church, which is still there today and under construction, Pere Antoine was the priest. He was cool because he gave communion to everyone, he totally understood the ambiguity: those free women of color in common-law marriages with already married men and their complex families and the bigamy and sex out of wedlock and slavery and Voudou and the Caribbean and Africa, and how tradition must evolve, must not be erased.

But, God, do not get me wrong—this was all pretty fucked up. In both the eighteenth and nineteenth centuries, Code Noir was used to police, not unlike Jim Crow, the limits of participation for people of color in public life, especially about marriages and transference of wealth. But people found ways, partly because of the common laws. Long says that most of the free people of color owned their own homes and made modest livings from carpentry, masonry, iron-working, as shopkeepers, barbers, tailors, hairdressers, etc. And so lots of people of color, lots of women, became property and business owners.

The Anglos were horrified because they were confused, threatened, supremacist—the usual. All this ambiguity was disturbing to the white ruling class who, as Long puts it, "were accustomed to the concept of slavery as a permanent condition appropriate to an inferior race and who considered free people of African descent an anomaly that threatened the stability of society." What complicates this from both ends is the question of slavery—for Anglos, it had to be either absolutely wrong or absolutely right. To find this society that wasn't fretting over these questions was an inconceivable horror.

Culture is not fixed. Everyone knows that now, I suppose. But American culture, in all of its newness, likes to prey on this myth of fixity. It's been the same for a seemingly endless number of years—generations, centuries—and it won't change now. It can't. This is what's normal. This is what's right. This is who belongs and who does not, and these are our values. This desperate attempt, this elaborate fantasy, of purity and continuity.

A few years ago I became interested in how American religion, especially American Christianity, had existed in so many thousands of iterations over time, despite its attempt to frame itself as forever fixed, full of continuity, with constant values and expression. But then, where I found women making religion—queering religion, if you will—I also found the ways or the moments when other big changes were afoot, or were forced to be.

Yes, it has just as often been the case that where women and queer people are worshipping, you will find a complete and actual vision of the afterlife: Case in point, the funeral of the drag queen in the movie version of *Angels in America*, the close-up on the drag queen gospel singer at the pulpit in the steepled church, then panning to old women, bitter parents, supportive siblings, queens, dykes, trans, black, white, and they're all singing and dancing. It's amazing! It's a vision of the worshipping world as God intended (or as Christ was talking about) in all its misfit paradox! That scene at the funeral—it's everyone, like how Belize describes it to Roy Cohn later on in the film. Cohn is dying, wandering around the hospital halls attached to an IV, haunted by the specter of Ethel Rosenberg. Cohn asks Belize, in a morphine daze, "What's it like, afta'?" Belize lights a cigarette, says, "Heaven or Hell?" But when Cohn doesn't specify, Belize says:

"San Francisco . . . mmm, a big city, overgrown with weeds, but flowering weeds, and on every corner, a wrecking crew, and something new and crooked going up catty-corner to that. Windows missing in every edifice like broken teeth, gritty wind, and a gray high sky full of ravens . . . Prophet birds, Roy. Piles of trash, but lapidary, with rubies and obsidian, and diamond-colored cowspit streamers in the wind. And voting booths. And everyone in Balenciaga ball gowns with red corsages, big dance palaces full of music and lights, and racial impurity and gender confusion. And all the deities are Creole, mulatto, brown as the mouths of rivers. Race, taste, and history are finally overcome. And you ain't there."

"And Heaven?"

Belize takes a drag of his cigarette. "That was Heaven, Roy."

"Voudou" becomes "voodoo" during Jim Crow. An old move—delegitimizing as response to threat of destabilization. And just like the religion, around this time, which is also around the time most of the Louisiana Writers' Project interviews are conducted, Marie Laveau herself becomes less a proper noun and more of a feeling, a memory, a legend, a spirit.

I go to the Voodoo Museum of New Orleans, just around the corner from Bourbon Street. The door is narrow and sticks when I open it, so I plunge into the small front room, squashed behind a small family of tourists who have also just arrived.

"Well, hi," says a woman in a bright yellow kaftan, smiling at me from a loveseat. "I'm so-and-so, the Voodoo Queen of New Orleans." Another woman sits bored at the messy ticket counter. She says nothing to me when I approach except the price of admission. Her counter, a schoolteacher's desk, really, is crowded with bits of things: candles, paper, a credit card machine. I fumble for my wallet, and she warns me that I should be prepared to leave cash for the spirits inside because they, unlike her, do not accept credit cards. I laugh as I hand her my credit card, but she does not. Then a white couple stumbles out from the museum exit, a curtained doorway just a few feet away. She turns to them. "That wasn't so scary, now was it? You have any scratches, any bleeding?" She cackles. "No? Well, all right then." And the Voudou priestess on the loveseat laughs loudly, nervously—"That's right, that's how it's supposed to be. 'Course there's no bleedin'."

There are shelves holding a variety of things for sale: Robert Tallant's *Voodoo in New Orleans*, gris-gris, Marie Laveau paper dolls by Tom Tierney where she looks like Natalie Wood in *West Side Story*, like a white person trying to look Puerto Rican. It's ridiculous.

And then I go through the curtained doorway.

I'm in a hot, narrow, windowless hallway covered in old wallpaper, and in true nineteenth-century fashion, not one inch of the wall is left uncovered. There are two oil paintings exposed to the elements—one of Marie Laveau as an adult and one of Marie Laveau, or Marie II, as an adolescent. There are images of Dr. John, framed articles, biographies of all the famous New Orleans Voudou mambos alive and dead. Lining the floor is Marie Laveau's original kneeler, bits of bracelets, gris-gris, piles of cigarettes, dollar bills, and plastic jewelry around its base. Connected to the hallway are two small rooms, both stuffed with ephemera: dusty bookshelves, altars, effigies, statues in the form of specific Iwa studded with more offerings—coins, cigars, candy, empty liquor bottles. The spirits, Iwa and ancestors alike, are capable of many earthly interventions and actions, with a few exceptions: They cannot eat, drink, smoke, dance, or have sex—they need humans to help facilitate that for them—and these offerings, and sometimes these activities, are the content of ceremonies, those by Lake Pontchartrain and others that I've been reading about.

I can barely explain how strange of a space it is—spatially, not the contents. Even though it's right off of Bourbon Street, the museum is refreshingly janky, a series of real shrines cast in a patina of devotional offerings, not any kind of sleek tourist shit.

In another room is a painting of a nude woman holding a writhing python high above a roaring fire: the Grand Zombi dance. There's an empty terrarium where the "spiritual python" once lived (a curled piece of paper taped to the glass says it died in 2004). Where I expect museum-style monographs, there are instead bits of paper stapled to the walls or tacked to the table, describing the Iwa's particular domain. Hokey music is piped in from all corners: "Love Potion No. 9" and cutesy songs about Marie Laveau.

There is a framed newspaper clipping about how Pope John Paul II said that African religions needed to be recognized as "in legitimate dialogue" with Catholicism. There is a pamphlet saying that in Voudou, "the only consistency is inconsistency." There's a biographical plaque of one of the contemporary local Voudou priestesses, and the copy ends by noting that she "is a practicing Catholic." Catholicism and Voudou were both seen as misfits by the Protestant Anglo ruling class, so it was easier to band together.

I leave a written prayer and some money and a few cigarettes with spirits I cannot even recall the names of.

When I get back to my rented room, I finally dig out my copy of Silko's *Ceremony* and find the passage I thought of when I was talking to the New Mexico boy on the train. It's a scene where the medicine man is speaking to the young Navajo protagonist, a WWII vet suffering from PTSD:

> "The people nowadays have an idea about the ceremonies. They think the ceremonies must be performed exactly as they have always been done, maybe because one slip-up or mistake and the whole ceremony must be stopped and the sand painting destroyed. That much is true. They think that if a singer tampers with any part of the ritual, great harm can be done, great power unleashed." He was quiet for a while looking up at the sky through the smoke hole. "That much can be true also. But long ago when the people were given these ceremonies, the changing began, if only in the aging of the yellow gourd rattle or the shrinking of the skin around the eagle's claw, if only in the different voices from generation to generation, singing the chants. You see, in many ways, the ceremonies have always been changing . . .
>
> At one time, the ceremonies as they had been performed were enough for the way the world was then. But after the white people came, elements in this world began to shift; and it became necessary to create new ceremonies. I have made changes in the rituals. The people mistrust this greatly, but only this growth keeps the ceremonies strong.

She taught me this above all else: things which don't shift and grow are dead things. They are things the witchery people want. Witchery works to scare people, to make them fear growth. But it has always been necessary, and more than ever now, it is. Otherwise we won't make it. We won't survive. That's what the witchery is counting on: that we will cling to the ceremonies the way they were, and then their power will triumph, and the people will be no more.

What rarely gets foregrounded is that Voudou is a religion of healing and a religion of resistance. It started in places like Haiti and New Orleans, where the religions of West Africa were coming in from the trans-Atlantic slave trade and ran up against the strictures of Catholicism. Yoruba deities find their double in saints—in the 1850s, there began to be Catholic stand-ins for Haitian Iwa, La Bas becomes St. Peter, Gran Bwa becomes St. Francis. Elements of ceremony start to look liturgical.

Voudou is a religion that emerged out of slavery, oppression, threat of erasure, and so it is, of necessity, a syncretic religion, incorporating elements from others, so that it no longer resembles from whence it came. New Orleans Voudou, says Long, is a mix of "Senegambian, Fon, Yoruba, and Kongo slaves with Haitian Voudou, Euro folk magic, and folk Catholicism," and it absorbs "the beliefs of blacks imported from Maryland, Virginia, and the Carolinas during the slave trade . . . [who] were English-speaking, at least nominally Protestant, and practiced a heavily Kongo-influenced kind of hoodoo, conjure, or rootwork." The ceremonies are passed down from person to person; sometimes they're used to rectify a troubled love affair, and sometimes they're used to heal the sins and scars of a landscape or a people.

We don't even know for sure that Marie Laveau was a hairdresser, though lots of Louisiana Writers' Project interviews account for it, and Tallant makes a compelling case for all the dirt it must have given her to work with:

Marie must have learned some amazing things. She probably discovered that many Creole marriages were pure business arrangements. She undoubtedly learned that Creole gentlemen almost invariably kept beautiful quadroon mistresses in cozy little cottages not far from Congo Square. She must have met grand ladies, who though they presided in their French opera boxes like duchesses and appeared with their husbands at great balls and certain soirees, spent much of their time weeping in their boudoir, or in giving way to secret alcoholism. All the family skeletons must have come out to dance for Marie: the family with a strain of insanity and the strange aunt kept locked in a room upstairs . . . The ladies talked and Marie listened.

Now that I am in New Orleans, I really begin to understand what Long means by the Laveau Legend.

I go to St. Louis Cemetery No. 1 on a rainy day, and I notice that the guide's story about Marie Laveau is full of certainty. So many of the stories I will hear are full of that same certainty, yet each is different. This guide says that Laveau's first marriage to Jacques Paris was arranged and that her family was "trying to make their way" in New Orleans after leaving Haiti—but as far as I know, she was something like a third-generation New Orleanian, her father was Haitian but white or white-ish, and she was born free, though her great-grandmother was an American slave. The guide continues, describing how Laveau was trained in Voudou ritual by her grandmother, how she offed her first husband, rose to power, and conducted ceremonies for rich scorned lovers, and how there were possibly four different people over the course of the nineteenth century posing as Marie Laveau.

He gestures for the group to follow him to the next tomb. One other girl and I, the only loners on the tour, wait until they've all gone ahead and then, one after the other, never making eye contact, we whisper prayers to the tomb, according to tradition.

In New Orleans the cemeteries look like cities of the dead, with tombs built aboveground because otherwise, when the rains came, the dead would float up all over the city, and you might find someone familiar, though all gaseous and dissolved. It has happened before. So now the tombs are like little houses, and they are often decorated to look like the dead people's former homes, complete with matching gardens and gates.

As the tour goes on, we stop briefly at the "heretic section," which basically means the Protestant section.

I walk into the New Orleans Healing Center with my heart pounding against my ribs, and then suddenly, finally—stillness. There are Persian-style rugs laid out across the polished concrete floor. Faux–Spanish moss hangs from all the old-timey sconces in the lobby. There are four young men inside the large foyer, each sitting on the floor against the wall, reading or writing. They look like crust-punks; two have dogs, one has a skateboard. They are white and black. I see the Marie Laveau shrine immediately to my right—it was constructed a couple of years ago for one of Sallie Ann Glassman's St. John's Eve ceremonies and placed here afterward with no particular intent, though almost immediately people began making pilgrimages, leaving things at her feet, paying respects.

I don't approach her yet. I don't even look at her straight on.

I walk around the center, a cooperative mixed-use galleria. I find it all oddly soothing. There's a barber, a church plant, a gym, an affordable wellness clinic, a clothing store, a food co-op. Two men breeze past me, and I turn to see their backs: one T-shirt says I AM PRESENT FOR PEACE and the other says CHANGING PLACES, CHANGING LIVES.

I'm still not sure how to approach the shrine—I'm self-conscious—so I find a spot against the wall in the room with the punks. Two women walk in, one after the other, and approach the shrine. They're both dressed in white. They sit nearby and write, they use the kneeler; one carries a plastic bottle of Mug root beer, which at first I think she is going to leave at the altar, but which she drinks from instead. I wait until they leave, then walk to her.

She's five or six feet tall, papier-mâché, swaddled in a pale blue shawl covered in stars, seeming both stiff and supple. Her red seven-pointed scarf is tied around her head, and she holds a bundle of magic objects in her arms: a skull, a plant, a vase. The X is everywhere, her signature. It is the X that devotees are compelled to etch onto her tomb, the X that marks her existence, the X, like G.K. Chesterton's description of the cross, which is the "signpost for free travelers," the X that comes up later during the civil rights movement: Malcom's X and others. It is also, plausibly, an X in the absence of her literateness.

I sit at the kneeler. Around the shrine are all kinds of things: saints, figurines, Jesus carrying a little boy, a St. Francis candle, a black serpent candle that says "*separar*," faux flowers, peace flags, bottles of brightly colored nail polish, brooches, prescription bottles, rocks, wine, toys, a horseshoe, playing cards, an empty Jameson bottle, a homemade Mother Mary shrine, paper notes, single beads, lots of blue. I unhook my grandmother's blue clay necklace and place it on the shrine. There's a note in a frame, beseeching a prayer of thanks for Marie Laveau's intercession on a miracle that took place April 29, 2016, when a Louisiana judge ruled that continuous glucose monitors must be covered by Medicare. So I pray for that too. I pray for intercession, healing, sleep, wisdom, restoration, hope. I race through the Apostles' Creed, say a few words of Creole French, but then my mind has wandered to some other place, some other commercial complex in some other city. When I open my eyes, I noticed that there are papier-mâché dragonflies everywhere, big and glittering.

I think of the giant dragonfly that threw itself against my window screen one night earlier this summer. It was the night before my grandmother died. I was up late in my studio, which has a panel of huge screened windows I can roll open. Outside it was silent and pitch dark. As always, there was a circus of insects bashing themselves against the screens, flitting their wings in panic and ecstasy. Then, all of a sudden, there was a series of heavy thuds against the screen: *Thud. Thud. Thud.* Almost no buzz. And there was a huge dragonfly—the biggest I have ever seen—throwing itself over and over against my screen, at one or two in the morning.

That same night I dreamed of dragonflies, tons of the small skinny blue kind. In the morning I looked up "dragonfly symbolism" and read about change, paradigm shift of the self, mental and emotional maturity, death making room for life. Later that day, I got a call from my sister that my grandmother had one hour left to live.

At the Island of Salvation Botanica, I thumb through clay tiles marked with Marie Laveau's X and saints' pendants and bottles of oil that have been blessed for particular spells. I find a sleeve of greeting cards printed with a white woman in a bowler hat sitting at a tea table with Marie Laveau. Then I notice the signature: Carolyn Morrow Long, the biographer. She's the white woman at the table. I buy the card, a bracelet, a St. Anthony pendant, a tile. The woman who rings me up is Sallie Ann Glassman, one of the city's best-known mambos. "What brought you to New Orleans?" she asks. I can feel my heart pounding again.

Yeah, what *am* I doing here? Did I say that out loud?

Other than orders placed with bartenders and waiters, and phone calls to Sweeney and Amber and my friend Lina, Sallie is the first person I've spoken to in days. "I took a train," I answer strangely. "From Portland, Oregon. It took three days." I swallow. "Um, do you know if this is the same Carolyn Morrow Long who writes about Marie Laveau?"

"Yes," Sallie says. "You would never guess, though, if you met her, that she's into this stuff."

She starts to place my purchases in a small paper bag, and I rush to explain.

"Well, I'm working on a book—about American women prophets, or some women prophets, or just spiritual celebrities, I guess. And of course Marie Laveau is one of them, so I'm doing some research. Or—just walking around."

"If you're still here in a couple of days," she says, handing me her business card, "you should come to my temple for a ceremony."

It isn't until I'm back in my rented room that I realize I don't have an address for the temple, don't know when the ceremony starts or what it is, or anything about the protocol. I email her, saying all of this, and she tells me to call the shop. I do, and she tells me that the ceremony will be for Gran Bwa, a tree spirit, the Iwa of the forest under the ocean, and that I should bring an offering that feels related to that. Some people bring plants, shells, food. She says I should arrive in either all red or all white, with a red headscarf.

L ina flies in for a night at the last minute. We go out walking and drinking all night long, eating fried oysters and grilled tuna and summer squash and succotash and gumbo. We walk into a tobacco shop just off of Frenchman Street where the guy looks genuinely surprised, even dismayed, to see customers. New Orleans continues to be strange that way: seemingly designed for tourism and yet averse to outsiders. We sit on a bench above the Mississippi and watch the Natchez roll back and forth. Bourbon Street is mayhem, crowded with teenagers and proselytizers and performers and mud and neon lights. A young man joins us on a stoop. He is from the Ninth Ward, had to leave after Katrina, moved to Mississippi, and has just come home again. We listen to him, sipping our neon-hued Green Grenades.

And then we keep drinking, deeper into the night, planning possible joint futures for ourselves—a residency in the Hudson Valley, a piece of land where all our friends and partners could live. As we talk, we pass by the old Ursuline Convent where a statue of Christ is backlit, casting a shadow thirty times his size onto a far wall. And then it's four o'clock in the morning, then a Pabst and a paper bowl of red beans and rice in a diner, and then we go home.

Though we are terribly hungover the next morning (Was it the Green Grenades? The shots of Fireball we made off with after three bros bought them for us at Larry Flynt's Hustler Club?), I insist we bike to Lake Pontchartrain. It looks close on Google Maps, but it takes us two or three hours to get there, and we have to walk our bicycles over the crumbling I-10 overpass. The minute we come up over a short hill, there are fireflies everywhere.

It is only upon arrival that I realize how big the lake is. I cannot see across. A causeway disappears into silvery infinity. And for such a big lake, it is very still. I realize that we should've gone straight to Bayou St. John where the Voudou ceremonies were traditionally held, but it's too late now. We're exhausted. The air is heavy and gray and so bright it hurts the eyes.

Later, on our way to Sallie Ann Glassman's temple, dressed all in red and sweaty, I realize we've forgotten an offering. We gather chinaberry branches that have fallen in someone's yard. Down a dead-end alleyway, there are murals mounting in intensity, and then a one-room wooden building. We walk in.

A few people have gathered already. There are elaborate altars on either side of the room, layered with offerings. In the middle of the room, a sanded-smooth tree trunk. A woman comes in holding a shopping bag full of corn, eggs, cake. Others have brought potted plants, saplings. They talk about the storm that's coming and the flooding already happening in the lower wards, though there is no trace of alarm in their voices. As more people gather and we wait for Sallie, two women smoke cigarettes out the back door. Lina and I sit on folding chairs and wait silently.

Then Sallie arrives, and the lights go out, and we begin.

The lead drummer is a white guy—he beats in a loud thumping rhythm. We stand in a circle, dancing, swaying from foot to foot. The drummer leads us in a call-and-response. We are moving clockwise, then we are moving toward each of the four directions. Between songs, Sallie says prayers in Haitian French. Each song marks a different round: inviting in Gran Bwa, and maybe other spirits, too; making space and setting intentions; extending our offerings. Sallie prays and very slowly draws four symbols on the ground in sand, in the four directions. We get on our knees, foreheads to the concrete. The spirit is in the house.

We continue dancing, singing. We offer ourselves for possession.

Sallie and a helper come around, smudging us with a rattle. We dance in a circle around the sanded-smooth tree. The possessions start to happen: a man tenses up his arms, a leg, cocks it back kind of like a flamingo then strikes it straight like a stick, his neck suddenly stiff, his eyes glazing over—he walks around, extends his arms like a toddler learning to balance, he laughs and laughs and falls over. Another woman, stricken too, starts to move quickly, collecting bits of things from the altar—palm leaves, a bit of rum, flowers, peanuts—and bundles them together, then gives the little packet, with an impish expression, sincere and mischievous, to another woman, who is crying because Gran Bwa embraced her.

These kinds of things, again and again, and everyone laughing, laughing, hysterical, laughing so hard they can't breathe, and then falling back into someone else's arms.

Sallie looks around and begins to slow things down, to find a resting place, but there is still one woman possessed. Her laugh is low and loud, and it is slowing, too. "I'm back," she pants.

I am hot and tired; we've been going for hours, I don't know how long. Then—I know this. I recognize this. I am sixteen, in a Lakota ceremony, a sweat lodge, a Sun Dance, a *yuwipi*: the rounds, the dancing, the water, the offering; instead of the rattle, sage; instead of possession, dialogue. The timbre of the lead drummer's voice, the blue-eyed blond young man, this ancient music, this ancient sound rising out of him.

It's my father.

When I wake up the next morning, I am back at the beginning.

SANCTUARIES

The yuwipi

I.

A man dying of brain cancer sits on the back steps of a Presbyterian church. He's slumped against a woman who is arranging a Pendleton blanket around his shoulders. With their knees drawn to their chests, their eyes scanning the gathering for cues, they remind me of children. When I walk by, the woman adjusts her glasses and introduces the two of them—husband and wife—and then asks, "So, have you been to a *yuwipi* before?" I tell them I have not, then settle one step higher on the staircase. The man redistributes his weight against my leg. He can barely move. The fishy, petrol smell of American hospice, mixed with sweet grass, rises from the back of his skeletal head.

The wife asks me how I got there.

"My father," I say, gesturing to the crowd, though I don't see him.

From our spot on the steps, we're facing a parking lot where Lakota and non-natives alike filter in for the *yuwipi*, a healing ceremony that a medicine man from Ashville, North Carolina, has been flown out to facilitate. The church we're waiting to enter is in a 1960s square brick building, bereft of windows, save for a few narrow stained-glass panels. The Whitedeer family, a Northwest hoop of the Lakota Sioux, regularly rents out its basement to hold ceremonies like this one.

Jay breaks away from the parking lot's growing assembly and wanders up to the steps. A year ago, just before my sixteenth birthday, he and I spent a week at a Sun Dance in southern Oregon, praying, singing, and swaying under the pine-and-brush arbor encircling the dancers, who, within that large circle we'd all created, fasted for five days and pierced their chests, connected by rope to the base of a cottonwood tree. Both Jay and my father sat at the spirit drum that summer, installed centrally among the community of supporters. They were responsible for guiding the songs, ushering in the ancestors, and keeping the beat the community echoed with their bare feet.

I'd watched Jay closely—he was among the youngest people there, just barely twenty-one. He had a rough, wry, big-bodied handsomeness. He didn't introduce himself to me until the end of the week, which culminated in a giant potluck dinner as a breaking of the dancers' fast. Jay and I sat next to each other in camp chairs, eating from paper plates, watching heat rise from the weary, sunburned community. Dancers reunited with their children and spouses and friends, though they still carried the residue of the ceremony: bits of paint flecking from their faces, notches cut in their arms from skin sacrifice, a bright, cloudy look in their eyes.

Jay was serious about the ceremony but dismissive of the preciousness some of the white people brought to it. We sat irreverently, joking about the breathy, middle-aged women who smiled at us, saying, "Well, Spirit says . . . Spirit says . . ." I asked him how he'd wound up getting involved in Lakota ceremony. "I was addicted to heroin," he said, "and in a recovery youth group, the leader suggested I go to a sweat. The rest is history." All the stories I'd heard that week bore some semblance to this: substance abuse, jail time, war tours, terminal illness, decades of melancholy.

The next day we packed up camp, and Jay, my father, and I stopped by Immigrant Lake for a swim. As Jay's body disappeared below the waterline, I watched the big gothic scrawl across his shoulder blades that said SOBER disappear, too.

Sitting next to me on the church steps, waiting for the *yuwipi*, Jay slaps my shoulder and says, "I was hoping to see you here." Then he looks down at my feet. "Girl—you've got some widely spaced toes."

I look down. I'm barefoot, which is part of the dress code for participation in most Plains Indian ceremony. For women, you also need a long cotton skirt; a loose T-shirt or something like a kaftan, mid-calf or longer; plus a shawl. All of my skin is covered, save for my ankles and wrists. Though the Whitedeers impose a strict code of female modesty, I've never been able to get a clear answer about its origin, except that it was likely a modification wrought by early contact with Christian missionaries.

I haven't washed these clothes since the last time I used them in a sweat lodge. The dying man next to me doesn't seem to mind the smell.

The Lakota believe that the world began in the Black Hills, not far from the site where Mt. Rushmore was drilled into granite cliffs, but some archaeologists claim that the Plains people actually came down from Canada sometime after the Spanish paid their fifteenth-century visit. I learned this a few weeks after I moved to Wyoming, when a couple of new friends took Sweeny and me on a treacherous canoe ride across one of Carbon County's desert reservoirs.

Our friends used a topographical map to guide us through back roads and dusty, unkempt stretches of public land to Seminoe State

Park. I thought about the life the Lakota might have carried out on land like this, overexposed but endowed with visual and spatial awareness of the open plains, allowing them to see enemies and bad weather far before it reached them. I wondered how the scrubby steppes had shaped the way they thought about God, and I thought of Native American activist Leonard Peltier decaying in his prison cell, and brawny American Indian Movement vigilantes, and Crazy Horse and Custer too. I could see the loss, in every divot and dike, like Jay's recovery tattoo slipping out of sight.

When we arrived at the edges of the big brown reservoir, we set up camp under the single cottonwood, drank a couple of beers, and then climbed into our friends' canoe. We were halfway across when a quick-moving storm cloud, carrying dirt and bits of shale, raced up the water's surface. It nearly capsized us as we reached the opposite shore.

While we were crouched behind a boulder to shield ourselves, we started talking about our childhoods. I told them about participating in Lakota ceremonies as a teenager with my father, and one of our friends, an archaeologist, said, "That whole Plains Indians idea we have, of them riding horses across the prairies in battle—that existed only after the Spanish brought horses here. The whole plains life, as we imagine it, was only possible after the horses came, and it lasted for only three hundred years or so. Before that, they were in southern Canada, the Great Lakes region."

It hadn't occurred to me till then—though it seems obvious—that the Lakota hadn't carried out a static spiritual or cultural existence. The creation stories I grew up hearing at Jim Whitedeer's elder talks were contingent on a confluence of both modern geologic and imperial circumstances. The Sioux tribes may not have even seen the Black Hills until their fifteenth-century mobility, though maybe an early medicine man had dreamed of them, holed up in the dark cool reaches of Canada. Lakota spirituality, after all, doesn't rely on continuity. It's dynamic, a framework rather than a doctrine: Respect the Great Spirit, call on ancestors for help. The fact that the dress code for the ceremony might have come from Christians, and that the Sun Dance started in the nineteenth century as a reaction to the violence of white settlement, doesn't undermine the credibility of Lakota spirituality. It's not bound to a set of practices frozen in the past only to be duplicated, like the Eucharist or Lent or Ramadan, because Spirit is always changing.

I was ten years old when my father first started "going down the red road," a pan-Indian term referring to embarking on a sacred life governed by the beliefs, ceremonies, and traditions of indigenous Americans. He took shamanic healing workshops from a woman named Jan, a tall, luscious former beauty queen with long curly black hair, who resembled Cher from the mid-1980s, except with a Southern accent. She hailed from a Texas Baptist tradition, and her own teenaged kids were certain she was going to Hell. I remember my dad coming home from her class one night while I was sitting awake in bed. I was in fifth grade. He came in to say goodnight, and when I asked him how the class had gone, he sat down on my floor and we started talking. Jan had walked them through vision quests that night, specifically to seek on a partner's behalf a loved one who had died. My dad said that his partner had seen his father, Stanley, that Stanley was turned away, sort of faint and confused, that he wanted to know how his son was, and that he was sorry for disappearing with his stepmother in those last years of his life.

At the time, I was joining my friend's family every week at a Baptist church, where I memorized Bible verses and was regaled with gruesome tales of heretical kings getting eaten alive by worms. I listened to my father, whose experience was as believable to me as anything else, and I wondered how I could reconcile this reality with a Christian one, which I barely understood anyway. I said something to that effect, and all he said was, "Well, one woman was upset recently after one of these workshops because Christ turned out to be her spirit guide, and she'd spent all this time and money trying to get away from her upbringing—which was traumatic. The quest ended, and she looked dour, and when Jan asked what she'd seen, she frowned and said, 'Jesus.'" Jan had then offered a disturbing vision story of her own in consolation, in which, during an early quest, she ended up in a shopping mall. It gave me pause, though the two didn't seem related.

The previous summer, I'd gone to a Baptist summer camp in Washougal, Washington. There was an hour of devotional reading of the King James Bible each morning on the blacktop, but other than that we spent our days in the river, in tetherball tournaments, or wrestling in industrial-sized sacks of flour that puffed out and got caked in our hair. On the final Sunday, we watched passion movies in the chapel and were invited into small rooms to be saved. A woman with a curly brown bob waited for me there, shut the door, and took out a pamphlet.

"Will you accept Jesus into your heart?"

My throat went dry. Whatever was being asked of me, I didn't want to do in front of her.

"I need to think about it," I said.

She looked concerned and started to describe the Acceptance prayer, opening the pamphlet to a cartoon girl being talked to just like me. "You see," she said, "your mom is going to come pick you up tomorrow, and if you get in a car crash on your way home and die, and you haven't said the prayer, you will go to Hell." She explained to me that her husband had not yet said the prayer, and that she worried for him daily.

I thanked her, said I understood, that I wasn't ready, and I hurried out of the room, though I repeated the prayer over and over and over to myself for weeks.

* * *

I grew up with a lot of cognitive dissonance. Each of my two households—my father's and my mother's—operated as though the other didn't exist, even though they lived only a mile apart. My bedroom at my mom's befitted the pink fairy dreams of a little girl, and my room at my dad's, where I had the conversation about the vision quest, was the simple quarters Of a monk, coarse wool blankets and all. I was both kid and grown-up, caught in the psychological and mystical dialectic of my secular social worker, musician, and union-organizing parents. The church, on the other hand, was mine alone, a structured space for thought and uncomfortable inner silence that nobody else could weigh in on—which is the same thing that I imagine, at least initially, drew my father to the Lakota.

Since around the time he started hanging out with the Whitedeer hoop, there's been an ongoing debate about whether or not—and also how—non-natives can participate in traditional Plains Indian ceremonies, with most members of First Nations now relegated to small, dilapidated reservations in eastern South Dakota. In 2003, a council of Cheyenne, Sioux, and Arapahoe held a meeting that adjourned after making the decision to prohibit non-natives from any degree of involvement, trusting that those in the middle of a four-year Sun Dance commitment would understand and terminate their vows. The concern had to do with the preservation of culture—an attempt to prevent sacrilegious appropriation or gross misconduct of ceremonies resulting from a lack of knowledge, and beneath that, a response to the unpaid debt of white imperialism. Angry elders made reference to the *Dances With Wolves*-inspired influx of white people seeking a fetishized version of Native American spirituality. Alfred Bone Shirt, a tribal member of the Rosebud Sioux in South Dakota, told the story of tying a sacred eagle feather to the alter during a Sun Dance, only to find out later that a white woman had naïvely taken it home with her as a souvenir.

Americans fetishizing spiritual practices is nothing new, from "Jesus is my boyfriend" evangelicalism to upper-class suburbia's Buddhism-lite. To believe that Christianity might be a means to an end of pleasant interaction and a sense of individual specialness, or that Nirvana is sought via a series of platitudes etched on fake rocks, is to take the blood and humility out of the submission these practices require. Is it possible for a white person to obtain a thorough understanding of a spiritual practice that emerged from environments and cultural trappings otherwise unrecognizable to them? Can a white person participate if they have not reckoned with white supremacy?

It must be possible, or at least there must be enough people who believe so, because in spite of the 2003 council, many Sioux communities maintain their openness to non-natives, which included all the ceremonies I attended as a teenager, but always under the conditions that participants follow the ceremonial protocol closely. These dissenters of the council decision argued that spiritual practices shouldn't be legislated, that they were to be taught, facilitated, and carried out for everyone who was called to come—which, in its democratized, come-one-come-all attitude, reminds me of an American Protestant ethos, though, of course, the Lakota aren't trying to convert anyone.

Over the next few years, I accompanied my father to ceremonies from time to time. He'd quickly risen as a drummer, singer, and transcriber important to the local hoop. When I was thirteen years old, I joined him for a weekend vision quest, both of us as supporters— people who, from a safe distance, gather to help aid the questers' spiritual passage. I was at that moment of adolescence when growing up is happening in real time, when you're filled with a fierce, present conviction that nothing is ever going to be the same, when one moment you're watching reruns of *The Wonder Years* in your friend's basement and then the next you go to your first punk show, or shotgun your first can of PBR, or just stay out later than usual, and everything changes permanently. Around that time, I distanced myself from all organized religion. It all seemed like a terrible hoax. Except these outings with my father.

A group of twelve of us camped out on a pretty piece of land in eastern Oregon at the base of a forested hill. At the beginning of the weekend, the questers went into the woods and constructed little altars called *hochoka*, tied with prayer ties, a bedroll, and a couple of blankets, and then they got to fasting and praying for a day and a half. The supporters sang them to their *hochoka* in an early-afternoon procession and left them there, and then we spent the next couple of days eating and caring for ourselves, as their proxies, and praying for them.

There was a spirit fire that needed to be tended throughout the night, in shifts, and I took one in the wee hours with the only other girl my age. I remember, very acutely, walking across a field to get to the small thicket clearing where the fire raged and feeling suddenly full of regret and despair, as though my whole life had been a waste. My life—probably eight or nine years of which I could actually retain memories of—played out before my eyes, and I felt jaded and robbed and useless.

But then, next to the fire, the feeling left, and in the morning it was as though the depression hadn't happened at all. When I described the feeling to my father the next day, he said, "You know, that's what most people up on the hill are feeling."

At the end of the weekend, a portly blond woman hugged me and said, "When you go back to your life this week, people are going to have a hard time understanding what you experienced. But you know the truth." And while I nodded and thanked her, I remember growing suddenly angry. What I'd experienced, I wanted to say, was a group of faithful people who gathered and allowed for miraculous happenings, and she seemed to want to name it, to codify it, to imply that ours was exclusive, that no one else had ever experienced something "truly" sacred. It reminded me so much of the Baptist counselor trying to squeeze out the Acceptance prayer at summer camp in that little chapel room, saying, "Either you repeat the prayer or you're going to Hell."

Every time I'd encountered religion up to that point, something had always gone awry, ultimately leaving me feeling alienated or frightened or angry. But I thought of that Baptist camp in Washougal, which I hadn't been back to since the summer before fifth grade, and I remembered an older girl who'd seemed very cool and sad, with deep-set blue eyes, who wore jelly bracelets and frayed jeans, whose attention I wanted very badly. When I confessed this to one of the Sunday school teachers, she'd said, "It'd mean a lot to her to hear that." And I so I told her, and I remember her toothy smile right before she hugged me, and how we took a walk toward one of the cabins and sat on a wobbly bench side by side, and her telling me about Jesus and her estranged mother whom she could visit only once a month. And at the end, right when the megaphone started calling us forth for dinner, she suggested that we pray.

II.

Some scientists theorize that the Shinnecock Indians came to North America on caribou hunts just as the ice caps were melting, although, as Reverend Michael Smith reminds me, their creation story is that they've been here all along. Since 1986, Smith has ministered to the Shinnecock Presbyterian Church in its small arched meeting house on the eastern shores of Long Island, that brackish, sandy hamlet known for Gatsby's galas, the crumbling Bouvier Beale fortune, and summer getaways for Manhattan's elite: the Hamptons. Since the mid-eighteenth century, the Shinnecock Indian Reservation has been gradually hemmed in on that body of land Walt Whitman once celebrated for its fated binding to the American continent.

I tell Smith, a lifelong tribal member, that I became a Presbyterian as an adult, which was only partially true at that moment and is not true at all now, and I do not mention that I grew up around American Indians. When I ask him whether he'd always planned on joining the ministry, he laughs and says, "Like many people in my situation, it happened by accident."

I want to understand at least one way that Christianity and indigenous religion might intersect, might make sense of each other, might not have to mean that Jesus appearing in a vision quest is like waking up in a shopping mall, or that calling on your ancestors with a stick of sweet grass is heretical. I want to understand, too—though I will not be able to articulate this for some time—how Christianity is a religion of liberation, of resistance to empire, and how any religious practice that lives that same hope is a sister in spirit.

Smith has records evidencing a worshipping body of Shinnecocks in his church as early as 1741. As the oldest Indian Christian congregation in the United States, this church might be a place to start.

Most New Yorkers recognize the name of the reservation only by the Shinnecock Hills Golf Course, which has hosted four U.S. Opens and remains part of a territory dispute that was reopened in 2005. The Shinnecock nation filed a lawsuit against the state seeking the return of nearly thirty-six hundred acres of tribal burial grounds. In a *New York Times* article from 1999, when the case was first surfacing, Smith told reporters:

> When you look at the real estate on the East End of Long Island, anybody in his right mind would be concerned. Let's face it, we're on a lucrative piece of property. There were once thirteen tribes on Long Island and now only two have maintained lands. The other eleven tribes have lost their lands through dishonesty and deceit on the part of those who came to colonize. That's the history of colonization. It's

one of the sadder parts of American history, and it's a reality that we live with every day.

The reservation's median annual income is $14,000, and in 2005 most of its roads remained unlighted. Many homes still have hand pumps for water, and because banks are unwilling to underwrite mortgages for houses on sovereign tribal land, many of the structures, built on plots passed down through generations, are cobbled-together cabins or prefabs.

A branch of the Algonquin and once close affiliates of New England's powerful Narragansett and Pequot, the Shinnecock offered unusually fraternal and peaceful use of their ancestral grounds to the first settlers, by whom they were later converted—with the first Bible ever translated into an American Indian language—and even later stolen from. Given that it's the oldest native-Christian church in the United States, I ask Smith whether he has to reconcile his faith with what I called "the very unique position he and his church occupy," but what I really mean is usurpation of land by the institution he belongs to, and the broader history of cultural and actual genocide.

He laughs and says that, as far as he's concerned, what the Shinnecock were practicing was not so far off from a Christian theology: Love your neighbor, care for the poor and needy, humble yourself unto the Great Spirit, and be stewards of all that you've been offered on the earth. "The tribal notion of land is that it's the gift of the Creator, and no one owns it, we all use it. And that's a very Biblical understanding of Creation." He tells me that while he was studying at Princeton Seminary in the early 1970s, his dissertation focused on these similarities. "Christianity comes from Judaism, which is a tribal religion. Their teachings and writings were fostered by the twelve tribes of Israel. This whole tribal ethos looks at the world much differently than contemporary Western ways of looking at it . . . So when settlers started moving in, the Shinnecock people were very generous with their land—'You want to use it, fine'—no deeds. But when the use became ownership, that was just a foreign concept."

He thinks about this for a minute. "I mean, they didn't know of the man Jesus Christ, but the tribal ethos was so similar to his teachings . . . You have to separate the Christian message from the Christian messengers who brought it. If you don't—or if you can't—then it makes no sense that I am Christian Indian." Though he doesn't say so, Smith's rhetoric sounds like that of destiny, that the Shinnecock people were uniquely poised to bear the cross—a deeply American sentiment held by pilgrims, immigrants, and all manner of evangelical Christians who thank God for this free land in which we live. No Pope, no monarch, no feudal lord—at least not in the way we're fearful of.

Until my early twenties, religious destiny was a sentiment that made me queasy, which was also true for everyone else I grew up with or among. When, as an adult, I told my father that I had started going to church again, he sighed and said, "I just don't understand a religion that's based on two thousand years of misreadings of things that one guy said. And what is it about everyone wanting to 'go home'? What's wrong with here"?

I wonder what my father would say to Smith. Perhaps that the Shinnecock had no choice but to convert, perhaps they'd been brutally coerced, because they obviously didn't need Christ to live productive and ethical lives. I wonder, too, what the Presbyterian minister of my old congregation in Brooklyn—a young man stewarding a community of twentysomething New York artists—might say. He might have been offended by Smith's use of historicity, because for him, like many evangelicals, conversion is never convenience or happenstance—it's a mystical, unifying call. I think also of the Ghost Dance, a nineteenth-century religious resistance movement passed from tribe to tribe in the form of a ceremony that would speed up the process of the apocalypse, make the white people go away, make them realize that Jesus was coming to save the colonized, not the colonizers.

When I ask Smith if traditional Shinnecock ceremonies inform his church services, he kind of shrugs off the thought and calls his church "by the book." "In fact, some of my peers even say, 'You're more Reformed than we are!'" by which he means the strict observance of liturgy and his emphasis on communion, infant baptism, continuous study of the scriptures and interpretation of doctrines, and, above all, the necessity of grace through faith in Jesus Christ. However, he tells me that the reservation does host Pow Wow Sunday every June, when Shinnecocks from all over New York will pilgrimage to Southampton for traditional songs, dances, and services. "And then we'll share a meal, in typical Indian fashion, because two things that Indians love to do is talk and eat," he says.

When Reverend Smith describes Pow Wow Sunday, he emphasizes that the most prominent part of the proceedings is this great, culminating feast. He grounds the importance of the feast in the continuity of native life—the giving away of goods, and thus the self, getting nourished from a common creator's bounty—but he also grounds it in the seven Jewish feasts, the Canaan wedding, the shores of Galilee, the Last Supper. "Within Reformed theology, the table is very significant also," he says.

"I think of Luke's story of the road to Emmaus, when Jesus joins two individuals walking along the road. These two men were so heavily involved in this conversation about what had just happened in Jerusalem that they didn't even recognize that *that* was Jesus, the risen Lord. And it wasn't until they invited him to have dinner, till they were *sitting* at that table, that they recognized him."

I wonder if Shinnecock Presbyterian adolescents struggle with the church in a more violent way than, say, the average white fourteen-year-old who falls from faith—who spits on prayer pamphlets, feigns possession in front of proselytizers, eats communion wafers with salsa—after that first inkling of deep distrust for all the mores and institutions they've been raised to revere. Surely, after that first taste of real colonial history education, when a Shinnecock kid becomes acutely aware of the implications of living on a reservation, they must question the validity of a faith brought by Europeans. Smith shrugs this suggestion off, too, saying that they leave for the same reasons any other disillusioned kid might. "I was one of those kids," he says. "I wandered away . . . It was a decision I had to make on my own."

He wandered away to school at SUNY Old Westbury, and then to Princeton, and in the 1980s found himself in Phoenix working for the American Indian Presbyterian Synod of the Southwest, which governed the region's reservation churches. One of the final projects he worked on before returning to Long Island was with the Sanctuary Movement, an effort to assist Guatemalans, Hondurans, El Salvadorians, and Nicaraguans, who, at the time, were crossing the Mexican border in droves, seeking exile in reservation Presbyterian Churches. "Most of the people who were making their way up there were indigenous people who'd been dispossessed, and so we said that the Navajo would be making a significant statement if they did this," Smith says, an irony he doesn't call further attention to but which reminds me of another: the U.S. government's involvement in arming all of those Central American coups that were sending citizens over the border in the first place. "One of the last things I was negotiating was with the Navajo presbytery chairman who was preparing to offer sanctuary to those who made it to the reservation. We were fairly close to having that done, when, like I said, I was called to come back home."

One winter in college, every time I thought about Christ, I'd start crying. I'd see something from the gospels printed on a subway advertisement or read one of Marilynne Robinson's biblical metaphors in her novel *Housekeeping* or see the Assembly of God missionaries preaching in front of their little storefront churches in Bed-Stuy and my eyes would well up. The feeling was unwelcome and thus disturbing. What business did I have sentimentalizing something that happened on the other side of the world two millennia ago? And do we even really know what He said, or what He meant? And what about all the terrible shit that's been done—that is still being done—in His name?

But then I began going to a Presbyterian church plant in Williamsburg, which held its services in a rented Puerto Rican Lutheran sanctuary within the densest hipster neighborhood in Brooklyn. When I was finally seated in its pews, listening to all the off-key voices joined in "Joy Is a Fruit" and the Apostles' Creed, and watching the cartoonishly large communion table sitting below the risen Christ on his cross, and listening to the two-thousand-year-old political histories of the Middle East, I suppressed the maniacal urge to laugh. I was always either laughing or crying. How could God, the Trinity, three-in-one, give a shit about this particular pageant or another? In her essay "An Expedition to the Pole," Annie Dillard describes her regular Catholic mass as being less polished than a high school play: "In two thousand years, we have not worked out the kinks. We positively glorify them. Week after week, we witness the same miracle: that God, for reasons unfathomable, refrains from blowing our dancing bear act to smithereens."

But there was something about the very improbability of us being there at all, in that old sanctuary in Williamsburg perched right above the Brooklyn-Queens Expressway, that I found moving. At the time, I was listening to as many different recordings of "Amazing Grace" as I could get my hands on, that beautiful old hymn written by a former slave trader in response to a revelation he had on the Atlantic—a revelation he didn't heed until after he was paid for each and every soul. It's fucked up. It's complicated. The writer was British, but the song was popularized by Americans, the tune created by Sacred Harp singers and slaves, reinvigorated in the mid-twentieth century by American soul singers and folk musicians. In my favorite verse it says, "'Twas Grace that taught me how to fear / and Grace my fears relieved." It's only after you recognize what a desperate situation you're in that you have anything to be relieved of.

One night I was listening to Joan Baez' live version, and I remembered being in a sweat lodge some years back, when the woman who was leading it asked, before the ancestors were sang away, whether we could join her in "Amazing Grace." She and I were the only ones who knew it, so we sang, in that hot dark space beneath the weight of wool blankets and bowed pine branches, Lakota-style, as loudly as we could, this song about the unequivocal mercy of God, in a ceremony that put no particular emphasis on sin, by a man who committed heinous crimes against humanity. I thought about that from my bedroom in Brooklyn and sang along to Baez, as her fans did from the crowd.

As the months went on, I read C. S. Lewis's *Mere Christianity* and felt myself inhabiting an architecture that made comforting, mysterious sense. That Christ's sacrifice was a gesture of freedom—to be free to be human, to learn to love without law, to live your life for someone else, to live against empire—was radical to me. I wrote a poem called "The Troubadour," which I completely forgot about and then found years later, its date just preceding my arrival at this church. "When He used to dream about the future, He dreamt this: to commit to / something is to careen late into the night passionately, obsessively late into the night and to let / go like 'all outdoors,' to risk breathing, stakes in your palms." Three years later I was baptized at a different church, though it was also a Reformed church, like the one in Williamsburg, and like Reverend Michael Smith's. These were churches born of Martin Luther's reformation but amended by John Calvin's doctrine of predestination—Luther and Calvin, who thumbed their noses at the Vatican, dropped the saints, the indulgences, the theatrical mummery, and ran about central and northern

Europe saying that we cannot earn God's favor, so worship obedi-
ently, read rigorously, live well, baptize your babies, and give thanks.
And oh, yes, also some of us are predestined for Heaven and others
are not, so don't kid yourself.

The Presbyterians in the U.S. were historically from the Isles,
Scotch-Irish especially. And the people of the Isles were also people
of a reservation, in a way, who were subjected to a genocide, who
lived in the windswept highlands, who had to build into the earth
in order to stay dry. The Reformed church sprung from a belief in
the free grace of God, which can't be earned by tithing or even good
works, but rather by being admittedly undeserving of it. That, to
Calvin, was the only thing that made sense. And the doctrine of Predestination attempts to affirm that, though it's mostly only known by
its negative identity—that not everyone is destined—though its uses
as a belief had much more to do with letting go of the conviction that
there was anything in particular you could do to win God's favor, that
His favor could be won at all.

When I moved to Providence, Rhode Island, I was finally baptized
in another church plant, in the basement of a vocational high school.
My self-selected baptismal gown was a vintage dress made of thin
green cotton from a thrift store in Warren. By weird chance, a couple
of my in-laws had come up to visit us the day before, and we'd stayed
up late drinking and playing bumper pool. I wondered if I looked
tired, if I had breakfast in my teeth.

The pastor, a born-again ex-punk normally theatrically confident
in his delivery, stumbled over the vows, looked me in the eye, and
said, "Well, then, little old me . . . baptizes you into the name of the
Father and of the Son and of the Holy Spirit," before he drizzled the
holy water over my scalp. Staring back at me while I took my vows
was a throng of lapsed Catholics and renegade Jews, my sister- and
father-in-law, two old friends, and a congregation of mostly charismatic Christians, bored Episcopalians, and snubbed Baptists, who'd

elected for the unwieldy, laborious, pedagogical homilies of this new church body where almost no one was over the age of forty.

Afterward we all got mussels and beer at the Trinity Brewhouse.

In the booth, my friend, a renegade Jew, threw his arm around my neck. "Well," he said, "is your hair still wet?"

"No," I said. "It dried."

He laughed. "Good answer."

I laughed, too, but why? Was it that the meaning, the import, of my baptism lasted only for a short moment and then was gone—or that I thought I knew what it meant until my hair dried, but now I wasn't sure? Something about his warm laughter seemed to imply all of this.

In that same Dillard essay, she offers a kind of coda for Christian pageantry and piety that rings as true to me now as it did right after my baptisim: "God does not demand that we give up our personal dignity, that we throw in our lot with random people, that we lose ourselves and turn from all that is not him. God needs nothing, asks nothing, and demands nothing, like the stars. It is a life with God that demands these things . . . you do not have to sit outside in the dark. If, however, you want to look at the stars, you will find that darkness is necessary. But the stars neither require nor demand it."

Of course, I would eventually leave this church because I moved. And later on, the church would fold. And for a couple of reasons, I would regret having been affiliated with that church, and the one before that, and all the ones before that. By then I was in Wyoming, dropping into and leaving churches with greater and greater frequency, as my dream of a religious home revealed itself to be just that. (Christians are always insisting that no church is perfect, no marriage is perfect, it is perfect because you love it; but some marriages, like some churches, are harmful.) Each church always appeared to me at first as a sort of promised land, then maybe as an oasis in the promised land (you know, it's a desert, after all), then later, just as a mirage, and

I'd find myself in the desert again, a very American pose—the American religion that Harold Bloom describes as "the American [walking] alone with Jesus in a perpetually expanded interval founded upon the forty days' sojourn of the risen Son of Man." The churches were always stopping places, always mobile, and, as far as I was concerned, Jesus would leave when I did.

Over the years, I have sat in so many churches, mostly with male pastors or priests, and sometimes they hit the mark, but sometimes they did not, and sometimes they betrayed what I thought we both believed. I cannot hold much against them without implicating myself. God knows, the journey is long. So what is a church, a religion, supposed to do? I find the easy answers—community, worship, love—to often be empty. Above all, it seems, a religion should demand crazy things of you, and enormous self-sacrifice, and it should stir doubt, leave you doubting your intentions, your altruism, your own narrow idea of what it means to give your time, yourself, to someone, and it should perpetuate this interrogation, this inquiry, until you pass to the other side. A Christian church in particular must know that it is a church against empire, against the cultural mores, a sanctuary to the misfits and most vulnerable, and it should face the strangeness of the parables, the contradictions in the epistles, be a place where you confess your fearing heart and not every tiny misstep. Missteps miss the point. Above all, a church must know that, like all churches, it is a sham, a faint and pathetic glimmer of an attempt to reconstitute the paschal feast. It must know that it is only ever going to do it wrong, and that only by accident, by miracle, will it inspire things like community, worship, love. (All these shoulds and musts; I contradict myself.) And yet, knowing all of this, a church must trudge on anyway, trying to do what it was always tasked with: to teach that you must give your life away, literally, to those who need it most and to those who deserve it least. I want what documentary filmmaker Alex Mar describes on her quest in *Witches of America* as a spirituality that leaves you feeling disturbed. In a good way.

Oh, and hope.

I don't mean the puerile American idea of hope. Theological hope is a long game, what we might call eschatological. It has nothing to do with progress; it betrays ideas of improvement, because humans will always do the wrong thing, because the various systems in place will always fail, because power will always corrupt. Theological hope, though, is not simply longing for Eden and accepting these things, but is rather, like Marilynne Robinson writes, "a mourning that will not be comforted," a longing that is mobilizing, resistant, that leads us to each other, and maybe to a garden, even if it is a long way off. True hope, deep hope, guarantees only continuous shift against oppressive forces, bizarre and extraordinary acts of love, irresolvable questions of resistance and submission, leaving and cleaving, surprise, play, like poet Wendell Berry's fox "who makes more tracks than necessary / some in the wrong direction," and like Berry himself urges: "so friends, every day do something / that won't compute."

Outside the church where the *yuwipi* is about to happen, the crowd calls itself to attention as the doors are opened. With his wife, I help the man with brain cancer to stand. I find my father, and we file into the darkened basement. It's the type of space usually used for things like AA meetings and tepid post-service luncheons, a place of warm shrimp salad and red sauce and gooey fruit pies. Other than the medicine man bound on the floor, it's an ordinary room with stiff blue carpet, wood paneling, shallow ceilings, with some folding chairs and tables pressed up against the back wall. A few couches and overstuffed chairs reserved for elders to sit in have been pulled into a circle around the medicine man, who sits in the center, tied up with rope, his arms pinned to his sides. He's surrounded by rattles and colorful prayer ties knotted together with twine in a long string. Excepting him and a few elders, the majority of the group are non-native.

I sit on the floor at the foot of Jim and Velia Whitedeer, who are cozied up on a loveseat. Velia winks at me.

There are six people sitting at the back, behind the bound medicine man, who have all requested healing of some kind. It's not until I see the dying man that I realize he was among those who called for the ceremony.

The lights go out. We're plunged into pitch darkness. The drummers, which include my father, begin beating the spirit drum, and everyone joins in singing, inviting the ancestors who come as intercessors to help carry messages to the Creator. We sing and drum in the dark and no one moves.

It's very difficult to describe what comes next. There are flashes of light, greens, blues, and the sound of shaking, the rattles, rattling all around the room, up near the ceiling, next to my ear, like they're flying, zipping across space. Everyone continues singing, and the drummers continue drumming, and I hear big bodies thumping around the perimeter of the room. I feel condensation on my arm from a big mammal breathing on it. There are crashes, thumps. The medicine man stops between songs and talks with the spirits in Lakota, and the shakers shake in response. This goes on for a while. The blue flashes crack closer and closer to my face. And then we sing the spirits away, a goodbye song, and the shaking stops.

When the lights go on, the medicine man has been unbound by the spirits; the cloth and rope lay around him. Hours have gone by. It's night and we're hungry. Some people step outside for a cigarette while others set up tables and bring out coolers of food from their cars. We eat.

CODA

There is a statue in my grandparents' living room and I wonder about it. It's Mary Baker Eddy, except it's not—but thinking it is is enough to send me searching. I go to Sun Dances and to Sunday school and to astrologers. I start reading Flannery O'Connor from a big cloth book my grandmother gives me. I pore over the pages of Linda Goodman's *Love Signs*. My brother goes crazy and my family fractures and goes silent, and there is no recourse. I move far, far away, and I find myself in churches in borrowed sanctuaries and high school basements, and I listen to a lot of men talking about what God is saying when He says "do my will," or when Jesus says it, and Jesus is God, but also Jesus is Jesus, we don't know, but we pretend to understand. I listen to the ecstatic sermons of Aimee Semple McPherson and fantasize about "going native" like Dennis Covington did while writing *Salvation on Sand Mountain*. I visit Lily Dale down the street from the Fox sisters' home and try to speak to the dead, and I go to the Salt Lake

City temple grounds to see if anyone is talking about Eliza Snow and the Mother in Heaven, and they are not. I get older and go further, and my family's sadness starts to wear on me like an old boot gone soft in the tongue. Somewhere in Rhode Island, I try to figure out what my aunt has been running from all these years, and all of these people silent on the issue of the afterlife, though at least half of us got here because of those wild Mennonites running from pitchforks to baptismal fonts, who survived with a modicum of continuity only because the women cooked porridge and made their children read the Bible. I am surrounded by Irish Catholic in-laws who are loudly principled, but anything goes—do drugs in their Westchester back-yards when you're seventeen or twenty-seven, and they'll still take you back, and they won't talk about it. It's not really until I start teaching that I realize how white my spiritual gaze has been. There's poet Claudia Rankine's open question in *The Guardian* to Jonathan Franzen, which is more generally directed at white people willing to face the answers: "What choices have you made in your life to keep yourself segregated?" The day I go to the mill where Sojourner Truth first got her powers after she'd said *Fuck all y'all* to literally everyone who had ever done her wrong, my grandmother dies. I sit in a small studio overlooking Edna St. Vincent Millay's wild meadows. "You had to go, though," my grandmother had said to me, cryptically, one night after I'd left the Pacific Northwest with no plan to return. My heart is so heavy—everyone's dying, or on the verge of dying, for a whole year: parents and grandparents, and my own family more remote than ever, and war rages on in the Middle East, more refugees than ever. America elects a fascist. I hop on a train hoping for clarity, and for three days I watch the country go by and by, having seen it now back and forth so many times, and I feel loss. I convalesce in a rented room in New Orleans, and I kiss Marie Laveau's grave. In the news that week, Miss Cleo dies. I find myself at a Voudou ceremony in a plywood temple I've ridden to on a bicycle, dressed all in red from

CODA

scraps I could find at Restoration Thrift ("All Things Made New"). And during the ceremony led by Sallie Ann Glassman, who is white and from Ukrainian Jewish stock settled in Maine long ago, I see that it is actually a lot like the Sun Dance, the *yuwipi*, the sweat lodge, from all those years ago. When I return to New York, I take myself to a church called New Day Methodist, an interracial, inter-class, boundary-crossing, social-justice ministry in the Bronx, a site of resistance. And for the first time ever, without feeling compromised, I think: *Here is an approximation of what Jesus might have meant.* (I also think of Marx saying, "I am not a Marxist.") A genderqueer person gives a guest sermon: "The gospel does not guarantee that love will protect us," they say. "It is, rather, up to us to protect love." I have just been to the chapel where the suffragists stated their resolutions and opened the operating line to God for women—well, *some* women— because of course on the drive back home we remember that within a few short years the suffragists and the abolitionists had split, and an angry Susan B. wrote racist diatribes, and the whole project went silent for a hundred years. The truth shifts. The end is always the beginning. Will you ever make it home? You feel a breeze pass your cheek and it means nothing, or it means something for a moment, and then just the faint glimmer of grace, like a rotten peach on the sidewalk, beseeching—*Whatta you gonna do with me now*? This is a living document. The statue of a pioneer wife comes to life in *Angels in America* when Mary-Louise Parker asks how can people change. "Well," the statue says, "it has something to do with God, so it's not very nice." It never is. Try asking a woman.

And in the last days it shall be, God declares, that I will pour out my
    Spirit on all flesh,
and your sons and your daughters shall prophesy, and your young
    men shall see visions,
and your old men shall dream dreams; even on my male servants
    and female servants
in those days I will pour out my Spirit, and they shall prophesy.

Acts 2:17–21

· ACKNOWLEDGMENTS ·

I owe more than I can say to—

Every scholar, archivist, and activist whose work made the very idea of a history of American women and religion possible, without whom or without whose patience, ethics, fortitude, and brilliance there would have been no way for me to write a book like this, and without whom we would have no way to reimagine the past, no way to make room for the future.

Anyone who read this work in its early stages: Beth Loffreda, Andy Fitch, and Frieda Knobloch; all of my peers and teachers in the MFA program at the University of Wyoming, as well as the American Studies program; Erin Forbes and Quincy Newell and their profoundly shaping course, "Religion & American Women Writers"; Ariel Gore, for reasons too numerous and going back too far in time to name.

Each friend, teacher, and voice in the wilderness who has read, edited, coached, inspired, been interviewed by me, or opened up this work or the thinking and writing that led to it, whether or not they know it: Amber Stewart (forever in her editing debt), Robert Balkovich, Chanelle Bergeron, Lina Misitzis, Lily Herman, Jennifer Stohlmann, Laura Henriksen, Hallie Flynn, Jess Monday, Susan Dewey, Seth and Jen Nelson, Michael Smith, Robert Snyderman, Yanara Friedland, Gabriella Hook, Molly Bernard, Sofi Thanhauser, Kelly Hatton, Rebecca Golden, Grace Kredell, Rachel Levitsky, Ellery Washington, Suzanne Verderber, Benjamin Lytal, Samantha Hunt, Cecilia Muhlstein, Sallie Ann Glassman, "Michael & the

Millays," and Deborah Yanagisawa. Thanks to Tom Robbins's generously corresponding with me all those years ago. Global thanks to the Pratt Institute BFA Writing Program where nearly everything began (eschatologically speaking) and then began again years later. Thanks also to every faith community that has ever welcomed me over the threshold and every student who has trusted me enough to transverse a whole semester by my side—me as captain, them as first mate. Special shout-out to the "Bad Girls" and to the senior thesis "heroesses," whose creative manuscripts were ushered into their final forms simultaneously to my own, and who modeled a depth of compassion, devotion, intelligence, and mutual support that I'm still being moved by.

The Millay Colony, whose nourishment came at the absolute right time—in spirit, in company, in space. The editing boot camps in "Bronkers" and Brooklyn.

The Pratt Faculty Development Fund for facilitating an important research trip to New Orleans that unexpectedly brought everything together.

New Day Methodist Church in the Bronx, which revealed for me, at the eleventh hour, how a Christian community can be a site of resistance.

My whole family—both of origin and my Sweeney in-laws—for their unflagging support and excitement, and especially to my parents, for being champions of my writing, and of my will to write, from the very beginning.

My husband, [Christopher] Sweeney, brilliant scholar of religion and fearless adventurer, who for ten years now has been my comrade and confidant through a thousand wild days and nights, and who (to take a phrase from Richard Rodriguez) "has read and edited every page of this book with a rigor and compassion that define for me the meaning of love."

ACKNOWLEDGMENTS

My agent (and wonderful writer) W. Ralph Eubanks, who *got* the work when not that many other people got it, and who connected me to a publisher he knew would get it, too.

My brave, visionary, and supportive team at Counterpoint Press, which has done the otherwise thought-to-be-impossible task of remaining an independent, author-centered publisher for fifty years: Jack Shoemaker, Jennifer Alton, Kelli Trapnell, Oriana Leckert, Megan Fishmann, Shannon Price, and Alisha Groder.

To the virtuosic editors I worked with before I knew I was working on a book: Mensah Demary, Yuka Igarashi, Austin Tremblay, Arvind Dilawar. Early versions of "Dear Linda" appeared in *The Airship*; "Our Bodies, Our Smoke" in the *Owl Eye Review*; and "This Building Is Yours" in *Catapult*.

My creative research assistants, Carliene Thompson and Anjette Rostock, both of whom are going to conquer the world.

Finally, to everyone who passed away during the final year of writing this book, for whom we are still grieving: my grandmother Gale Adair, my grandmothers-in-law Peggy Rodway and Patricia Sweeney, Uncle Dean Stickler, Uncle Johnny Billington, and lifelong family friend Pat Parker.

Adrian Shirk was raised in Portland, Oregon, and has since lived in New York and Wyoming. She's a columnist at *Catapult*, and her essays have appeared in *The Atlantic* and other publications. She has produced radio stories for Wyoming Public Media and Pop Up Archive, and she holds an MFA in nonfiction from the University of Wyoming in Laramie. Currently, she teaches women's studies and creative writing at Pratt Institute. She lives on the border of the Bronx and Yonkers with her husband, Christopher Sweeney, and Quentin the cat.